Paläoklimaforschung · Pal

Akademie der Wissenschaften und der Literatur

Paläoklimaforschung
Palaeoclimate Research Volume 7

Special Issue: ESF Project
"European Palaeoclimate and Man" 2

Editor: Burkhard Frenzel

Associate Editor: Birgit Gläser

1992

European Science Foundation
Strasbourg

Akademie der Wissenschaften
und der Literatur · Mainz

European climate reconstructed from documentary data: methods and results

Edited by Burkhard Frenzel

Co-edited by Christian Pfister & Birgit Gläser

64 figures and 15 tables

SEMPER BONIS ARTIBUS

Gustav Fischer Verlag · Stuttgart · Jena · New York · 1992

Der vorliegende Sonderband wurde mit Mitteln der European Science Foundation (Straßburg) und der Akademie der Wissenschaften und der Literatur (Mainz) gefördert. Die Verantwortung für den Inhalt dieser Veröffentlichung liegt bei den Autoren.

Anschriften der Herausgeber:

Prof. Dr. Dr. h.c. Burkhard Frenzel, Institut für Botanik 210 der Universität Hohenheim, Garbenstraße 30, D-7000 Stuttgart 70, F.R.G.

Prof. Dr. Christian Pfister, Historisches Institut der Universität Bern, Engehaldenstraße 4, CH-3012 Bern, Switzerland

Dr. Birgit Gläser, Institut für Botanik 210 der Universität Hohenheim, Garbenstraße 30, D-7000 Stuttgart 70, F.R.G.

Bibliographische Bearbeitung: Dipl. Agr.-Biol. Mirjam Weiß, Hohenheim/ESF
Graphische Bearbeitung: Erika Rücker, Hohenheim
Technische Redaktion: Dr. Birgit Gläser, Hohenheim/ESF

Die Deutsche Bibliothek — CIP-Einheitsaufnahme

European climate reconstructed from documentary data :
methods and results / ed. by Burkhard Frenzel. Co-ed. by
Christian Pfister & Birgit Gläser. — Stuttgart ; Jena ; New York
: G. Fischer, 1992
   (Palaeoclimate research ; Bd. 7 : ESF project "European palaeoclimate
   and man" ; Special issue 2)
   ISBN 3-437-30701-0 (Stuttgart ...)
   ISBN 1-56081-361-X (New York ...)
NE: Frenzel, Burkhard [Hrsg]; Paläoklimaforschung / ESF project
   "European palaeoclimate and man"

ISBN 3-437-30701-0
ISSN 0930-4673

CONTENTS

ADDRESSES OF THE AUTHORS

Dr. V. Banzon, I.F.A. (Ist. di Fisica dell'Atmosfera), C.N.R., p. le L. Sturzo 31,
I-00144 Roma, Italy

Dr. J. Boryczka, Department of Climatology, Faculty of Geography and Regional Studies,
Warsaw University, ul. Krakowskie Przedmieście 30, PL-00-927 Warsaw, Poland

Prof. Dr. R. Brázdil, Department of Geography, Masaryk University, Kotlářská 2,
CS-611 37 Brno, Czechoslovakia

Dr. D. Camuffo, Consiglio Nazionale delle Ricerche, I.C.T.R., Padova, Italy

Dr. M. Chernavskaya, Institute of Geography, Academy of Sciences, Staromonetny 29,
Moscow 109017, Russia

Prof. Dr. E. Chrysos, Department of Byzantine History, University of Ioannina,
GR-451 10 Ioannina, Greece

Prof. Dr. T. Dunin-Wąsowicz, Institute of the History of Material Culture, Polish Academy
of Sciences, Świerczewskiego 105, PL-00-140 Warsaw, Poland

Dr. S. Enzi, Consiglio Nazionale delle Ricerche, I.C.T.R., Padova, Italy

Dr. G. de Franceschi, I.N.G. (Ist. Nazionale di Geofisica) via di Villa Ricotti 42,
I-00161 Roma, Italy

Dr. R. Glaser, Geographisches Institut der Universität Würzburg, Am Hubland,
D-8700 Würzburg, F.R.G.

Prof. Dr. G. P. Gregori, I.F.A. (Istituto di Fisica dell'Atmosfera), C.N.R., p. le L. Sturzo 31,
I-00144 Roma, Italy

Dr. A. T. Grove, Geography Department, Downing Place, Cambridge, U.K.

Dr. J. M. Grove, Girton College Cambridge, U.K.

Dr. J. Guiot, Laboratoire de Botanique Historique et Palynologie, CNRS UA 1152,
Faculté de St-Jérôme, F-13397 Marseille cédex 13, France

Dr. M. Gutry-Korycka, Department of Hydrology, Faculty of Geography and Regional Studies, Warsaw University, ul. Krakowskie Przedmieście 30, PL-00-927 Warsaw, Poland

Dr. J. Kynčil, Ruská 298, CS-431 51 Klášterec nad Ohří, Czechoslovakia

Dr. A. Lauterburg, Oberdorfstraße 124, CH-9100 Herisau, Switzerland

Dr. J. Munzar, Geographical Institute of the C.A.S., Mendlovo nám. 1, CS-662 82 Brno, Czechoslovakia

Dr. M. Pavese, I.F.A., C.N.R., Istituto di Fisica dell'Atmosfera, p.le L. Sturzo 31, I-00144 Roma, Italy

Prof. Dr. C. Pfister, Department for Regional and Environmental Studies at the Institute for History, University of Bern, Engehaldenstr. 4, CH-3012 Bern, Switzerland

Prof. Dr. J. Piontek, Department of Human Evolutionary Biology, Adam Mickiewicz University, Fredry 10, PL-61-701 Poznań, Poland

H. Schüle, Department for Regional and Environmental Studies at the Institute for History, University of Bern, Engehaldenstr. 4, CH-3012 Bern, Switzerland

G. Schwarz-Zanetti, Florastraße 29, CH-8620 Wetzikon, Switzerland

W. Schwarz-Zanetti, Florastraße 29, CH-8620 Wetzikon, Switzerland

Dr. H. Salvesen, University Library, University of Tromsø, N-9000 Tromsø, Norway

Dr. I. Telelis, Department of Byzantine History, University of Ioannina, GR-451 10 Ioannina, Greece

Dr. L. Rácz, Centre for Regional Studies of the Hungarian Academy of Sciences, Rákóczi ut. 3, Pf. 261, H-6001 Kecskemét, Hungary

Preface

Christian Pfister

There is growing evidence that over the last 100 to 150 years human activity has had a significant impact on our climate. Describing the evolution of the climate system in terms of a transition from conditions only insignificantly influenced by man to a state in which human activity becomes at least temporarily dominant is thus of great importance. There are only few regions in Europe where instrumental measurements go back far enough to document the last phase of a mostly "natural" state of climate.

The goal of the European Palaeoclimate Programme EPC is the reconstruction of the European Climate since the last glaciation and its interpretation in terms of natural and human influences. Due to its long tradition in palaeoclimatic research, European scholarship could make a significant contribution to reconstruct past climate, to interpret the present trends, and to improve model calculations for scenarios. In addition to time series, palaeoclimate maps of continental Europe and the adjacent oceans for specific time slices are needed.

The most detailed record of past weather and climate may be obtained for the last 800 years. Within this long period documentary data are of great value, in particular for mapping extreme events in particular years and for comparing the incidence of anomalies in the past with their frequency and magnitude in the instrumental period. Moreover, documentary data may improve the quality and the time resolution of time series and the quality of palaeoclimatic mapping, if they are cross calibrated with high resolution proxy data from natural archives such as tree-ring or pollen evidence.

It is true that compilations of weather and hazard reports contained in documentary sources and reconstructions of weather and climate from those sources have a long tradition in Europe. However, even in recent studies the sources have not been critically evaluated. There is no established scientific community working in this field, yet. As a consequence, research work is carried out by individual scholars, a generally recognized methodology is lacking and the results obtained from different studies are not coherent and may not easily be compared.

In order to improve this situation, the Scientific Coordinating Committee of EPC has advanced the idea of a workshop on methodological problems in historical climatology. Scholars from 14 countries of Europe and from Japan convened at the Academy of Sciences and Literature in Mainz from March 1-3, 1990. The participants of the Mainz workshop were not satisfied with the presentation and discussion of papers. During the last day they agreed on an agenda for further common research which includes the following six steps:

(1) collecting and compiling all the relevant evidence, especially in areas where gaps exist;
(2) mathematical and geophysical consideration of the data;
(3) estimating temperature and precipitation trends within the "similo-fluctuative zones" in Europe;
(4) mapping and interpretation of the major climatic shifts and large-scale anomalies;
(5) deciphering man's influence on the "natural" climatic variability;
(6) processing and publishing an extensive record of all the source materials that have been used in the analysis.

As a prerequisite for cooperation, a common research strategy has been agreed upon. The known techniques of historical source evaluation have to be applied to the data. Moreover a data bank to store, merge, process, print and map the evidence should be created at a convenient place. This data bank should be maintained by a staff prepared to introduce historians to the facilities and to adapt the programmes to their particular requirements. On a secondary level of analysis interdisciplinary teams of historians and scientists should be called in. This level of analysis has to include the wealth of additional data which can be obtained from biology, geology, glacial history, palaeo-ecology, sedimentology, isotope studies etc.

The articles contained in this volume are intended to provide methodological guide-lines for the on-going interdisciplinary research efforts:

Teresa Dunin-Wąsowicz gives a summary of some literature with special reference to Poland. Sources are discussed and presented in the following papers: Marco Pavese demonstrates how information on past environments can be obtained from Latin epigraphs; Ioannis Telelis and Evangelos Chrysos deal with the pitfalls inherent in the interpretation of Early Medieval Byzantine records; Gabriela and Werner Schwarz-Zanetti display some of the wealth of detailed information contained in South German weather diaries for the time around 1500; Jean and A.T. Grove focus on source material available from Crete in order to shed light on anomalies in the Eastern Mediterranean region in the late sixteenth century; Ian Munzar presents a list of weather records from late sixteenth century Bohemia, and Jiří Kynčil describes some flood hazards in the North Bohemian Ore Mountains from the late eighteenth century.

Two papers focus on the interpretation of documentary data: Dario Camuffo and Silvia Enzi have disentangled the different styles of dating that were in use in Late Medieval and early modern Northern Italy; Rudolf Brazdil has evaluated some methodological and data problems inherent in climate reconstructions from the example of Bohemia and Moravia, such as record density, the intensity of the phenomena described, and the quantitative interpretation of written records.

Three papers introduce proxy data from natural or material archives: Margarite Chernavskaya demonstrates the value of dendrological data for climate reconstructions from the example of the Russian plain. Joël Guiot has assembled information available from dendrological and documentary data for the Western Mediterranean area. Janusz Piontek introduces the biological structure of skeleton populations as an environmental indicator from the example of Polish evidence.

Examples of detailed climate reconstructions were provided by Rüdiger Glaser for Southwest Germany and by Lajos Racz for Hungary, both for the early modern period.

Mathematical and statistical handling of documentary data is important: Filter techniques suited for the analysis of this kind of data are presented by Viva Banzon, Giorgana Franceschi & Giovanni P. Gregori and M. Gutry-Korycka & J. Boryczka. Christian Pfister and Andreas Lauterburg have defined areas of similar year-to-year fluctuations of temperature and precipitation in Europe using cluster analysis in order to obtain spatial units in which the evidence may be summarized. Hannes Schüle and Christian Pfister then give an outline of the EURO-CLIMHIST data base which is being created and point to the advantages of this approach for the individual scholar and for the research community. Gabriela and Werner Schwarz-Zanetti and Christian Pfister explain the computerized procedure which was used to create the nucleus of this data base from the example of the period 1270-1525.

From a Nordic point of view, Helge Salvesen contributes to the old discussion as to how far climatic impacts may have had a bearing upon economic, social and political actions.

The Mainz meeting has born fruit beyond the publication of this volume. Important steps have already been taken for putting the guide-lines of the first workshop into action.

Climatic changes in Medieval Poland: methods and investigation

Teresa Dunin-Wąsowicz

Summary

The author presents the twentieth century literature of climatic changes in Medieval Europe, especially in Poland.

Résumé

L'auteur présente un coup d'oeil sur la littérature du XXe siècle concernent les changements climatiques en Europe médiévale spécialement en Pologne.

1. Introduction

Already a first glance at the literature of the twentieth century concerning climatic changes in Medieval Europe shows that an attack of those problems by the humanists alone is almost impossible because of the rapid developments in the exact sciences.

From the times of BRÜCKNER (1912), BERG (1914), SEMKOWICZ (1922), and SULIMIRSKI (1934), the historians' and archaeologists' interests became more extended but their methods have changed but little. On the contrary, the climatologists have restricted their interests as far as research subjects and specialization are concerned, but they have developed their scientific equipment further. These new methods provided them with some new perspectives and opened up new ways of research. An important common policy of basic research for historians and geographers has also evolved, i.e. archaeological sources (KURNATOWSKI & WISLAŃSKI, 1966) have become better known over the last few years. They offer the possibility of verifying the new methods used by palaeogeographers and of properly understanding the preserved written documentary fragments.

The renowned English climatologist BROOKS (1950) considers some sources as fundamental to the study of climatic relations in historical times. These are:

- the results of instrumental meteorological observations;
- the ancient weather chronicles;
- the information concerning the unusual atmospherical and hydrological events known from historical literature and archival documents.

2. Instrumental records and weather diaries

The beginning of instrumental meteorological observations in Europe can be dated to the second half of the seventeenth century (although they had been carried out earlier in India, Palestine, and Korea). Among the earliest observations of this kind are those from Florence and Pisa (1654) and from Warsaw (1655). In South America the earliest observations were made in 1738, but the establishment and development of a regular network of meteorological stations only started in the second half of the nineteenth century (ROJECKI, 1956).

The situation is very similar as far as measurements and hydrological observations of water-levels are concerned. Although the first hydrological measurements in the Nile valley are known from the fourth millennium B.C., the first reliable hydrological observations in Europe appear in the eighteenth century (e.g. in Russia they have been carried out in the mouth of the Neva river since 1807, and the first water gauge was installed there in 1715).

The earliest results of systematic hydrometrical observations on Polish territory are known from Wrocław (from 1717), Gdańsk (from 1739 and the following years), and Toruń (from 1760-1772). In the preceding period there were only some occasional visual observations of the Vistula river concerning the events of freezing and ERNDTEL's statements about high water-levels from the years 1725-1728. The actual setting up of hydrological stations with large-scale observations also began in the second half of the nineteenth century. Therefore, detailed studies of climatic and hydrological processes were only possible in the last two centuries, although sometimes one can reach back to the seventeenth century.

Fragmentary notes about weather and several hydrological events are provided by so-called weather chronicles - collections of more or less systematic notes concerning atmospherical and, sometimes, hydrospherical phenomena. The oldest known notes were taken by WILIAM MERLE in Dryby near Oxford in 1337-1344 and published in 1891. Second come notes dated to the second half of the fifteenth century and the first half of the sixteenth century taken by some professors of the Cracow University and in particular by a priest MARCIN BIEM who started to note his visual meteorological observations in Cracow sporadically from 1490 and in a systematic way in the years 1502-1517 (then, from 1525-1540 he continued his observation in Olkusz). Those results have not been completely published yet. As to the more recent weather chronicles - only very few of which concern Poland - it is important to mention the 62-year series of visual observations carried out in Oleśnica since 1536, as well as the remarks by J. KEPLER noted in Zagań in 1628-1630. The following times (1755-1763) are referred to in the diary of JERZY DAWIDSON - a merchant from Warsaw. This diary included notes on weather and was damaged in 1944 in the Krasiński's Library in Warsaw.

There are perhaps other manuscripts with information about the weather, e.g. RACIBORSKI's notebook from 1797 discovered in the State Archive Registry in Cracow.

Since historical weather chronicles are fragmentary and regionally scattered, one can use them only for some parts of Europe. As for Poland, studies of this kind are being prepared for the region of Cracow.

3. Historical records

The historical written sources (chronicles or documents) are much richer in information about hydro-atmospherical phenomena. Though being fragmentary, they can give - if combined - an interesting picture of several regions (HENNIG, 1904). Much information from these sources is, however, not exact and sometimes even fantastic but their critical choice and analysis in comparison to geological, geomorphological, botanical, and archaeological data could provide valuable information concerning the hydrography and climate of the last millennium.

At the Congress of Directors of Meteorological Services in Innsbruck in 1905 (CLOUZOT, 1907) it was suggested that the countries belonging to the International Meteorological Organisation should undertake investigations to gather information about unusual and catastrophic meteorological and hydrological events, e.g. inundations, floods, rigorous winters, strong tempests etc. This proposal has been, however, realised in different ways (SEMKOWICZ, 1922). Several historians have simply added this subject to their research questionnaires. But there were also works written by non-specialists, more or less dilettantes, and this is why several elaborations are only faulty compilations, without any data about the source of information. There are, however, some important works connected with this initiative of 1905: "Einige Bemerkungen über das Klima der historischen Zeit", by NORLIND (1914) and "Elementarereignisse in Gebieten Deutschlands", by WEISS (1914), including data sources up to 1900. It seems that some other books edited after the First World War are a result of the same initiative: "Chronique des événements météorologiques en Belgique jusqu'en 1838", by the Belgian meteorologist VANDERLINDEN (1924) and "Les hivers dans l'Europe occidentale" by the Dutch meteorologist EASTON (1928). With the same set of works the elaboration by POLACZKÓWNA (1925) should be ranked, concerning historical references in the Polish descriptive documents on the climatic-meteorological changes in the Middle Ages. The initiator of this work, ROMER (1962) - the author of valuable dissertations concerning climatology - wanted to introduce historical data to the scientific equipment of Polish climatology. The specifications carried out by POLACZKÓWNA are waiting to be completed and interpreted on the basis of this broadening scientific background. The same applies to later works by ALEXANDRE (1987).

The study "Quellentexte zur Witterungsgeschichte Europas von der Zeitwende bis zum Jahre 1850", by WEIKINN (1958), edited after the Second World War in Berlin, has the same aim. The first part of this work deals with hydrography and consists of four volumes: the first of them gives information from the written documents and elaborations up till 1500, the second volume the data from the period 1501-1600, the third data from 1601-

1700, and in the last volume there are sources for the years 1701-1750. With this work a series "Quellensammlung zur Hydrogaphie und Meteorologie" has started, edited by the Deutsche Akademie der Wissenschaften zu Berlin (Institut für Physikalische Hydrographie). For Polish readers, and especially for Polish students of geography, an extract from this book has been compiled and completed with Polish studies by ROJECKI (1965). The utility of this issue for historians will be tested in the course of research work focussing on different regions. It seems that only the confrontation between narrative references and the whole context of sources could provide an exact picture of climatic changes in a given region. Whereas the narrative sources only concern specific climatic events but do not refer to constant and systematic changes, the file sources sometimes can give - in my opinion - a much more complete picture of changes in a relatively small territory.

Other guide-lines in the studies of climate and climatic changes in historical times can be observed in the nineteenth century's economic-historical research. The problems of climatic changes and the disasters connected with them were pointed out mainly in the works of German economic historians at the end of the nineteenth century. Among others should be mentioned: LAMPRECHT (1886), who gives a chronicle of disasters in the Mosel region; SCHULTZ (1889), who deals - among other things - with climatic changes between 1110-1295; and CURSCHMANN (1900), who includes the climatic changes up to the fourteenth century in his study of famines in the Middle Ages.

Studies undertaken by BUJAK constituted an important continuation of the research on the problems of disasters on Polish territory. In his lecture "Remarks concerning the necessities of economic history" (edited in 1918), he pointed to the indispensability of elaborating disaster chronicles as an auxiliary medium to economic historical research. Some years later he succeeded in including into this work some other persons: WALAWENDER (1932) to elaborate the chronicle of disasters in 1450-1586; WERHACKI (1938) for the period 1587-1648; NAMACZYŃSKA (1937) for the period 1649-1700, and SZEWCZUK (1938) for the period 1772-1848. The preceding period concerning the Polish Middle Ages has not been elaborated separately, because of POLACZKÓWNA's work, edited in Lvóv in 1925. Also in BUJAK's opinion the data base for this period in Poland was too fragmentary to create such a chronicle which could be an additional source. In his work WALAWENDER collected an enormous amount of material from descriptive sources and POLACZKÓWNA's publication is used as a background for climatic studies in Poland in the Middle Ages.

There are two especially important approaches aiming at the elaboration of general problems of Medieval climate which were published in the interwar period. One of these approaches was carried out by the historian SEMKOWICZ (1922) and the second by the archaeologist SULIMIRSKI (1934). Although it would be difficult to completely accept their results they undoubtedly made a big step forward in assessing the history of climate, the methods used in its investigation, and in summarizing the contemporary state of research. Both these attempts were important achievements towards a European level of science in that epoch. And even today, in spite of criticism, they have not been replaced by any better work. On the basis of geographical investigations both authors rightly pointed to the difficulties resulting from the location of Polish territories between two climatic zones: the Atlantic and the Continental zone. An attempt to reconcile and to combine information concerning this climatic transitional zone is supposed to make the presentation of its picture for both authors difficult. It seems that climate research in its historical development should not be based on state territorial boundaries but rather on limits of physiographical regions, e.g. the European Lowland, the Baltic or Subcarpathian regions etc.

The research of climate history during the last thirty years (BUCZEK, 1960; BEAUJOUAN, 1968) undoubtedly comprises a separate chapter for representatives of exact sciences as well as for humanists interested in climatic problems: historians and archaeologists. It is necessary to emphasize here that some attempts of comprehensive presentation of climatic changes during the last millennium made by French (LE ROY LADURIE, 1983) or Swedish historians (UTTERSTRÖM, 1955) are interesting but need to be treated with care. New perspectives of historical climate research have been opened up by particular disciplines introducing their own methods of investigation. Among the most interesting approaches are the investigations of the team "Spectrum of Time", managed by the English astronomer SCHOVE (1955), and the works of Dutch geographers (e.g. BAKKER, 1958), introducing the methods of physical geography and geology to historical geography. Interesting attempts of palaeobotanists trying to reconstruct the natural environment and climate on the basis of pollen analyses (MAMAKOWA, 1966; OLDFIELD, 1983) should be ranked here.

It seems that these new methods and the sometimes scant written sources should, for the study of Medieval settlement groups, be used selectively: the results obtained for these microregions (e.g. BAKKER's results for the Netherlands and the investigations of BOHÁČ for Bohemia) could be a basis for further generalisations. Otherwise they lead to premature general statements as we can see in the interesting articles by LE ROY LADURIE (1959, 1979) or by UTTERSTRÖM (1955) and, most of all, in the studies of OLAGÜE (1963), which are sometimes past the bounds of reality. The studies on climate and hydrological conditions of selected regions during the Subatlantic period and especially the last millennium should also be closely connected with our knowledge about the settlement processes in the given region, because these processes point to changes in hydrography which indirectly testify the climate (cp. FLOHN, 1968, for Germany; KURNATOWSKI & WISLAŃSKI, 1966, for Poland; PFISTER, 1984, for Switzerland). This long and laborious way of assessing the climatic fluctuations in the Holocene through settlement studies and by using the results of palaeogeographical research seems, however, to be the only one known today and a reliable way of grasping approximately the hydrographic and climatic changes in Europe before the fourteenth century (DUNIN-WĄSOWICZ, 1974, 1975, 1984; TYSZKIEWICZ, 1981).

References

ALEXANDRE, P. (1987): Le climat en Europe au Moyen Age. Contribution à l'histoire des variations climatiques de 1000 à 1425, d'après les sources narratives de l'Europe occidentale. Ecole des Hautes Etudes en Sciences Sociales, Paris, 827 p.

BAKKER, J. P. (1958): The Significance of Physical Geography and Pedology for Historical Geography in the Netherlands. Tijdschr. Econ. Soc. Geogr. 10/11

BEAUJOUAN, G. (1968): Le temps historique. In: L'histoire et ses méthodes. 52-57, Paris

BERG, L. (1914): Das Problem der Klimawanderung in geschichtlicher Zeit. Geographische Abhandlungen 10/2

BROOKS, C. E. P. (1950): Climate through the Ages. A study of the climatic factors and their variations. London

BRÜCKNER, E. (1912): Klimaschwankungen und Völkerwanderung. Almanach der Wiener Akademie der Wissenschaften, Wien

BOHÁČ, Z. (1988): Historical-ecological aspects of the Bohemian Feudal State Economy. Historical Ecology I, Praha, 11-59

BUCZEK, K. (1960): Ziemie polskie przed tysiącem lat (Polish Territories Thousand Years Ago). Wrocław

BUJAK, F. (1918): Uwagi o potrzebach historii gospodarczej (Remarks Concerning the Necessities of Economic History). In: Nauka polska, jej potrzeby, organizacja i rozwój (Polish Science, its Needs, Organisation and Development), Vol. 1, 275-286

CLOUZOT, E. (1907): Histoire et Météorologie. Bull. Hist. Phil. Com. Trav. Hist. Sci. 117-175

CURSCHMANN, F. (1900): Hungersnöte im Mittelalter. Leipzig

CZŁOWIEK i środowisko w pradziejach (Man and Environment in Prehistory) 1983, Warszawa

DUNIN-WĄSOWICZ, T. (1974): Zmiany w topografii osadnictwa wielkich dolin na niżu środkowoeuropejskim w XIII wieku (Changes in the Topography of the Settlement of the Big River Valleys on the Central European Lowland in the 13th c.). Wrocław

DUNIN-WĄSOWICZ, T. (1975): Climate as a factor affecting the human environment in the Middle Ages. J. Eur. Econ. Hist. 4/3, 691-706

DUNIN-WĄSOWICZ, T. (1984): L'Environnement et l'habitat: la rupture d'équilibre du XIIIe siècle dans la grande plaine européenne. Annales E.S.C. 35, 1026-1045

EASTON, C. (1928): Les hivers dans l'Europe occidentale. Leyden

FLOHN, H. (1968): Le temps et le climat. Paris

HENNIG, R. (1904): Katalog bemerkenswerter Witterungsereignisse von den ältesten Zeiten bis zum Jahre 1800. Abh. Königl. Preuß. Meteorol. Inst. 2/4, Berlin

KURNATOWSKI, S. & WISLAŃSKI, T. (1966): Rola archeologii w badaniach historyczno-przyrodniczych nad przemianami środowiska geografiznego (The part of archaeology in historic-natural research of changes of natural environment). Studia z dziejów gospodarstwa wiejskiego 8, 49-55

LAMB, H. H. (1982): Climate, history and the modern world. London

LAMPRECHT, K. (1886): Deutsches Wirtschaftsleben im Mittelalter. Leipzig

LE ROY LADURIE, E. (1959): Histoire et climat. Annales E.S.C. 14, 3-34

LE ROY LADURIE, E. (1970): Pour une histoire de l'environnement: la part du climat. Annales E.S.C. 25, 1459-1470

LE ROY LADURIE, E. (1983): Histoire du climat depuis l'an Mil. Paris

MAMAKOWA, K. (1969): Postęp badań nad wpływem osadnictwa prehistorycznego na szatę roślinną (Progress in Research of the Prehistoric Settlement Influences on the Vegetation). Archeologia Polski 11/1, 107-115

NAMACZYŃSKA, S. (1937): Kronika klęsk elementarnych w Polsce i w krajach sąsiednich w latach 1649-1696 (Chronicle of Disasters in Poland and in Neighboring Countries in the Years 1649-1696). Lwów

NORLIND, A. (1914): Einige Bemerkungen über das Klima der historischen Zeit. Leipzig

OLAGÜE, I. (1963): Les changements de climat dans l'histoire. Cah. Hist. Mond. 7/3, 637-674

OLDFIELD, F.; BATTARBEE, R. W. & DEARING, J. A. (1983): New approaches to recent environmental change. Geogr. J. 149/2, 167-181

PEDELABORDE, P. (1957): Le climat du bassin parisien. Essai d'une méthode naturelle de climatologie physique. Paris

PFISTER, C. (1984): Klimageschichte der Schweiz 1525-1860. Das Klima der Schweiz von 1525-1860 und seine Bedeutung in der Geschichte von Bevölkerung und Landwirtschaft, 2 vols. Bern, 3rd. ed. 1988

POLACZKÓWNA, M. (1925): Wahania klimatyczne w Polsce w wiekach średnich (Climatic Fluctuations in Poland in the Middle Ages). Prace Geogr. Wyd. przez Prof. E. Romera, Lwów, 1-80

ROJECKI, A. (1956): O najdawiejszych obserwacjaxch meteorologicznych na ziemiach polskich (The Most Ancient Meteorological Observations on Polish Territories). Przegl. Geograf. 1/9, No. 3/4

ROMER, E. (1962): Wybór prac. Selected Papers. Vol. II, Warszawa

SCHOVE, D. J. (1955): The Sunspot Cycle, 649 B.C. to A.D. 2000. J. Geophys. Res. 60, 127-146

SCHULTZ, A. (1889): Das höfische Leben zur Zeit der Minnesänger. Leipzig

SEMKOWICZ, W. (1922): Zagadnienie klimatu w czasach historycznych (The problem of climate in historical times). Prz. Geogr. 3, 18-42

SULIMIRSKI, T. (1934): Osadnictwo i ruchy etniczne a klimat (Settlement, ethnic migrations and climate). Roczniki Dziejów Społecznych i Gospodarczych 3, 1-56

SZEWCZUK, J. (1938): Kronika klęsk elementarnych w Galicji (Chronicle of disasters in Galicia), 1772-1848. Lwów

TYSZKIEWICZ, J. (1981): Człowiek w środowisku geograficznym Polski średniowiecznej (Man in his environment in Medieval Poland). Warszawa

UTTERSTRÖM, G. (1955): Climatic fluctuations and population problems in early modern history. Scand. Econ. Hist. Rev. 3/1, 3-47

VANDERLINDEN, E. (1924): Chronique des événements météorologiques en Belgique jusqu'en 1834. Mém. Acad. Roy. Belg. VI/1

WALAWENDER, A. (1932): Kronika klęsk elementarnych w Polsce i w krajach sąsiednich w l. 1450-1586. T. 1: Zjawiska meteorologiczne i pomory. (Chronicle of disasters in Poland and in neighbouring countries in the years 1450- 1586, Vol. 1: Meteorological events and epidemics.) Lwów

WEIKINN, C. (1958): Quellentexte zur Witterungsgeschichte Europas von der Zeitwende bis zum Jahre 1850. Hydrographie 1, Berlin

WEISS, J. (1914): Elementarereignisse im Gebiete Deutschlands. Wien

WERHACKI, R. (1938): Klęski elementarne w Polsce w latach 1587-1647, cz. I: Zjawiska meteorologiczne, stan urodzajów i pomory (Disasters in Poland in 1587-1647, Part I: Meteorological events, harvest states and epidemics). Spraw. Tow. Nauk. 18/3, Lwów

WYJĄTKI ze źródeł historycznych o nadzwyczajnych zjawiskach hydrologiczno-meteorologicznych na ziemiach polskich w wiekach od X-XVI (Extracts from historical sources concerning the extraordinary hydrological and meteorological phenomena on Polish territories in the 10th-16th centuries). Selected and translated into Polish by Ryszard Girgus and Witold Strupczewski, with introduction and management of Ananiasz Rojecki (1965), Warszawa

WORLD Climate from 800 to 0 B.C. (1966) Proc. Int. Symp. held at Imperial College, London 18 and 29 April 1966, London

Address of the author:

Prof. Dr. T. Dunin-Wąsowicz, Institute of the History of Material Culture, Polish Academy of Sciences, Świerczewskiego 105, PL-00-140 Warsaw, Poland

Latin epigraphy and environment: a proposal for an investigation

Marco P. Pavese

Summary

For studies of the history of the environment epigraphic material can be useful both for checking the reliability of and for completing the data series provided by other sources. Unlike the information related to the Nile or to the Chinese carved oracle bones, the wealth of the Latin epigraphs does not seem to have ever been suitably scanned and interpreted from the climatological and environmentological viewpoint. Though these epigraphs do not provide a continuous and homogeneous record either in time or space (i.e. only a few and sporadic events are reported), the intrinsic reliability of such information is considerably higher than that of literary sources. Therefore, it appears worthwhile to scan the large amount of published inscriptions and to search for those epigraphs which contain some information on the environment. As for methodological aspects, the current methods of epigraphical research can be applied. A few interesting examples of Latin inscriptions are presented in the following.

Zusammenfassung

Epigraphisches Material kann für die Erforschung der Umweltgeschichte von großem Nutzen sein, und zwar sowohl im Hinblick auf die Ergänzung von Datenreihen aus anderen Quellen als auch in bezug auf deren quellenkritische Überprüfung. Im Gegensatz zu den Aufzeichnungen aus dem Niltal und den chinesischen Orakelknochen scheinen die lateinischen Inschriften niemals kritisch gesichtet oder unter klimatologischen bzw. umweltgeschichtlichen Gesichtspunkten ausgewertet worden zu sein. Obwohl die Inschriften weder eine räumlich noch zeitlich lückenlose Dokumentation ermöglichen (nur wenige und vereinzelte Ereignisse wurden festgehalten), ist die Verläßlichkeit der hieraus abgeleiteten Information deutlich größer als die der literarischen Quellen. Aus diesem Grunde scheint es durchaus lohnend zu sein, die große Zahl der veröffentlichten Inschriften kritisch zu sichten und systematisch nach klima- bzw. umweltrelevanten Inschriften zu suchen. Die Untersuchungsmethoden können hierbei problemlos aus dem Bereich der Inschriftenkunde übernommen werden. Einige interessante Beispiele lateinischer Inschriften werden im folgenden vorgestellt.

The environmental and geophysical phenomena of the Ancient World are not as well investigated as those of Medieval and modern times, although some studies do exist on the climate of ancient times and on its influences on mankind (e.g. CARPENTER, 1966; WRIGHT, 1968; MCGHEE, 1981; SHAW, 1981; DESANGES, 1986; FREI STOLBA, 1987). Several differences distinguish the studies concerning the environment of Antiquity from those on the later historical periods. A very important aspect deals with the source availability and the specific methods needed to use them (INGRAM et al., 1981; RABB, 1983). Other differences are related to this one. Archaeological evidence and the literary works by Greek and Latin writers certainly represent the most important data source on ancient geophysical and environmental phenomena. But, unlike for the later periods (with the important exception of Egypt and its papyrus documentation), there are relatively few documents available for checking and comparing with the literary sources the reliability of which is often debated by historians and philologists.

A different and independent source able to provide specific information useful for the study of the geophysical phenomena in Antiquity are ancient inscriptions. These epigraphic materials can be considered as a viable and reliable source of the history of the environment (INGRAM et al., 1981), both in view of the search for completeness, and of checking the information's reliability. Unlike the information related to the Nile (BELL, 1970, 1971) and to the Chinese climate (CHU PING-LAI, 1968; CHU KO-CHEN, 1973), the wealth of Latin epigraphs does not seem to have ever been adequately scanned and interpreted from the climatological and environmentological viewpoint, with a few exceptions (BURNAND, 1984; GUIDOBONI, 1989). Information derived from epigraphs cannot be expected to provide a continuous and homogeneous record either in time or space, as only some sporadic events are reported. Nevertheless, with regard to its high reliability, such information constitutes an important reference-point for all other investigations. Useful data can be provided by almost every kind of Latin inscriptions. The various categories, according to the standard definitions by epigraphists' classification (CALABI LIMENTANI, 1973), are as follows:

Kind of inscriptions	Kind of data potentially related to geophysics and environment
Religious inscriptions	Forms of worship devoted to natural phenomena and their catastrophic manifestations (e.g. PIETRANGELI, 1951, concerning thunderbolt inscriptions, and ALFÖLDI, 1989, concerning an eclipse)
Tomb and honorary inscriptions	Professional activities or offices of the dead. E.g. *curatores alvei Tiberis et riparum* (LE GALL, 1953)

Public buildings records	Construction, and in particular restoration due to damages caused by natural disasters (BURNAND, 1984; LEPELLEY, 1984; see below)
Juridical epigraphy	Laws and decrees; documents on public administration; deeds among privates (e.g. *CIL* XI, 1147 = *ILS* 6675 concerning land property increased by alluvial accumulation).
Fasti and calendars	Exceptional events. E.g. *Fasti Ostienses (II* XIII, 1, 207 = VIDMAN, 1982: 51; see below)

To show the potential usefulness of Latin epigraphy for geophysical and environmental studies, a few examples are presented. The text of two twin inscriptions found in the south of the Roman province of Numidia (Africa), at a site named *Ad Maiores (Oasis Nigrensium Maiorum)* in Antiquity and subsequently Besseriani-Negrîn, is as follows *(CIL* VIII, 2480-2481 = 17970, following in particular n. 2481 for a few differences between the two versions):

Pro salute d(ominorum) n(ostrorum duorum) [- - - ar]cu[m ex HS - - - m(ilibus)] n(ummum) hoc [loco muni]cipio n(ostro), / quem Clodius Victor, Pomponius Macia[nus ob honorem duovi]ratus promiser[ant post terra]e mo[tum, quod patriae Paterno e[t] Arcesilao co(n)s(ulibus) hora noc[tis (illa) somno f]essis contigit, dedi[c]ante v(iro) p(erfectissimo) Flavio Fla[vi]/ano p(raeside) n(ostro), Clodius Victor f(ilius), Flavius Paulinianus f(ilius) fecerunt, curante [C]occeio Donatiano [e(quite)] R(omano) c(uratore) reip(ublicae).

Translation: "For good health of our two emperors... the arch that Clodius Victor and Pomponius Macianus had promised for the honour of their office after the earthquake that, in the year in which Paternus and Arcesilaus were consuls in Rome, in the... hour of the night befell on the tired persons who were sleeping, was built in this place of our town by Clodius Victor son, Flavius Paulinianus son, with... thousands sesterces; Flavius Flavianus, *vir perfectissimus*, our governor, dedicated it being curator Cocceius Donatianus, *eques Romanus, curator reipublicae*".

This inscription bears testimony to an earthquake which occurred in Roman Numidia; the consular dating allows us to assign the occurrence of the event to the year 267 A.D. (*CIL* VIII, sub 2480-2481, cfr. *PIR*, III 15, 116). As pointed out earlier, Latin epigraphy can effectively contribute to the study of the ancient seismic phenomena, both by referring to evidences directly mentioning earthquakes, and by exploiting indirect sources which generally refer to reconstructions of buildings; by using such data sources it is sometimes possible to get hints at the extension and the intensity of the earthquake (LEPELLEY, 1984; BURNAND, 1984; GUIDOBONI, 1989).

On other occasions, a Latin inscription can provide information on river floods. This is the case of *CIL* VIII, 2661 = *ILS* 5788, found at *Lambaesis*, later Lambèse, in the Roman Numidia:

Aquam Titulensem, quam ante annos / plurimos Lambaesitana civitas in/terverso ductu vi torrentis amiserat, / perforato monte, instituto etiam a / solo novo ductu, Severinius Apronianus v(ir) p(erfectissimus), p(raeses) p(rovinciae) N(umidiae), pat(ronus) col(oniae), restituit, cur(ante) Aelio Rufo v(iro) e(gregio), fl(amine) p(er)p(etuo), cur(atore) r(ei) p(ublicae).

Translation: "Severinius Apronianus, *vir perfectissimus*, governor of the province of Numidia, patron of the colony, with the curatorship of Aelius Rufus, *vir egregius, flamen perpetuus, curator reipublicae*, after having tunnelled the mountain and rebuilt a new conduit over the ground, restored the *Titulensis* aqueduct that several years earlier the people of *Lambaesis* had lost owing to the rush of the torrent that diverted the previous conduit".

From this text it is possible to infer that the ancient town of *Lambaesis* suffered from the rush of a torrent (which is likely to be what was subsequently named Oued-Tazzout or also Oued-Batna supérieur) that once was strong enough to divert the conduit of the aqueduct. The dating of the event is not punctual, but we know that Severinius Apronianus, governor of the Roman province of Numidia, was active from 276 to 282 A.D. (*PLRE*, I, p. 87, Apronianus 7) and the expression *ante annos plurimos* can perhaps refer to the first half of the third century.

Sometimes other inscriptions give additional information about events already known from other sources. According to the *SHA* (Ant. 9: *fuit et inundatio Tiberis*, maybe coincident with M. Aur. 8: *sed interpellavit istam felicitatem securitatemque imperatoris prima Tiberis inundatio quae sub illis gravissima fuit*; LE GALL, 1953: 29) a severe Tiber flood occurred during the princedom of Antoninus Pius, without any further chronological specification. A line of the *Fasti Ostienses* (*II*, XIII, 1, 207 = VIDMAN, 1982: 51) which are a list of magistrates and of important events found at Ostia, close to Rome, allows to assess the date of the inundation. In fact, after the names of the consuls of 147 A.D. the following sentence is reported:

[-]X K. April. aqua magna fuit

Besides the year, the epigraph reveals also that the flood occurred in the month of March, on a day which the gap at the beginning of the line allows to indicate close to the 23rd (cp. also LE GALL, 1953: 30).

The last example concerns an environmental datum. A long inscription of *Thugga* in the Roman *Africa Proconsularis* (*CIL* VIII, 26517 = *ILS*, 6797) dated between January 25th (48 A.D.) and January 24th (49 A.D.) mentions, with reference to the career of a magistrate of the town, a previous position of office. In some readings of the text it was proposed to be *IIvir cur(iae) Lucusiae* (HOMO, 1899) or *IIvir, cur(ator) Lucusiae* (SESTON, 1967), which was thought to indicate an office related to a town named Lucusia. In a more recent study, however, the reading *cur(ator) lucustae* already accepted in the *CIL* has been confirmed. Such an interpretation is in agreement with the literary sources which refer to the frequent invasions of migratory locusts into Roman Africa. This provides a geographical and chronological reference for the study of such a kind of events (DESANGES, 1976).

These few examples are sufficient to illustrate the potential importance of epigraphic sources to the history of environmental and geophysical phenomena. Therefore, it appears worthwhile to attempt a scanning of the large amount of published inscriptions, and to search for all epigraphs containing relevant environmental data. The methodological aspects should not present particular difficulties, since standard procedures already used for current epigraphical research can be safely adopted.

Acknowledgements

The author is very grateful to Professor P. A. Février of the University of Aix-en-Provence for having called the attention on *CIL* VIII, 26517; to Professor G. Mennella of the University of Genova for his relevant comments and suggestions; and to Viva Banzon for her careful reading and English editing of the paper. This investigation has been accomplished in partial fulfilment both of a research grant from a CEE program on climatology, and of the Strategic Program by the Italian C.N.R. on "Climate and Environment in Southern Italy". This activity was also performed in the framework of an ESF program on the history of climate in Europe.

Acronyms

CIL = *Corpus inscriptionum Latinarum* consilio et auctoritate academiae litterarum Borussicae editum, Berolini
  Vol. VIII, *Inscriptiones Africae Latinae. Pars I, Inscriptiones Africae Proconsularis et Numidiae*, coll. G. WILLMANS, ed. T. MOMMSEN 1881 (1960). *Supplementi pars I, Inscriptiones Africae Proconsularis*, edd. R. Cagnat, I. Schmidt, 1891
  Vol. XI, *Inscriptiones Aemiliae, Etruriae, Umbriae, Latinae*, ed. E. Bormann. *Pars I, Inscriptiones Aemiliae et Etruriae comprehendens*, 1888 (1966)
II = *Inscriptiones Italiae*, Academiae Italiae consociatae ediderunt, Roma. Vol. XIII, *Fasti et elogia; Fasciculus I, Fasti consulares et triumphales*, cur. A. Degrassi, 1947
ILS = *Inscriptiones Latinae selectae*, ed. H. Dessau, Berolini 1892-1916

PIR = Prosopographia imperii Romani saeculi I, II, III, vol. III, consilio et auctoritate
academiae scientiarum regiae Borussicae, edd. P. de Rhoden et H. Dessau, Berolini
1898

PLRE = A. H. M. JONES, J. R. MARTINDALE, J. MORRIS, The Prosopography of the later
Roman Empire. Vol. I: A.D. 260-395, Cambridge 1971

SHA = Scriptores Historiae Augustae, ed. E. Hohl, Leipzig, Teubner, 1927; add. et corr.
C. Samberger - W. Seyfarth, *ibid.*, 1965

References

ALFÖLDI, G. (1989): Epigraphische Notizen aus Italien III: Inschriften aus Nursia (Norcia).
Z.. Papyr. Epigraph. 77, 155-180, in particular 161-167

BELL, B. (1970): The oldest records of the Nile floods. Geogr. J. 136, 569-73

BELL, B. (1971): The Dark Ages in ancient history. I. The First Dark Age in Egypt. Am. J.
Archaeol. 75, 1-26

BURNAND, Y. (1984): Terrae motus. La documentation épigraphique sur les tremblements
de terre dans l'occident romain. In: Helly, B. & Pollino, A. (eds.) (1984): Tremblements
de terre; histoire et archéologie. IVᵉˢ Renc. Int. Arch. Hist. d'Antibes (2-4 novembre
1983, Association pour la promotion et la diffusion des connaissances archéologiques),
Valbonne, 173-182

CALABI LIMENTANI, I. (1973): Epigrafia Latina. 3ʳᵈ ed., Cisalpino-Goliardica, Milano,
550 p.

CARPENTER, R. (1966): Discontinuity in Greek Civilisation. Cambridge Univ. Press, Cambridge

CHU KO-CHEN, (1973): A preliminary study on the climatic fluctuations during the last
5000 years in China. Scientia Sinica 16, 226-256

CHU PING-LAI, (1968): Climate of China, English language version. 2ⁿᵈ ed., Washington,
DC, US Department of Commerce, 621 p.

DESANGES, J. (1976): Un curateur de la sauterelle sur la pertica de Carthage en 48-49 de
notre ère. Eos 64, 281-286

DESANGES, J. (1986): De Timée à Strabon, la polémique sur le climat de l'Afrique du Nord
et ses effects. Histoire et Archéologie de l'Afrique du Nord, Actes du IIIᵉ Coll. Int. Paris
C.T.H.S., 27-34

FREI STOLBA, R. (1987): Klimadaten aus der Römischen Republik. Mus. Helv. 44, 101-117

GUIDOBONI, E. (1989): I terremoti prima del mille in Italia e nell'area mediterranea.
Bologna

HOMO, L. (1899): Les suffètes de Thugga, d'après une inscription récemment découverte.
Mélanges de l'Ecole Française de Rome 19, 297-306

INGRAM, M. J.; UNDERHILL, D. J. & FARMER, G. (1981): The use of documentary sources
for the study of past climates. In: Wigley, T. M. L.; Ingram, M. J. & Farmer, G. (eds.)
(1981): Climate and history. Cambridge Univ. Press, Cambridge, 180-213

LE GALL, J. (1953): Le Tibre, fleuve de Rome dans l'Antiquité. Presses Universitaires de France, Paris, 367 p.

LEPELLEY, C. (1984): L'Afrique du Nord et le séisme du 21 juillet 365: remarques métho-dologiques et critiques. In: Helly, B. & Pollino, A. (eds.) (1984): Tremblements de terre; histoire et archéologie. IVes Renc. Int. Arch. Hist. d'Antibes (2-4 novembre 1983, Association pour la promotion et la diffusion des connaissances archéologiques), Val-bonne, 199-206

MCGHEE, R. (1981): Archaeological evidence for climatic change during the last 5000 years. In: Wigley, T. M. L.; Ingram, M. J. & Farmer, G. (eds.) (1981): Climate and his-tory. Cambridge Univ. Press, Cambridge, 162-179

PIETRANGELI, C. (1951). Bidentalia. Atti della Pontificia Accademia Romana di Archeo-logia. Ser. III, Rendiconti 25-26, 37-51

RABB, T. (1983): Bibliography to accompany "Climate and society in history": A research agenda. In: Chen, R. S.; Boulding, E. & Schneider, S. H. (eds.) (1983): Social science research and climatic change. D. Reidel Publ. Comp., Dordrecht, 77-114

SESTON, W. (1967): Des "portes" de Thugga à la "Constitution" de Carthage. Rev. Hist. 237, 227-237

SHAW, B. D. (1981): Climate, environment, and history: the case of Roman North Africa. In: Wigley, T. M. L.; Ingram, M. J. & Farmer, G. (eds.) (1981): Climate and history. Studies in past climates and their impact on man. Cambridge Univ. Press, Cambridge, 379-403

VIDMAN, L. (1982): Fasti Ostienses. Acad. Sci. Bohem., Pragae, 163 p.

WRIGHT, H. E. Jr. (1968): Climatic change in Mycenaean Greece. Antiquity 42, 123-7

Address of the author:

Dr. M. Pavese, I.F.A., C.N.R., Istituto di Fisica dell'Atmosfera, p.le L. Sturzo 31, I-00144 Roma, Italy

The Byzantine sources as documentary evidence for the reconstruction of historical climate

Ioannis Telelis & Evangelos Chrysos

Summary

This paper presents an attempt to evaluate the significance of the Byzantine historical sources to historical climatology and the potential contribution of climatological evidence from these sources to the reconstruction of the Medieval climate of the Eastern Mediterranean basin. A net of methodological observations on the difficulties inherent in the various types of the narrative sources and the trustworthiness of the climatological information deriving from them, is generally outlined as it arises from the *corpus* of information developed by a research project still in progress at the University of Ioannina. The historical and philological efforts necessary to approach in a scientific way climatological evidence from the Byzantine sources are demonstrated by an example: in the winter 763/64 A.D. the Black Sea froze and big ice-drifts covered the surface of the Bosphorus, up to the Marmara Sea. This extraordinary meteorological phenomenon is documented by contemporary and Later Byzantine chronographers whose trustworthiness is tested and correlated with accounts from Latin annals and chronicles of the same and later periods.

Zusammenfassung

In diesem Beitrag wird versucht, die Bedeutung der Byzantinischen Quellen für die historische Klimaforschung und für die Rekonstruktion des mittelalterlichen Klimas im östlichen Mittelmeerraum darzustellen. Im Rahmen eines an der Universität von Ioannina gegenwärtig laufenden Forschungsprojektes konnten wertvolle Informationen über die zahlreichen methodischen Probleme, die mit der Auswertung überlieferter Quellen verbunden sind, und über die Verläßlichkeit der daraus abgeleiteten Klimainformationen gewonnen werden. Die bei der wissenschaftlichen Auswertung der Byzantinischen Quellen in bezug auf die darin enthaltene Klimainformation gebotene, sorgfältige Anwendung historischer und philologischer Methoden wird anhand eines Beispieles verdeutlicht: Im Winter 763/64 A.D. froren Teile des Schwarzen Meeres zu und mächtige Eisschollen trieben durch den Bosporus bis ins Marmarameer. Dieses bemerkenswerte meteorologische Phänomen wurde durch zeitgenössische und spätbyzantinische Chronisten beschrieben. Die Verläßlichkeit dieser Berichte wurde getestet, indem sie mit zeitgenössischen und späteren lateinischen Annalen und Chroniken verglichen wurden.

1. Introduction

In the flourishing international cooperation for the reconstruction of the European climate in historical times (ALEXANDRE, 1987; PFISTER, 1988), there has so far been no serious attempt for making use of the information hidden in Greek Medieval historical sources. Only sporadic evidence has been available to scholars from the time of NEUMANN & PARTSCH (1885) and the less known Russian geographer, count of TCHICHATCHEF (1864), and to later compilers such as EASTON (1928), HENNING (1904) or WEIKINN (1958), who usually repeat each other without studying the evidence itself. The reason for this is, of course, to be found in the Medieval expression "Graeca sunt non leguntur" or in its American version: "it's Greek to me"!

In 1987 D. METAXAS, the meteorologist at the University of Ioannina, joined a European community project (contract EV-0028-GR/TT) on "The reconstruction of past Mediterranean climate in historical time". His interest to close the just mentioned gap in climatological scholarship with his contribution to the project caused him to seek the cooperation of the Historical Department at the same University. In this department, though we had so far no experience in this type of research, we accepted his proposal for the following reasons:

(a) an increasing awareness of the climatological problems of our times (greenhouse effect etc.) and the wish or the obligation to support any attempt tackling these problems;
(b) our expectation that through this cooperation and the attempt to reconstruct the historical climate, we may find answers to some crucial historical questions such as the ups and downs in the development of the Medieval society, the political changes, and the material culture, for which the narrative historical evidence is not sufficient for providing definite answers. For instance we lack sufficient evidence to explain the decline of the Late Antique economy and culture in the sixth century or the impressive wealth we meet in the ninth century in Eastern and Western Europe;
(c) last but not least: in many aspects historical research has reached a deadlock. After her devotion to the study of the role of personages in historical developments, due to given political patterns, *historia* as a scientific discipline turned her head towards the study of political structures, states, and statehoods. Then came MARX who demonstrated the necessity of studying the economic and social aspects influencing the historical phenomena. In the last decades we grew more interested in analyzing the position of the individual in history and studied the behaviour and the mentality of the average citizen. Now one has the feeling that we should start facing more consciously questions concerning the impact of nature on political, social and economic developments - questions we have forgotten to ask in the past.

1.1   The research project at the University of Ioannina

Responding to D. METAXAS' invitation two graduate students of the Byzantine Department (Mr. TELELIS and Mrs. MOYSIDOU) were appointed to undertake the task of reading thoroughly all the Byzantine sources from 300 to 1500 A.D. in original Greek, which promised to offer information of climatological value. The project was enlarged by asking F. NOTORA, University of Athens, to provide us with material from marginal notes in Greek manuscripts - she has made a compilation of approximately 5,000 Greek manuscript notes - and, finally, we gained the cooperation of Dr. RADICA of the Serbian Academy of Sciences at Belgrade, who has studied the Early Slavonic sources up to 1500 A.D.

Until now we have studied and excerpted around 60 large historical works, 11 church histories, 80 chronicles, 5 geographical surveys, and around 50 Saints' Lives. As a result of this effort, approximately 600 concrete pieces of meteorological and parameteorological evidence and about 700 further accounts referring to this evidence have been obtained so far.

We still have to read and study a number of sources: approximately 150 Saints' Lives and a number of collections of correspondence. We also intend to study in a special section the theoretical cosmological and agricultural treatises which, even if not providing concrete meteorological evidence, will nevertheless help to elucidate the sensitivity and knowledge of the Byzantines about the impact of nature on man in Medieval times. Due to reasons of academic discipline our team has not studied yet any documentary sources for the period after 1500 A.D. with the exception of some secondary works and compilations, although we expect that the material from this later preinstrumental period will certainly provide us with much more useful information especially for the Little Ice Age (GROVE, 1988).

Nevertheless, we hope that soon we shall be able to excerpt all other Greek sources of the Classical, Medieval and Postbyzantine times with the support of the new "Thesaurus Linguae Graecae", available as a computer programme called IBYCUS, developed at the University of California at Irving. We hope that with some hundred keywords and the proper "Find Command" all references to natural phenomena will be at our disposal thanks to a software programme called "Pandora". (This will soon be our Pandora box!)

1.2   Methodological aspects concerning documentary evidence of climatological value from the Byzantine narrative sources

As for the reconstruction of historical climate we cannot claim that the results of our research are satisfactory so far. The direct meteorological evidence providing data on changes in temperature or humidity, adequate for quantification in terms of standard meteorological variables and for constructing meteorological time series to introduce long-term fluctuations, is very scarce and fragmentary. More often we have accounts on parameteorological phenomena such as famines, epidemics etc., usually not offering any explanations about possible climatological causes. Thus, we must underline that our information does not go much beyond the general observations made by INGRAM et al. (1978: 332): "Most historical information is not so readily quantifiable in terms of meteorological variables, as the data are discontinuous, non-homogeneous, and show a marked bias towards the recording of extreme events."

Of course, there is a number of extreme individual meteorological events recorded in the Byzantine and Oriental sources. One such event, like the severe winter 763/64 A.D. is described further below. However, these extreme events belong to the category described by FARMER & WIGLEY (1983: 180): "Although individual events such as gales and thunderstorms may cause considerable damage to harvests, their effects can be very local and their severity need have no bearing on the general evolution of the climate".

Although the study of the available sources has not been completed yet, we have come to the conclusion, disappointing though not despairing as it may be, that the contribution of the Byzantine, Oriental, and Slavonic sources to the reconstruction of the European climate for the period before 1500 A.D. is not expected to be substantial but rather secondary and merely supportive to the efforts of other methods and disciplines. As a matter of fact we shall have to rely basically on the results of other sorts of proxy data research such as tree-ring evidence, pollen and sediment analysis etc. which, contrary to other parts of Europe, have not been sufficiently developed in Greece and the other Southeastern European and Middle East countries.

With regard to our documentary evidence, for a reliable use of our information we have to overcome some difficulties inherent in the type of the sources providing them. The Byzantine narrative sources belong actually to three different literary genres (HUNGER, 1978; KRUMBACHER, 1958):

(1) The actual historical writers such as AMMIANUS MARCELLINUS, ZOSIMUS, and PROCOPIUS or the later MICHAEL PSELLUS, ANNA COMNENE, or IOANNES CANTACUZENUS;
(2) the chronographers who write universal chronicles starting from the Creation of the World up to their days, such as IOANNES MALALAS (sixth century), THEOPHANES (ninth century) or IOANNES ZONARAS (twelfth century);
(3) The church historains such as EUSEBIUS, SOCRATES, EUAGRIUS or NICEPHORUS CALLISTUS XANTHOPULOS.

Because of certain norms in literary tradition of writing historical works, the authors in these three different genres obey to well established rules: the historians imitate the model of the classical Greek writers, mainly THUCYDIDES, and they are interested in demonstrating the initiatives or the deeds of their heroes who are usually their benefactors. For this reason they are less interested in describing meteorological phenomena which according to their sophisticated attitude are irrelevant to the political events they want to describe. The philological study of stereotype expressions describing meteorological phenomena such as "severe winter", "much snow" etc. may prove to be very helpful for the assessment of the trustworthiness of this sort of evidence.

More useful are the accounts offered by the chronographers. Their aim is to demonstrate the steady and powerful interference of God in the development of human history under a concrete eschatological scope. Because of this, they are more interested in recording physical phenomena (famines, epidemics, earthquakes or meteorological events) which they present as God's acts of educational punishment of His people. Opposite to what BELL & OGILVIE (1978: 333) observed concerning the western Latin Medieval universal chronographers, namely that "they were unable to distinguish fact from legend, the accurate from the erroneous, or to identify contemporary and non-contemporary sources", we must underline that the Byzantine and Oriental chronographers are usually more trustworthy and do provide some reliable information; of course, only if it is analyzed carefully. The information offered by Byzantine and some Oriental chronographers is of particular value because quite often they give us a rather accurate chronological frame on an annual basis, although they unfortunately fail to offer us more precise dates.

Some useful information is found, thirdly, in the writings of the ecclesiastical historains who stand between the political historians of the Classical type and the chronographers of the Medieval type in their aims and intentions in literacy and in exactness.

Furthermore, there existed a vast amount of Saints' Lives (*Vitae Sanctorum*) of the Byzantine Church - HALKIN (1957) counted 4,500 published Lives of Greek Saints. As a matter of fact these writings have minor importance as historical sources. Nevertheless, they are much more trustworthy when they mention physical phenomena occurring during their heroes' lives. But unfortunately, they usually offer no chronological reference to these events and this diminishes, of course, their value. However, this conclusion is not meant to support the decision of FARMER & WIGLEY (1983), who rejected *a priori* all Saints' Lives "as their composers were necessarily subject to too many distortions".

2. The winter 763/64 A.D. General description and sources' overview

One of the most astonishing meteorological phenomenon for the Black Sea, Bosphorus, and Constantinople area, occurred in 763/64 A.D.: the northern shores of the Black Sea froze and large ice-drifts moved towards the south, crossed the Bosphorus and crashed against the city walls of Constantinople, the capital of the Byzantine Empire, causing serious damage. Meanwhile the surface of the sea between the European and the Asiatic coast of the Bosphorus froze and was converted into a passable dry land. In March an exceptional period of drought allegedly followed causing the stagnation of springs and rivers.

This climatological phenomenon is documented by two of the most important Byzantine chronographers (THEOPHANES, 1883: 434-435; NICEPHORUS, 1880: 67-68), who claim to be eye-witnesses. The same event is described by eight further posterior Byzantine sources (cp. Fig. 1 for a stemma of these sources and table 1 for a list of them). The winter of 763/64 is furthermore described as very severe by thirty Latin annals and chronicles (cp. table 1).

2.1   Classification of the historical sources

The historical sources providing us with information about this meteorological event can be classified as following, according to the philological genre they belong to, the probable comtemporaneity of the authors to the event, and the geographical place and time in which the authors lived and wrote (INGRAM et al. 1981).

Concerning the philological genre of the sources we should mention that all sources are chronicles. This can be explained by the fact that the period of the eighth and ninth centuries in the Byzantine History is covered mainly by chronicles and Saints' Lives written in later time (KARAYANNOPULOS & WEISS, 1982: 337; HUNGER, 1978: 331).

On the other hand, we must stress the fact that only two out of a total of ten Byzantine chronicles and additionally two out of thirty Latin annals and chronicles can be designated as contemporary to the severe winter.

Such a classification of authors and sources into contemporary and later ones is of great importance because we can approach their evidence with greater or lesser "suspiciousness", taking into consideration that the later authors, as a rule, copy in a more or less faithful way the anterior sources, usually without questioning and testifying their material. Thus, the percentage of evidence rejected as deriving from later sources is high, unless they can provide us with additional information which they gained from sources lost or unknown to us. Unfortunately this did not happen in our case. Likewise, the question why later chronographers were so very interested in recording this exceptional event may be useful for our research because it indicated the impression this extraordinary event made on them.

The third parameter for the historical and philological scrutiny of our sources concerns their geographical origin: it is self-evident that a chronicle written in Constantinople (THEOPHANES, 1883: 434-435), is most trustworthy when it speaks about ice-drifts in the Bosphorus and also of extreme importance is the fact that this indigenous source harmonizes to a Latin annal originating from Central Europe (*Annales Regni Francorum*, 1950: 22), because both speak about the same winter at two very different and remote places. But let us examine our sources more closely.

2.2   The accounts of the contemporary sources

The two chronographers contemporary to the event, who offer us information through their parallel reports, are: THEOPHANES THE CONFESSOR, who was born in Constantinople in 760 and wrote his Chronicle between 810 and 814 (HUNGER, 1978: 335), NICEPHORUS, later patriarch of Constantinople, who was born in 758 and wrote his Brevarium between 775 and 787 (HUNGER, 1978: 344). Although it is accepted that the two writers did not know each other, so the probability of a mutual copying should be excluded (KRUMBACHER, 1958: 343), the resemblance in the course of their information and the fact that nothing significant differs, is changed, added or removed by THEOPHANES remains indisputable. THEOPHANES (1883: 434-435) has the following story to tell about the winter of that year:

<434> "In the same year it was bitterly cold after the beginning of October, not only in our land, but even more so to the east, west, and north. Because of the cold, the north shore of the Black Sea froze to a depth of thirty cubits a hundred miles out. This was so from Ninkhia to the Danube River, including the Kouphis, Dniester, and Dnieper Rivers, the Nekropela, and the remaining promontories all the way to Mesembria and Medeia. Since the ice and snow kept on falling, its depth increased another twenty cubits, so that the sea became dry land. It was travelled by wild men and tame beasts from Khazaria, Bulgaria, and the lands of other adjacent peoples.
By divine command, during February of the same second indiction the ice divided into a great number of mountainous chunks. The force of the wind brought them down to Daphnousia and Hieron, so that they came through the Bosphoros to the city and all the way to Propontis, Abydos, and the islands, filling every shore. We ourselves were an eye-witness and, with thirty companions, went out onto one of them and played on it. The ice-bergs had many dead animals, both wild and domestic, on them. Anyone who wanted to could travel unhindered on dry land from Sophianai to the city and from Chrysopolis to St. Mamas or Galata. One of these icebergs was dashed against the harbour of the acropolis, and shattered it. Another mammoth one smashed against the wall and badly shook it, <435> so that the houses inside trembled along with it. It broke into three pieces, which girdled the city from Magnaura to the Bosphoros, and was taller than the walls. All the city's men, women and children could not stop staring at the icebergs, then went back home lamenting and in tears, at a loss as to what to say about this phenomenon.
In March of the same year a great many stars were seen falling from the sky, so that everyone who saw them suspected this was the end of the age. There was also a bad drought, and even springs dried up." (TURTLEDOVE, 1982: 123-124).

In a few points this text is different from the parallel text of NICEPHORUS. For instance, THEOPHANES gives his own personal recollection of the severe winter, remembering that he himself with thirty of his playmates climbed on the top of one of the icebergs that had floated down the Bosphorus (THEOPHANES, 1883: 434). This detail lacks, of course, in the passage of NICEPHORUS. Another point more serious and critical for the assessment of the trustworthiness and the acceptability of the material presented by THEOPHANES, is that of the drought which in March of the next year allegedly caused the stagnation of the springs (THEOPHANES, 1883: 435).

Table 1   The sources for the severe winter 763/64 A.D.

B y z a n t i n e	L a t i n
1) *Theophanis, Chronographia*	1) *Einhardi Annales*
2) *Nicephori archiepiscopi Constantinopolitani, opuscula historica*	2) *Annales Regni Francorum*
	3) *Annales Laureshamenses*
	4) *Annales Petavianorum continuatio*
3) *Georgii Monachi, Chronicon*	5) *Annales Iuvavenses Minores*
4) *Leonis Grammatici, Chronographia*	6) *Annales Laurissenses*
	7) *Annales Laurissenses Minores*
5) *Georgii Cedreni, Historiarum Compendium*	8) *Annales Xantenses*
	9) *Annales Sancti Emmerammi*
6) *Ioannis Zonarae, Epitome Historiarum*	10) *Annales Alamanici*
	11) *Annales Mettenses*
7) *Michaelis Glyca, Annalium*	12) *Annales Breves Fuldenses Antiquissimi*
8) *Ephraemii monachi, Imperatorum et Patriarcharum*	13) *Annales Weissemburgenses*
	14) *Annales Fuldenses sive Annales Regni Francorum Orientalis ab Einhardo*
9) *Constantini Lascari, Compendium Historiarum*	15) *Annalium Tilianorum*
10) *Chronicon breve*	16) *Regionis Abbatis Prumiensis Chronicon*
	17) *Annales Sangalenses Breves*
	18) *Annales Sangalenses Maiores*
	19) *Annales ex Annalibus Iuvavenisibus Antiquis Excerpti*
	20) *Annales Altahenses Maiores*
	21) *Ekkehardi Chronicon Wirziburgense*
	22) *Annales Sancti Amandi continuatio*
	23) *Annales Sangalenses Baluzii*
	24) *Annales Laubacensium continuatio*
	25) *Annales Mellicenses*
	26) *Sigeberti Chronica*
	27) *Annalista Saxo*
	28) *Annales Hildesheimenses*
	29) *Annales Guelferbytani*
	30) *Annales Nazariani*
	31) *Lamperti Annales*

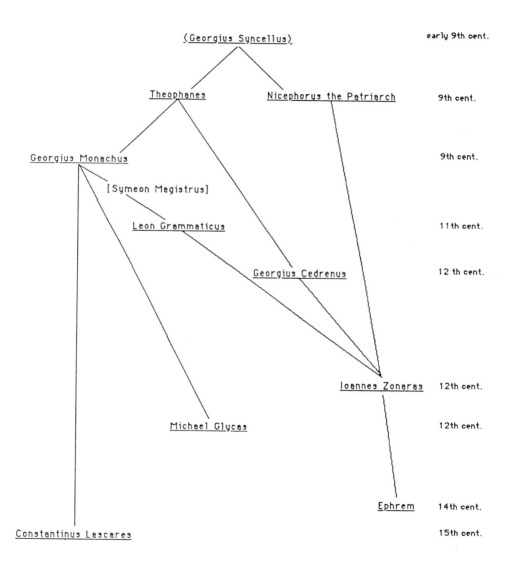

Fig. 1   Stemma of the Byzantine sources as it regards the accounts of the severe winter 763/64 A.D.

2.3   The trustworthiness of the contemporary sources. The hidden chronographer

The question is where the two chronographers could have collected their impressively identical and detailed information from. Do they both narrate some recollection of their childhood, as it is explicitly mentioned by THEOPHANES, and from which source do they supplement their material?

The key to answer these questions is hidden behind the year of birth of the two writers and in the conclusions of modern scholarship concerning the origin of the writings of THEOPHANES and NICEPHORUS and their possible common sources.

In the year of the severe winter 763/64 THEOPHANES must have been four years old and thus, it is doubtful whether a child of that age could have been allowed by his anxious mother to climb with his friends of the same age and walk on top of strange and dangerous objects such as the icebergs in front of the coasts of Constantinople (MANGO, 1978: 16). And if we accept literally THEOPHANES' personal recollection, the only answer we are able to give to the question where from he collected all those details about the geographical extent of the freezing, the dimensions of the ice or the precise depth of the snow, is that he found this information many years later, when he used some unknown oral or written sources which must have been the same as those which NICEPHORUS obviously used when he wrote his "Brevarium" (KRUMBACHER, 1958: 350; OSTROGORSKY, 1934: 2129; ALEXANDER, 1958: 159).

However, the personal recollection of the severe winter takes a new meaning if we attribute the Chronicle known as that of THEOPHANES not to THEOPHANES but to another author. Though this seems strange, it has recently been done in an absolutely persuasive and convincing way (MANGO, 1978, 1986; SPECK, 1988).

It is beyond the scope of this paper to elaborate on details about this. It should only be mentioned that a bulky dossier of notes and records - a complete chronographical material - was collected by GEORGIUS SYNCELLUS (a chronographer of the early ninth century). This material was used by NECEPHORUS, who extracted information from it and used it for the composition of this chronicle, and later it was given to THEOPHANES. It is believed now that GEORGIUS SYNCELLUS, who was close to his death in around 811, asked THEOPHANES to transcribe this dossier into a chronicle which would be the continuation of his own chronography that he expected to remain unfinished because of his imminent death. However, THEOPHANES never succeeded in making this composition. What is known as THEOPHANES' Chronography is nothing more than the text compiled by the copyist of the "archetypus" codes of his Chronography at the end of the ninth century. But no more details.

What is here interesting is the fact that the person who remembers the severe winter in THEOPHANES' passage and who stands as the author behind the relative account of NICEPHORUS is the same one: GEORGIUS SYNCELLUS.

So, the question asked about the documentary or the oral background of the evidence in the case of THEOPHANES can be transferred to that of GEORGIUS SYNCELLUS, whose trustworthiness should not be disputed, because he spent his childhood in Constantinople and we know, though not exactly, that he had used local oral and documentary evidence in order to supplement his chronographical material (HUNGER, 1978: 331 pp.)

Concerning THEOPHANES' account of the drought after March 764 A.D. (THEOPHANES, 1883: 435), we note that it sounds rather arbitrary. In his passage the drought is closely connected with a celestial phenomenon which took place shortly before and made anyone who saw it be afraid that this was the end of the age: obviously stars were seen falling from the sky; a fall of meteors.

If we consider that this account of the meteors is also found in the text of NICEPHORUS, however not related to any drought but combined with other historical events at an earlier chronological point (NICEPHORUS, 1880: 65), we can imagine that here we have to do with a false arrangement of the material on the one hand, and with the insertion of fictitious information on the other. For the author of THEOPHANES' chronicle hardly escaped from the very common motive in Byzantine chronographical writings to connect the appearance of stars, comets, and meteors to famines, pests, plagues, droughts, and similar mundane misfortunes (cp. CUMONT & BOLL, 1904: 1 50).

Let us now come back to the winter 763 and examine the information of the two basic accounts more closely. Though the assertion in the passages of THEOPHANES and NICEPHORUS that "it was bitterly cold after the beginning of October, not only in our land (Byzantine Empire) but even more so to the east, west, and north" sounds excessive, we have found a good number of Latin annals and chronicles contemporary or later to the event, originating from Central Europe, which are in agreement with the Byzantine sources and confirm them, so that the chronology of the event and the geographical dimension of the phenomenon are verified by these independent sources.

As a matter of fact, both the "*Einhardi Annales*" (1826: 145) and the "*Annales Regni Francorum*" (1950: 22) stay chronologically very close to the event and can be considered as trustworthy according to the rigourous comparative analysis of the annals and chronicles from Central Europe of the ninth to thirteenth centuries, carried out by FARMER, WIGLEY, and others (1983: 205 pp.) from the Climate Research Unit of East Anglia University.

2.4   Comment on the later accounts

Furthermore, these contemporary primary Byzantine and Latin chronicles served as sources for the later ones. Despite their minor differences, these chronicles rely on the primary sources of the ninth century. It is not the proper place here to put side by side authors' names and statements coming from various Byzantine and Latin texts in order to show that the small differences among the later testimonies do not question the trustworthiness of the primary information and that they simply owe their existence to the manner with which each later writer used the chronographical material that he received from the anterior sources, according to his personal style, his capability of recompiling the texts he read as well as the attention he paid when he was copying them. The output of the historical-philological comparison of the Byzantine sources quoting the event is shown in table 1.

2.5 Summary of the pure data

After this analysis, a résumé of the pure data should be offered, enabling the climatologist to make any quantifications necessary for the reconstruction of past Mediterranean climate:

It should be clear from the evidence of the contemporary Byzantine sources which were verified by contemporary Latin ones that a severe winter with harsh cold set in already in October 763 A.D., not only at the northeastern parts of the Balkan peninsula but also in Central Europe. The Black Sea froze up to a distance of about 100 miles off the shores and to a depth of about 13 m. This happened along the northern coasts including the mouths of the big rivers Dnieper and Dniester, along the eastern coast from the mouth of the Sea of Azof (Kerts) to the edge of the Caucasus and along the western coasts, from the mouth of the Danube to the shores of Eastern Thrace.

The snowfall which followed the harsh cold caused the development of a new thick ice-layer above the previous one about 9 m thick. After this, the sea became a passable frozen surface in the northern and western parts of the Black Sea.

In February 764 A.D. the ice broke into large ice-drifts which were pushed by the force of the winds and the streams to the southern (obviously unfrozen) extension of the Black Sea, floating down through the Bosphorus and covering the surface of the sea between the European and the Asiatic coasts to the Marmara Sea. The cold and the snowfalls that probably followed contributed to the formation of a new frozen passable surface.

2.6 Comment on the reliability of the quantitative information of the contemporary accounts

Perhaps, we should not take the quantitative elements of the evidence word by word because Medieval chronographers are usually fond of exaggerating. Such a suspicion would be legitimate if this freezing of the Black Sea and the Bosphorus had been unique in history. However, we happen to know of about 15 cases of similar freezings from 7 to 1862 A.D. (401, 739, 763, 800, 928, 934, 1011, 1232, 1454 A.D.; MIONI, 1980), 1620, 1669, 1755, 1823, 1849, 1862 (these chronologies were provided by TCHICHATCHEF, 1964: 268 pp.). If we correlate these events to the deduction of modern climatology for the region of the Black Sea (BORISOV, 1965: 127 pp.; Meteorological Office, 1963: 74 pp.), we should consider the quantitative information coming from the historical evidence as approximately true, provided that we attribute it to an exceptional case.

Of course, we should not forget the expected tendency of the iconophile chronographers NICEPHORUS and THEOPHANES to connect this severe winter with the "dark" political circumstances of their time, when the Iconoclast Emperor Constantine V was on the Byzantine throne (LOMBARD, 1902: 94). But the existence of this tendency obviously does not put under dispute the fact that the phenomenon took place really; although the authors may well exaggerate. The ice-drifts seem to have appeared in the Bosphorus and crashed on the walls on Constantinople, but their size or the damage they produced can have been less than what the chronographers record.

On the other hand, the details about the frozen wild and domestic animals on the icebergs should be evaluated as significant for the trustworthiness of the whole evidence, if we take into consideration that such a sight fits better to a polar or at least northern landscape than to a Mediterranean one and, as a matter of fact, it must have been unknown as visual impression to the Mediterranean man.

This severe winter was perhaps either the earliest of a series of very cold winters which indicate the development of a significantly colder climatic regime at the end of the first millennium in Europe, or an isolated climatic event as LAMB (1982: 157) observes. Anyway it did not have any effects on the economy of the period. Our sources do not let us come to any such conclusion. None the less, it is a good example to show in which way historical documentary sources of varying geographical origin can supplement each other providing simultaneous information which can be analyzed and interpreted in various manners.

Acknowledgements

The authors are pleased to put on record their indebtedness to the following: Prof. Dionysios Metaxas, Department of Astrogeophysics, University of Ioannina, Greece, project leader of the EEC research programme still in progress (contract EV-0028-GR/TT) "Reconstruction of past Mediterranean climate in historical time", which is undertaken by the Department of Astrogeophysics in collaboration with the Department of Byzantine History at the University of Ioannina, Greece; Prof. Florentia Evangelatou Notara, Department of Byzantine History, University of Athens, for providing the reference of the freezing of the Black Sea in 1454, and Dr. Sylvia Enzi, Consiglio Nationale della Richerche Padova, Italy, for reference to western sources.

References

ALEXANDER, P. J. (1958): The patriarch Nicephorus of Constantinople. Clarenton Press, Oxford, 287 p.

ALEXANDRE, P. (1987): Le climat en Europe au Moyen Age. Contribution à l'histoire des variations climatiques de 1000 á 1425, d'après les sources narratives de l'Europe Occidentale. Ecole des Hautes Etudes en Sciences Sociales, Paris

BORISOV, A. A. (1965): Climates of the USSR. (Ed. by C. A. Halstead, translated by R. A. Ledward), Oliver & Boyd, Edinburgh and London

CUMONT, F. & BOLL, F. (1904): Catalogus Codicum Astrologorum Graecorum. Vol. 5, Pars 1, Bruxellis

EASTON, C. (1928): Les hivers dans l'Europe occidentale. Etude statistique et historique sur leur temperature, E. J. Brill, Leiden

FARMER, G. & WIGLEY, T. M. L. (1983): The reconstruction of European climate on decadal and shorter time scales. Final Report and Progress Report for the period March-August 1982 to the Commission of the European Communities Contract No. CL-029-81-UK(H), Climatic Research Unit School of the Environmental Sciences, Univ. East Anglia, Norwich

GROVE, J. (1988): The Little Ice Age. Methuen, London and New York

HENNING, R. (1904): Katalog bemerkenswerter Witterungsereignisse von den ältesten Zeiten bis zum Jahre 1800. Abh. König. Preuß. Meteorol. Inst. 2/4, Berlin

HUNGER, H. (1978): Die hochsprachliche profane Literatur der Byzantiner. Handbuch der Altertumswissenschaften XII/5, Bd. 1/2, München

INGRAM, M. J.; FARMER, G. & WIGLEY, T. M. L. (1981): Past climates and their impact on man: a review. In: Wigley, T. M. L.; Ingram, M. J. & Farmer, G. (eds.): Climate and history. Cambridge Univ. Press, Cambridge

INGRAM, M. J.; UNDERHILL, D. J. & WIGLEY, T. M. L. (1978): Historical climatology. Nature 276, 329-334

INGRAM, M. J.; UNDERHILL, D. J. & FARMER, G. (1981): The use of documentary sources for the study of past climates. In: Wigley, T. M. L.; Ingram, M. J. & Farmer, G. (eds.): Climate and history. Cambridge Univ. Press, Cambridge

KARAYANNOPULOS, J. & WEISS, G. (1982): Quellenkunde zur Geschichte von Byzanz (324-1453). 2 Vols., (Schriften zur Geistesgeschichte des östlichen Europa 14), Wiesbaden

KRUMBACHER, K. (1958): Geschichte der Byzantinischen Literatur von Justinian bis zum Ende des Oströmischen Reiches (527-1453). Vol. 1, (2nd edition of the original publication in München 1897), Wiesbaden

LAMB, H. H. (1982): Climate, history and the modern world. New York

LOMBARD, A. (1902): Constantin V, Empereur des Romains (740-775). Paris

MANGO, C. (1978): Who wrote the chronicle of Theophanes. Zbornik Radova Vizantoloskog Instituta 18, 9-17

MANGO, C. (1986): The breviarium of the patriarch Nicephorus. In: Byzance. Hommage à André N. Stratos, Vol. 2, Athens, 539-552

METEOROLOGICAL OFFICE (1963): Weather in the Black Sea, London

MIONI, E. (1980): Una inedita chronaca Byzantina (dal Marc. gr. 595). Rivista di Studi Byzantini e Slavi 1, 71-87

NICEPHORUS (1880): Nicephori archiepiscopi Constantinopolitani opuscula historica. Breviarium ed. Carolus de Boor, Leipzig

OSTROGORSKI, G. (1934): Theophanes. In: Wissowa, G.; Kroll, W. et al. (eds.): Pauly's Real-Encyclopädie der classischen Altertumswissenschaften 5 A 2 (2nd series). Stuttgart

PERTZ, G. H. (ed.)(1826): Einhardi Annales. MGH, Scriptores Rerum Germanicarum 1, Hannoverae

PERTZ, G. H. & KURZE, F. (eds.)(1950): Annales Regni Francorum. MGH, Scriptores Rerum Germanicarum 6, Hannoverae

PFISTER, CH. (1988): Klimageschichte der Schweiz von 1525-1860 und seine Bedeutung in der Geschichte von Bevölkerung und Landwirtschaft. Academica Helvetica 6, 3rd ed., Paul Haupt, Bern, Stuttgart

SPECK, P. (1988): Das Geteilte Dossier: Beobachtungen zu den Nachrichten über die Regierung des Kaisers Herakleios und die seiner Söhne bei Theophanes und Nicephoros. (Ποικιλα Βυζαντινα 9, Freie Universität Berlin, Byzantinisch-Neugriechisches Seminar) Bonn

TCHICHATCHEF, P. DE (1864): Le Bospore et Constantinople. Paris

THEOPHANES (1883): Theophanis Chronographia. Ed. Carolus de Boor, Vol. 1 text, Leipzig

WEIKINN, K. (1958): Quellentexte zur Witterungsgeschichte Europas von der Zeitwende bis zum Jahre 1850. Hydrographie 1, Vols. 1-4, Akademie Verlag, Berlin

Addresses of the authors:

Dr. I. Telelis, Department of Byzantine History, University of Ioannina, GR-451 10 Ioannina, Greece
Prof. Dr. E. Chrysos, Department of Byzantine History, University of Ioannina, GR-451 10 Ioannina, Greece

Simultaneous weather diaries - a unique body of evidence for reconstructing the climate history of Southern Germany from 1480 to 1530

Gabriela Schwarz-Zanetti & Werner Schwarz-Zanetti

Summary

At least ten weather diaries were kept in Southern Germany over the period 1480 to 1530. The motivation of noting down the daily weather is discussed and the quality of the evidence is assessed by considering the writers' style and by cross checking the information.

Zusammenfassung

In Süddeutschland sind mindestens zehn Witterungstagebücher aus der Periode 1480-1530 überliefert. Die Motive zur Aufzeichnung dieser Beobachtungen werden diskutiert, und die Zuverlässigkeit der Aussagen wird sowohl quellenkritisch als auch im Quervergleich überprüft.

1. Introduction

This paper presents some intermediate results of an on-going attempt of a geographer and a historian, at reconstructing the history of climate and its impacts upon the social environment for the western part of Central Europe in the High and Late Middle Ages (SCHWARZ-ZANETTI & SCHWARZ-ZANETTI, in prep.). The present focus is upon non-instrumental weather diaries, which MANLEY (1953) classified among the five most valuable types of evidence for investigating climatic change. The authors of those diaries noted down the weather in a more or less daily sequence at different levels of detail. If a diary was kept for some time and if the gaps are not too numerous, it may be explored using various methods and the results obtained may be compared to other types of proxy data. This allows getting a picture of the weather patterns with a considerable degree of accuracy (cp. SCHWARZ-ZANETTI, PFISTER, SCHWARZ-ZANETTI & SCHÜLE, this volume).

2. First class sources for climate history

ALEXANDRE (1987) was the first to submit historical evidence from the Middle Ages to an exemplary criticism of sources, since it is a *conditio sine qua non* of any climate history based upon documentary data. Considering first class sources, for which the author is an eye-witness or at least a contemporary, the place of observation, the date and the vocabulary need to be analyzed, as the reliability of a climate history depends directly on the quality and density of the underlying sources.

Weather diaries were kept for several reasons. Firstly, people were well aware to which extent daily life depended on the outcome of the harvest and thus on the weather. Secondly, the invention of printing promoted the circulation of astro-meteorological predictions contained in ephemerides, calendars and prognostics. From Antiquity, and again in the Middle Ages, astro-meteorological predictions were often called in question, as for some alert people it was quite obvious that they were casual in nature. A famous example is the satirical prognosis of SEBASTIAN BRANT in 1494. Quite often, critical minds therefore began keeping their own weather observations. Some hoped finding the secret of the correct planet constellations which were supposed to influence weather patterns, or discovering the length of a weather-cycle, others had already a scientific idea about weather.

Weather diaries can easily be quantified by counting the frequencies of events such as rain, snow, thunderstorms etc. Whether it pays to attempt the cumbersome operation of counting depends on the quality of the observation. Comparisons of frequencies based on qualitative data with frequencies based on measurements provide a useful check of reliability. We may rely on the assumption that the meteorological framework does not change dramatically over time. A comparison of the yearly averages of days with precipitation obtained from the weather-logs of careful observers from the late seventeenth century with the frequencies of precipitation based on measurements (they include all days with more than 0.3 mm of precipitation) mirrors only minor differences. The quantified historical data may therefore be interpreted with regard to the statistics of the twentieth century from the same or from a neighboring station (PFISTER, 1984, 1992).

In Southern Germany, quite a few weather diaries have been discovered from the time of the late fifteenth century (table 1). They were mostly kept by clergymen, astronomers, and lawyers.

Fig. 1 displays a page from the almanac, in which the Prior KILIAN LEIB noted down his weather observations for July 1515 in the monastery of Rebdorf near Eichstätt. On the right of the planet constellations published for every day there is some space left in which the owner of a calendar could fill in personal notes. In this month LEIB had noted down "*pluvia*" or "*pluit*" on more than twenty days. The second example is a page from a diary for December 1508 (Fig. 2), which is supposed to have been written by JOHANNES STOEFFLER in Tübingen. This author uses Latin abbreviations, such as "*fri*" for "*frigus*" - coldness. Ten snowfalls ("*nix*") may be counted for this place, which is situated at 324 m a.s.l.

Table 1 Weather diaries kept in South Germany in the late fifteenth and early sixteenth centuries (KLEMM, 1973, 1979)

Observer	Place of observation	Period
ROTENHAN VON, ANTONIUS	Bamberg	1481 - 1486
BERNHARD, WALTHER	Nürnberg	1487
SCHOENER, JOHANNES	Gemünden	1499 - 1501
	Hallstadt	1501 - 1504
	Karlstadt	1504 - 1506
KRAFFT, PETER	Regensburg	1503 - 1529
STOEFFLER, JOHANNES (?)	Tübingen	1507 - 1530
ROSE, HIERONYMUS	Ingolstadt	1508 - 1518
AVENTINUS (TURMAIR), J.	München and Landshut	1510 - 1531
LEIB, KILIAN	Rebdorf near Eichstädt	1513 - 1531
INDAGINE (ROSENBACH) J.	possibly Mainz	1513 - 1522
WERNER, JOHANNES	Nürnberg	1513 - 1520

3. An astonishing density of evidence

This high density of evidence within a relatively small region of quasi homogeneous climate (Fig. 3) is certainly unique for the early sixteenth century. It is still open to debate, whether this unusual attention paid to the weather is rooted in a local tradition, whether it is the product of chance or whether it is an outflow of a period of climatic and economic hardship. In any case parallel records of this kind allow mutual control of the way in which the observations were made. In some months the daily weather was recorded by no less than six different observers.

Fig. 4 and 5 compare the observations made by three different individuals for December 1518. The first ten days of this month were cloudy, foggy, icy, and dark; it snowed on December 22nd and 23rd ("*nix*"). At the end of the month there is an example of "Christmas-prognostications": observations which are needed for the following year, it was believed that long-term prognostics for the twelve months of the coming year could be derived from the weather on Christmas day and on the following eleven days.

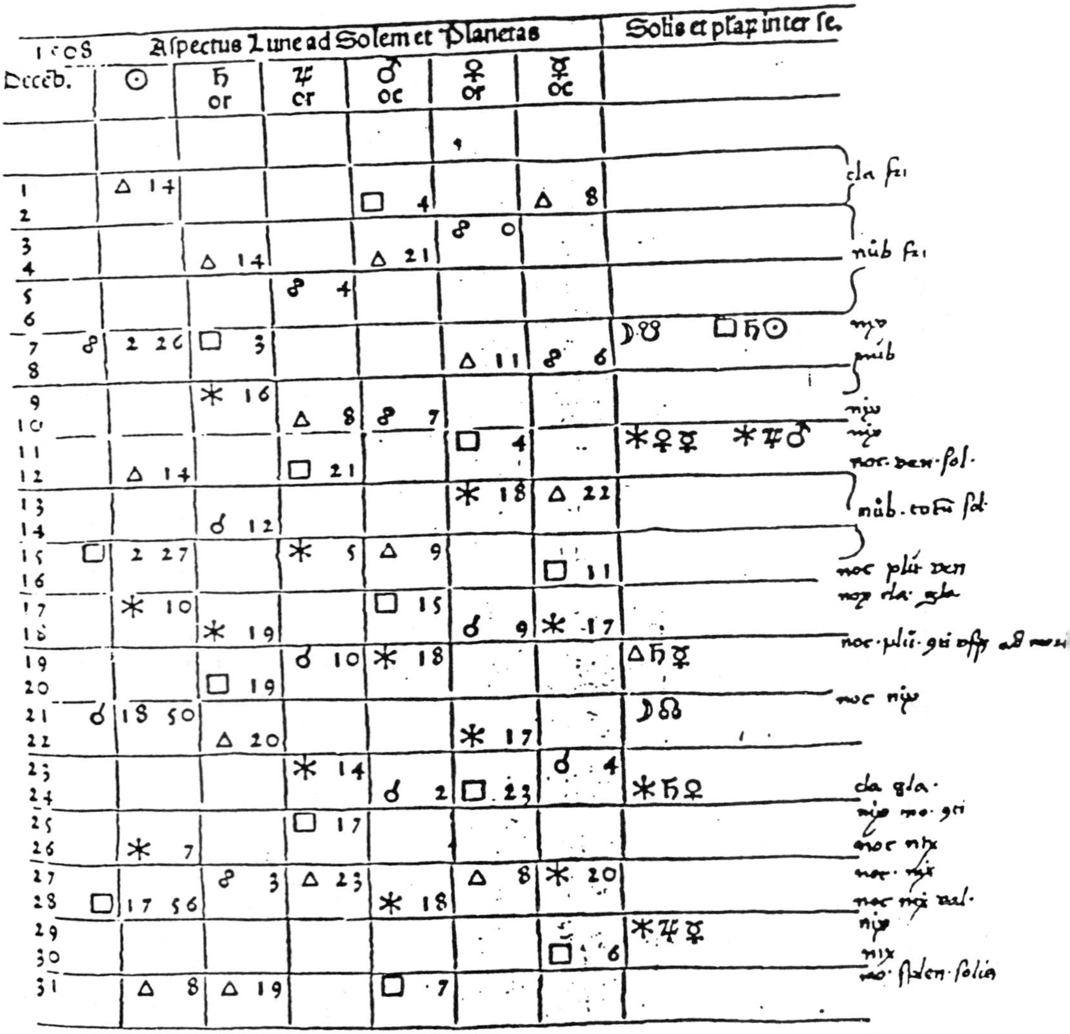

1508 Deceb.	Aspectus Lune ad Solem et Planetas ☉	♄ or	♃ cr	♂ oc	♀ or	☿ oc	Solis et plaꝫ inter se.	
1 2	△ 14			□ 4		△ 8		cla fri
3 4		△ 14		△ 21	☍ 0			nub fri
5 6			☍ 4					
7 8	☍ 2 26	□ 3			△ 11	☍ 6	☽☋ □♄☉	nix nub
9 10		✱ 16	△ 8	☍ 7				nix
11 12	△ 14		□ 21		□ 4		✱♀☿ ✱♃♂	nix nor. ven. sol.
13 14		☌ 12			✱ 18	△ 22		nub. cofu sol.
15 16	□ 2 27		✱ 5	△ 9		□ 11		noc plu ven
17 18	✱ 10	✱ 19		□ 15	☌ 9	✱ 17		nop cla gla noc plu gri
19 20		□ 19	☌ 10	✱ 18			△♄☿	noc nix
21 22	☌ 18 50	△ 20			✱ 17		☽☊	
23 24			✱ 14	☌ 2	□ 23	☌ 4	✱♄♀	cla gla
25 26	✱ 7		□ 17					nix no gri noc nix
27 28	□ 17 56	☍ 3	△ 23	✱ 18	△ 8	✱ 20		noc nix noc nix val
29 30						□ 6	✱♃☿	nix nix
31	△ 8	△ 19		□ 7				no sflen solia

Fig. 1 Example of a page from the weather diary of KILIAN LEIB in Rebdorf: July 1515

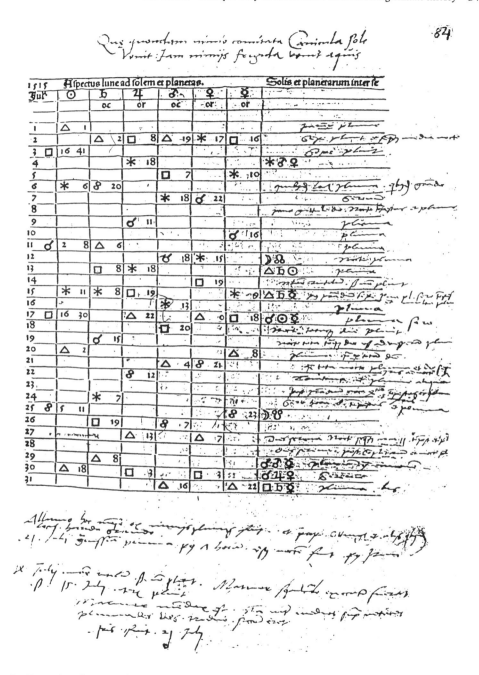

Fig. 2 Example of a page from the weather diary kept by JOHANNES STOEFFLER (?) in Tübingen: December 1508

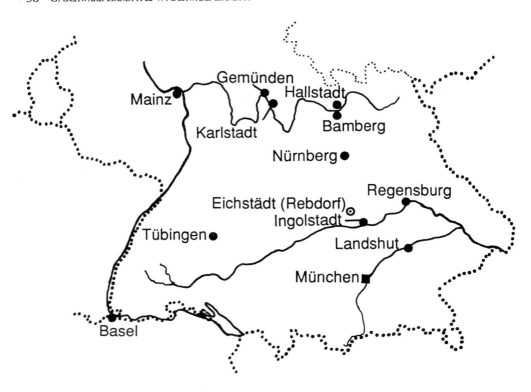

Fig. 3   Weather diaries: Map of the places of observation

4. Evaluation

It is obvious that the number of entries for a particular day are different, even if one single observer is considered. Nevertheless, more than 15.000 daily observations are counted for this period on a whole (table 2) with Kilian Leib and Johannes Stoeffler having got the lion's share.

The observations were made in different ways. Rose from Ingolstadt uses whole sentences, whereas the style of Stoeffler is cut down to a few abbreviations. If the observant lived in a monastery, such as the Prior Kilian Leib, he may have followed the weather sequences almost round the clock. At the end of every year he provides a summary of its main weather patterns including extreme events.

The spectrum of reported phenomena includes most of the observations that can be made without instruments. It is obvious, that not every single element can be interpreted in itself. For instance, observations of similar features such as "*gelu*", "*frigiditas*", and "*pruina*" (i.e. ice, cold, and frost) have been taken together in the codebook that was used (cp. SCHWARZ-ZANETTI, PFISTER, SCHWARZ-ZANETTI & SCHÜLE, this volume).

Table 2 Number of daily observations

Name	Number of observations
ROTENHAN	500
WALTHER	100
SCHOENER	100
KRAFFT	100
STOEFFLER (?)	5.500
ROSE	2.000
AVENTINUS	1.200
INDAGINE	1.000
LEIB	5.200
WERNER	100

These observations will be submitted to statistical analysis and compared to the long-term average of the present period. For example, FLOHN (1979) obtained an average of 165 days with precipitation for the period 1513-1531 from the LEIB diary, compared to 185 days (of >=0.1 mm) in the instrumental period 1891-1930. This suggests that LEIB was quite alert in observing daily weather for almost two decades.

Table 3 compares the average number of snowfalls noted down in Tübingen and Rebdorf for the same period 1517 to 1524. Both locations are situated at almost the same altitudes. It is obvious from those date, that LEIB has observed more carefully than his colleague STOEFFLER.

Table 3a Snowfall in Tübingen (324 m a.s.l.) 1517-1524 (Jul. cal.) observed by Johannes Stoeffler (?)

Year	J	F	M	A	M	J	J	A	S	O	N	D
1524	4		2								3	
1523	3	3									4	9
1522	4	2								1	3	3
1521	3		3	1								3
1520	2	3	3		1				1		3	5
1519	8	5	2							2	3	5
1518	5	5	7								3	3
1517	5	1	1	1							6	4
∅	4	2	2	0	0	0	0	0	0	0	3	3

Table 3b Snowfall in Rebdorf (Eichstädt, 388 m a.s.l.) 1517-1524 (Jul. cal.) observed by Kilian Leib

Year	J	F	M	A	M	J	J	A	S	O	N	D
1524	10	10	2							5	5	7
1523	8	4	5							1	4	13
1522	7	4	1							4	3	8
1521	6	6	11	3							2	6
1520	5	5	10		1				1	1		4
1519	8	12	2							4	4	12
1518	10	9	10	1							5	4
1517	9	1	2	2						1	3	9
∅	8	6	5	1	0	0	0	0	0	2	3	8

However, the late snowfall in May 1520 and the early snowfall in September 1520 are contained in both sources. This suggests that most early observers were focussing on spectacular weather events at the expense of "ordinary" weather. More work will be needed to assess the reliability of those diaries and to compare the statistics obtained from them to present-day averages.

1518 12 3 03 8857 // 32 (Kol. 62/63)
Veranderlich: Kurzere Periode mit Bewolkung
21. Dezember: nocte pluvia die instabilis
22. Dezember: nocte pluvia die instabilis
23. Dezember: nix
24. Dezember: nocte glacies
25. Dezember: nocte clarum glacies et die
26. Dezember: nox clarum frigor valida die nubes
27. Dezember: nocte nix die dissolutio
28. Dezember: nivosulum (?) solutio
29. Dezember: nbues solutio
30. Dezember: nubes
31. Dezember: nubes

1518 12 3 02 8858 // 06 (Kol. 62/63)
Unbekannt: Kuerzere Periode mit Bewoelkung
22. Dezember: sero aliquantum nivis decidit
25. Dezember: noxque diesque serenaque gelidaque
26. Dezember: dies nubilus sero nocteque nix non modica
27. Dezember: nubilosa dies
28. Dezember: nubilum tenuissime pluit quasi nebula decidens
29. Dezember: nocte parum nivis dies nubilus et lenis
30. Dezember: dies nubilus
31. Dezember: nubilus dies ut proximus

1518 12 3 05 8859 // 30 (Kol. 62/63)
Veranderlich: Unbekannt
21. Dezember: dunckel
22. Dezember: idem
23. Dezember: vor mittag schon abentz schne
24. Dezember: kalt apertio valida drucken
25. Dezember: fast apertio kalt und schon
26. Dezember: dunckel klatt eyss sud wint
27. Dezember: dunckel neblicht
28. Dezember: idem dam...
29. Dezember: dunckel nord wint
30. Dezember: idem feucht lufft
31. Dezember: sued wint dunckel
Zusatzliche Beobachtungen auf einem Einlageblatt:
25. Dezember: am cristag fast kalt und schoner sonnen schon
          mit einem ersten wind
26. Dezember: sant steffang fgr... die son uff gleich wulckelt sich der
          ... mit liechten wulcken in lenger je dunckler und
          ... den mittag wart sich der wynt suden dess obentz
          nach /5/ regent ess ein wenig und wart glat eyss
27. Dezember: sant Johand tag gantz dunckel neblicht mit kleynem
          rystl... und regens glat eyssig suden wynt
28. Dezember: der kindlin tag dunckel neblich feucht lufft und
          d... sud wint
29. Dezember: mitt... auch dunckel und neblich und wart der
          wint nord
30. Dezember: Dorstag neblicht dunckel nord windt feucht lufft
31. Dezember: freitag sued windt dunckel

Fig. 4 Examples of annotations of three sources for December 1518 in the computer-output: 8857: JOHANNES STOEFFLER (?), Tübingen; 8858: KILIAN LEIB, Rebdorf; 8859: JOHANNES DE INDAGINE, Rosenbach, Mainz

1518 12 1 03 8857 // 20 (Kol. 62/63)
Vorwiegend bewolkt: Unbekannt
1. Dezember: nubes glacies
2. Dezember: nubes glacies
3. Dezember: nubes glacies
4. Dezember: nubes glacies
5. Dezember: nubes glacies
6. Dezember: nubes glacies
7. Dezember: nubes glacies
8. Dezember: nubes glacies
9. Dezember: nubes glacies
10. Dezember: nox clarum frigor

1518 12 2 03 8857 // 30 (Kol. 62/63)
Veranderlich: Unbekannt
11. Dezember: pluvia nix aqua
12. Dezember: solutio nubes
13. Dezember: solutio
14. Dezember: nocte glacies modica
15. Dezember: glacies nubes
16. Dezember: glacies nubes
17. Dezember: nox clarum frigor valida die pluvia
18. Dezember: nox pluvia solutio
19. Dezember: nox ventus maximus
20. Dezember: nubes

1518 12 1 02 8858 // 70 (Kol. 62/63)
Vorwiegend Nebel: Unbekannt
1. Dezember: nebule densissime et dufft ingens
2. Dezember: nebule densissime et dufft ingens
3. Dezember: nebule densissime et dufft ingens
4. Dezember: nebule densissime et dufft ingens
5. Dezember: nebule densissime et dufft ingens
6. Dezember: nebule densissime et dufft ingens
7. Dezember: nebule densissime et dufft ingens
8. Dezember: nebule densissime et dufft ingens
9. Dezember: nebule densissime et dufft ingens

1518 12 2 02 8858 // 03 (Kol. 62/63)
Unbekannt: Vereinzelt Schnee oder Schnee und Regen
11. Dezember: mane rutilum deinde parum pluvie et nivis
13. Dezember: dies lenis quo nix tectis solvebatur ...
17. Dezember: nox serena frigida mane rutilum vespere parum pluvie ventusque
18. Dezember: nocte pluvia dieque
19. Dezember: dies lenis

1518 12 2 05 8859 // 32 (Kol. 62/63)
Veranderlich: Kurzere Periode mit Bewolkung
11. Dezember: vor mittag regen feuchte luff nach
12. Dezember: dunckel etwz windig
13. Dezember: dunckel
14. Dezember: kalt
15. Dezember: regen und schnee
16. Dezember: dunckel apertiu obentz hel
17. Dezember: morgens etwz kalt nacht windig
18. Dezember: feuchter lufft windig
19. Dezember: dunckel fast windig
20. Dezember: dunckel feucht windig

1518 12 1 05 8859 // 55 (Kol. 59/60)
Kalt:
1. Dezember: dunckel
2. Dezember: idem und etwz kul
3. Dezember: dunckel neblicht kuel
4. Dezember: idem dunckel und kalt
5. Dezember: idem, doch kein eyss
6. Dezember: idem, doch kein eyss
7. Dezember: idem, doch kein eyss
8. Dezember: idem, doch kein eyss
9. Dezember: idem, doch kein eyss
10. Dezember: nass kalt feuchte lufft neb.

Fig. 5 Examples of annotations of three sources for December 1518 in the computer-output: 8857: Johannes Stoeffler (?), Tübingen; 8858: Kilian Leib, Rebdorf; 8859: Johannes de Indagine, Rosenbach, Mainz

Acknowledgement

This research is supported by the Swiss National Science Foundation and by the Swiss Bundesamt für Bildung und Wissenschaft (COST Programme). Besides, we would like to thank David Spencer of Swiss Federal Institute of Technology in Zurich and to Christian Pfister for correcting the style and for making helpful suggestions.

References

ALEXANDRE, P. (1987): Le climat en Europe au Moyen Age. Contribution à l'histoire des variations climatiques de 1000 à 1425, d'après les sources narratives de l'Europe occidentale. Ecole des Hautes Etudes en Sciences Sociales, Paris, 825 p.

FLOHN, H. (1979): Zwei bayerische Wetterkalender aus der Reformationszeit. In: Mayer, H.; Gietl, G. & Enders, G. (eds.): Festschrift für A. Baumgartner., Wiss. Mitt. 35, Meteorologisches Institut der Univ. München

KLEMM, F. (1973): Die Entwicklung der meteorologischen Beobachtungen in Franken und Bayern bis 1700. Annalen der Meteorologie, (Neue Folge) 8, Selbstverlag des Deutschen Wetterdienstes, Offenbach a.Main

KLEMM, F. (1979): Die Entwicklung der meteorologischen Beobachtungen in Südwestdeutschland bis 1700. Annalen der Meteorologie, (Neue Folge) 13, Selbstverlag des Deutschen Wetterdienstes, Offenbach a.Main

LEIB, K. (?): Wettertagebuch für die Jahre 1513-1531 in einem Stoefflerschen Almanach. Staatsbibliothek München, Sign.: 4 L impr. c. n. mss 73

MANLEY G. (1953): The mean temperature of central England, 1768-1952. Quart. J. Roy. Meteor. Soc. 79, 242-261

PFISTER, C. (1984): Klimageschichte der Schweiz 1525-1860. Das Klima der Schweiz von 1525-1860 und seine Bedeutung in der Geschichte von Bevölkerung und Landwirtschaft (Bd. I). Bevölkerung, Klima und Agrarmodernisierung 1525-1860 (Bd. II)

PFISTER, C. (1992): Monthly temperature and precipitation patterns in Central Europe from 1525 to the present. A methodology for quantifying man-made evidence on weather and climate. In: Bradley, R. S. and Jones, P. D. (eds.): Climate since 1500 A.D. (in print)

SCHWARZ-ZANETTI, G. & SCHWARZ-ZANETTI, W. (in prep.): Klima- und Umweltgeschichte des Hoch- und Spätmittelalters in Mitteleuropa

STOEFFLER, J. (?): Wettertagebuch 1507-1530, in einem Stoefflerschen Almanach. Württembergische Landesbibliothek Stuttgart, Sign.: R 16 Stoe 1

Addresses of the authors:

G. Schwarz-Zanetti, Florastraße 29, CH-8620 Wetzikon, Switzerland
W. Schwarz-Zanetti, Florastraße 29, CH-8620 Wetzikon, Switzerland

Little Ice Age climates in the Eastern Mediterranean

Jean M. Grove & Alfred T. Grove

Summary

The climatic history of the Eastern Mediterranean has been relatively neglected but important archival collections in Venice, Constantinople and Heraklion, concerning Crete and some of the smaller Greek islands, can provide relevant data, the nature of which is discussed. The instrumental record from Crete is introduced. The archival record could be supplemented by glacial history from Turkey and possibly by dendroclimatological series.

Résumé

L'histoire climatique de la Méditerranée orientale a été negligée relativement, mais il y a des archives importantes à Venice, Constantinople et Heraklion, qui concernent Crète et quelques-unes des îles Greques plus petites, et qui peuvent fournir des informations importantes, qui sont discutées. Les données méteorologiques de l'île de Crète sont introduites. L'histore glaciaire en Turquie et peut-être les séries dendroclimatiques sont d'autres sources d'informations qui peuvent servir comme suppléments pour des documents archivales.

1. Documentary sources

The climatic sequences which have affected the Mediterranean during the last five or six centuries have received less attention than those which affected Northwestern Europe. The gap in knowledge is particularly pronounced as far as the Eastern Mediterranean is concerned. A decision to sample the climate of the Little Ice Age in Southern Europe by investigating conditions in the 1590s and 1690s, that is in two of the decades known to have been particularly severe further north, has revealed the existence of important data sources. In practice some data has already been collected for the period 1500-1700; most of this comes from Crete, a little from other Greek islands. It is hoped eventually to extend the project to a larger region including some of the smaller Greek islands and to build up a data base for the period from 1500 to 1910, permitting comparison with the period since instrumental observation began.

The most lengthy and continuous Venetian records apart from the Cretan come from Cephalonia, occupied from 1500-1797, Cerigo or Kithira (1363-1797), Corfu (1386-1797),

Tinos (1390-1715), and Zante, or Zakinthos, occupied from 1482-1797 (MARGARITIS, 1978). Crete is of particular interest because of its southerly position in the Eastern Mediterranean; data from the other islands would offer the possibility of sampling conditions in the Ionian and Aegean Sea areas.

The Venetian administration of Crete lasted from 1204 to 1669. From 1500 onwards written "relazione", and other reports and letters accumulated in the Venetian archives. Venetian administration was tightly controlled from the centre and so a particularly substantial documentation remains which does not appear to have been utilised for climatic reconstruction.

The Dukes of Crete had to provide "relazione" or accounts of the whole kingdom for which they had overall responsibility at the ends of their terms of office, which lasted about two years. A number of these have been transcribed and translated into Greek by SPANAKES (e.g. SPANAKES, 1949, 1950, 1953). Affairs discussed included such matters as the crops grown, harvest conditions and food availability. The "provveditors" or military governors also reported back, even more frequently. Their reports are dated to the day and specify the place where they were written. Some of these contain accounts of climatic conditions experienced over whole seasons or several months together. For example the Provveditor GENERAL FRANCESCO MORESINI reported on the "disastrous event...which happened in 1626, the first year of my term of office. This was the extreme drought resulting from the lack of rain and the frequent south winds which scorched the whole countryside." This drought caused grain to be short but "the greatest deficiency in Candia was the lack of water, and in 1626 the drought not only burned the greater part of the countryside but inside the city the 140 cisterns dried up and there was not a drop of water" (translated from Archivio di Stato, Venice, Relazione LXXX in SPANAKES, 1950).

Other letters to the authorities in Venice contain information about the weather over shorter time periods or individual events. ONORIO BELLI, a botanist who was physician to the Provveditor of Candia, in a letter written in Canea on January 22nd 1596 wrote of "the terrible drought we have had this autumn and winter; in November it was hotter than August and there was no rain until 6th of December old style. There was therefore great fear about because until that time they had not begun to sow, an extraordinary thing in this climate... There is no meat to be found because from the past drought the animals died of starvation; usually they are always kept in the country where all the winter they eat the grass that grows with the October rains. But until now everything has been parched; there is no grass to be seen except where it sprouts through the earth now and then." (Fol. 391-2 of Mss. 122. Ambrosiano Library, Milan, in MORGAN, 1955).

Each of the three main administrative divisions into which Crete was divided was headed by a "rector". Some of these also reported separately and some of the accounts written by Provveditors distinguish between conditions in different parts of the island. There seems therefore to be some possibility of acquiring knowledge of regional differences, crop failure or success and the incidence of drought or unusual precipitation in various parts of Crete at least for some years. Fortunately, when the last Duke of Crete, ZACCARIA MOCENIGO, was allowed by the Turks to leave the island in 1669, he took with him such records as had been kept in Candia (Heraklion). As a result, the Archives of the Dukes of Crete, collected in 95 large volumes, rest safely in the Archivio di Stato in Venice and are reported to be in good condition and readable in Latin and the Venetian idiom. There is also a huge collection of correspondence, the Senato Mar', which is likely to contain relevant information (MARGARITIS, 1978). One of the difficulties which has to be faced is the very large amount of documentation which should ideally be consulted.

The administration of the Ionian islands of Corfu, Cephalonia and Zante though not identical, was run along essentially similar lines (MARGARITIS, 1978). Overall authority was vested in the Provveditore GENERAL DEL LEVAANTE, or Captain of the Gulf who was seated in Corfu. The Governor or Bailly of Corfu, and the Governors of Zante and Cephalonia, entitled Provveditores, were appointed for two year stints and when they returned to Venice they too had to provide an account of their stewardship as well as reporting back by letter during the appointments. Amongst the taxes imposed were the tithes on all cereals, oil and other products. Tithe records have not yet been considered but offer obvious possibilities in conjunction with the many accounts of the reasons for shortages and surpluses, which differentiate between such factors as war and piracy inhibiting cultivation near coasts on the one hand and drought, too much rain in the planting season or hail at harvest time on the other.

There is no doubt that there is a mass of original documents from which information useful for climatic reconstruction can be extracted. Those examined so far have included the name of the author, the exact date and the place of writing. The need for verification appears minimal, but wherever possible it is intended to check the statements of officials against other local informants such as doctors or the consular records which survive in other archives such as those of France (TRIANTAFYLLIDOU-BALADIE, 1988) or England.

The use of Turkish records may well turn out to present more difficulty than those of Venice, though it is a source of encouragement that the archives in Istanbul have recently been opened to foreigners. Those documents relating to Crete were retained in the island at the end of the period of Turkish domination and are held in the Vikelea Library, Heraklion. So far we have only made use of the fraction of the great mass of Turkish documents which have been translated into Greek and so are far more accessible than the originals written in an obsolete script and in Ottoman not modern Turkish (STAURINIDES, 1976, 1978, 1984). These records include many "firmen" or edicts of the local Pashas, some of which have direct climatic implications, or reports to Istanbul, such as that of the newly appointed Dephterdares of Crete, MEHMET EFENDIS, on August 19th 1696 to the effect that it had not been possible to levy the "muskata" tax on grain or olives because of drought (Turkish Archives, Irakleion, Codex 11 in STAURINIDES, 1978: 108). One element recorded in some of the Turkish documents is the date at which bread was first brought to Heraklion from monastic estates, this signalling in some cases the completion of the barley harvest, in others the start of the wheat harvest. Thus, on April 23rd 1692 (Gregorian Calendar) "Today, Friday the 18th of Sabon 1104, barley bread was brought from the Monastery of Toplo in the region of Kainourgio, testifying that the harvest has finished" (Turkish Archive of Irakleion, Codex 7, p. 1, STAURINIDES, 1976: 429), while on May 11th 1696 "Today, the 8th of Seval in the year 1107 bread was brought from the region of Kainourgio from wheat from the new harvest; so let it be known that the harvesting time has begun. Recorded on the same day" Turkish Archive of Irakleion, Codex 7, p. 52, STAURINIDES, 1975, Vol. 3, p. 171). It is not yet known whether there is enough of this data to form a yearly record but it is intended to pursue this possibility. There are also letters to Constantinople explaining the great shortfalls in taxes collected in specified years with confirmation of the truth of the explanations given in terms of climatic difficulties.

We have at present no idea of the density of data which we may eventually hope to gather and accordingly we have made no decisions concerning the best way to handle the material when more of it has been collected. It is already clear however that we shall be able to identify some groups of years or clusters of seasons during which pronounced drought, prolonged rain or unusually timed rain occurred. It is hoped to compare the incidence of extreme climatic events in the past with their frequency and magnitude during the period of instrumental observation.

2. The instrumental record

The recent instrumental record for Crete is quite abundant though short. We have records from 60 rainfall stations, 15 evaporation stations and 8 temperature stations, but the records are brief, most of them beginning between 1969 and 1970. Only 5 stations have unbroken records since 1953. All the records have wartime breaks and only three stations go back over 60 years: Heraklion to 1909/10, Sitia to 1916/17 and Anoyia to 1919/20. The values are given for hydrological years running from September to August.

The distribution of the mean annual rainfall over the island can be explained, 75% in terms of altitude, latitude and longitude. It should be possible to provide an index for the total precipitation over the whole island and for its variation from year to year, at least as far back as 1960 and possibly somewhat earlier. This island precipitation index could be of considerable significance especially at the present time, as agriculture is now very dependent on irrigation using sub-surface water. Much of the precipitation infiltrates and percolates down into limestones which underlie most of the island.

Records exist of the water level in and around a sinkhole in the upland basin of Lasithi. When these records have been procured it may be possible to compare them with the variations in the island precipitation index.

The availability of instrumental records for the smaller islands has yet to be investigated.

3. Tree-ring data

It is hoped to supplement the archival material with tree-ring values. Material from the Aegean area collected in the course of a major project run by P. KUNIHOLM of Cornell University (KUNIHOLM & STRIKER, 1983, 1988) has been made available. KUNIHOLM, who extended his investigation to Crete in 1989 has so far been mainly concerned with chronology and with using tree-rings, mainly from oakwood, for dating buildings such as old Byzantine churches.

In Crete A. T. GROVE and his colleagues first cored various species to assess their relative usefulness. The two most promising species were deciduous oaks and cypress. The oaks are very tough to bore and several increment corers broke in them. Furthermore, specimens more than 150 years old were found to be rotten in the middle. However, in the absence of alternative sources of information about nineteenth century climate, further attention to the oak record would probably be justified.

Cypress near the north coast were mostly less than 50 years old and generally exhibited two rings for each year of growth. Recently attention has been concentrated on ancient cypress, immediately below the treeline at 1500 m on the southern slopes of the White Mountains and on Mount Idi south of the Nida plain. Discs cut from coppiced trees have as many as 940 rings and it seems possible that some of the older stumps which ceased to grow after they were cut are much older than this. Successive generations may allow the record to be carried back to much earlier times; ^{14}C dating could assist in confirming the age of the earlier material. On the other hand, the difficulties involved in procuring a climatic record from this source must be recognised: it is not known as yet what climatic variables control ring thickness, and ring thicknesses are not easily measured because occasional groups of individual rings are found to converge; several specimens therefore have to be measured and the results compared.

4. Glacial history

The possibility arises of identifying the timing of glacier fluctuations in the Taurus and other mountains of Anatolia (ERINC, 1952). The methods used would include identifying moraine sequences on the ground and dating them by a combination of lichenometry and ^{14}C dating of associated organic deposits. Repetition of earlier surveys, such as that of Erciyas Dagi (38°30' N, 35°30' E; MESSERLI, 1964, 1967) where they exist, and a comparison of air photos and ground photos of various dates could provide quantitative information on change in area and volume (GROVE, 1988). It is recognised that it may prove to be impossible to use air photographs in this region, but the work would be much easier if they could be obtained.

Acknowledgements

Work so far carried out has been in connection with EC Contracts EVHC 0044 (U.K.) H and EVHC 0073 (U.K.) H. Translation from Greek to English was all by Thomas de Waal.

References

ERINC, S. (1952): Glacial evidence of the climatic variations in Turkey. Geograf. Ann. 34, 89-98

GROVE, J. M. (1988): The Little Ice Age. Methuen, London, 498 p.

KUNIHOLM, P. & STRIKER, C. (1983): Dendrochronological investigations in the Aegean and neighbouring regions, 1977-1982. J. Field Archaeol. 10, 389-398

KUNIHOLM, P. & STRIKER, C. (1988): Dendrochronological investigations in the Aegean and neighbouring regions, 1983-1986. J. Field Archaeol. 14, 389-398

MARGARITIS, S. (1978): Crete and the Ionian Islands under Venetian Rule. Leontiadis, Athens, 113 p.

MESSERLI, B. (1964): Der Gletscher am Erciyas Dagh und das Problem der rezenten Schneegrenze im anatolischen und mediterranen Raum. Geogr. Helv. 19, 19-34

MESSERLI, B. (1967): Die eiszeitliche und gegenwärtige Vergletscherung im Mittelmeerraum. Geogr. Helv. 22, 105-228

MORGAN, G. (1955): The Canea earthquake of 1595. Kretika Chronika 9, 75-80

SPANAKES, S. (1949): E ekthese ton Douka tes Kretes Ioanni Sagredo (1604). (The Report of the Duke of Crete, Ioanni Sagredo (1604)). Kretika Kronika 3, 519-533

SPANAKES, S. (1950): Francesco Moresini, Provveditor General et Ingegner del Regno; Relazioni di Candia, 1629. Mnemeia tes Kretikes Istorias 2, 17

SPANAKES, S. (1953): Filippo Pasqualigo, Capitano di Candia et Provveditor della Canea; Relazione, letta nell' Eccelentissimo Senato, 1594. Mnemeia tes Kretikes Istorias 3 XVI, 182

STAURINIDES, N. S. (1976): Metaphraseis Tourkikon engraphon eis ten istorian Kretes. Engrapha tes periodou 1672-94 (Turkish documents relating to the history of Crete. Documents of the period 1672-94) 2, Vikelaia Vivliotheke, Irakleion, 480 p.

STAURINIDES, N. S. (1978): Metaphraseis Tourkikon engraphon aphorounton eis ten istorian Kretes. Engrapha tes periodou 1694-1715 (Turkish documents relating to the history of Crete. Documents of the period 1694-1715) 3, Vikelaia Vivliotheke, Irakleion, 480 p.

STAURINIDES, N. S. (1984): Metaphraseis Tourkikon engraphon aphorounton eis ten istorian Kretes. Engrapha tes periodou 1715-54. (Turkish documents relating to the history of Crete. Documents of the period 1715-52) 4, Vikelaia Vivliotheke, Irakleion, 409 p.

TRIANTAFYLLIDOU-BALADIE, Y. (1988): To emborio kai e oiconomia tes Kretes apo tis arches tes Othomanikes Kuriachias eos to telos tou 18[ou] aviona (1669-1795). (The trade and economy of Crete from the beginning of Ottoman rule until the end of the 18th century (1669-1795)), Vikelaia Vivliotheke, Irakleion, 335 p.

Addresses of the authors:

Dr. J. M. Grove, Girton College Cambridge, U.K.
Dr. A. T. Grove, Geography Department, Downing Place, Cambridge, U.K.

Weather patterns in Czechoslovakia during the years 1588-1598

Jan Munzar

Summary

This contribution attempts to reconstruct the weather patterns on the territory of today's Czechoslovakia at the end of the sixteenth century. From the results of this reconstruction of eleven years it is not possible to show the existence or even the climax of the "Little Ice Age" around the year 1590 in this region, as it is defined for Western Europe.

Zusammenfassung

Das Ziel des Beitrags ist ein Versuch, das Wetter in der Tschechoslowakei am Ende des 16. Jahrhunderts aufgrund schriftlicher Quellen zu rekonstruieren. Die Ergebnisse dieser Rekonstruktion für die elf angeführten Jahre können die Existenz bzw. den Höhepunkt der "Kleinen Eiszeit" um 1590 in diesem Gebiet nicht bestätigen, wie für Westeuropa angeführt ist.

1. Primary sources

Only one historical source gives direct or indirect information about the weather in all the eleven years under discussion: Czech written memories from KNĚŽOVSKÝ, concerning the city of Slaný in Central Bohemia. Practically the whole period 1588-1598 (with the exception of 1592) is covered by the chronicle of the town of Litoměřice (KATZEROWSKY, 1886).

As for the information density of the individual years, most is contained in two diaries which, however, cover only a shorter period of time. KAREL OF ŽEROTÍN left notes about the weather on individual days from January to December 1588 (in Latin), from January to April 1589 (in Czech) and from April to December 1591 (in Latin) (MUNZAR, 1984, 1989; IPOLYI, 1887).

Almost ten years after this, MATHIAS BORBONIUS of Borbenheim made similar visual observations between 1596-1598 (Latin) and in 1622 (Czech). Like ŽEROTÍN, BORBONIUS often travelled. For this reason the records from March 1596 cover the weather in Basel, Switzerland, from June 1597 to August 1598 the weather in Moravia, and from September to December 1598 the weather in Bohemia. The Basel records are published *in extenso* (PEJML & MUNZAR, 1968a, b).

The submitted synthesis is related to the critical reconstruction of the weather carried out by PEJML more than 20 years ago which was concentrated on the vineyards and hop regions of Northwestern Bohemia (PEJML, 1966). In part, it fills in information about weather in other areas of Bohemia, Moravia and Slovakia. Least of all, according to RÉTHLY (1962), weather information was obtained from Slovakia - the former Upper Hungary - however, only one record, concerning winter 1594, was of practical use.

In the following reconstruction, dated with the Gregorian calendar, it is not possible to reproduce all the sources in detail, due to their extent. However, this goes along with the progressive supplement of the catalogue and its future publication, including references (MUNZAR, 1988). The exact location of events will be given, as usual, only in case of differing weather patterns in various parts of the studied country. The simplification of the reconstructed sequence results from the fact that isolated weather phenomena (i.e. local hailstorms, local downpours) are not included, because they do not necessarily reflect the conditions of a more extensive area.

2. Summarizing account of the weather conditions in Czechoslovakia between 1588-1598

1588

Cold, rainy summer (until 15th August), a late harvest. Pretty good crop of wheat but losses during and after the harvest. Early frosts in autumn - vine froze before the vintage. Small yield and poor quality of wine - grapes not ripened.

1589

A hard winter from Christmas (1588) until 9th March. Cold and rainy from 8th June to 6th July. A hot summer (TRUTNOV) and a very dry year - it did not rain for the whole summer and winter (Jestřebí, Česká Lípa). In Bohemia bad wheat crop. Poor grape harvest, "as never seen before" - small yield and sour wine. An early winter (after 11th November) - hard with heavy snow.

1590

Hard winter with snow until 24th January ("such as has not been in 40 years"), after this cold period recurrent freezing and thawing from February until the beginning of April. A very hot and dry summer from the beginning of June, 2 to 3 months almost without rain (dried-up rivers, water shortage). With the exception of the area around Louny insufficient wheat. A good vintage (good yield as well as excellent quality, "such as has not been since 1540").

1591

A winter with changing weather, practically without snow. A dry spring, at the beginning of summer downpours and flooding. During the harvest a number of weeks with rain and bad weather, causing losses in the wheat yields. The grapes were small and sour. A relatively warm autumn.

1592

Winter practically without snow until the end of February. Frost until the last quarter of January and from the end of February. A late harvest, but good wheat crop (low prices). Again a poor grape harvest (there was little and sour wine). Winter started 11th November.

1593

A long winter. Cold, rainy summer (June-July). A late harvest and a small crop (higher prices). Sunny, warm autumn and beginning of winter. Small grape harvest, but better quality of wine than in 1592.

1594

Warm winter from Christmas until 6th January. After that frequent snow (but snow cover soon disappeared) and much rain until the beginning of February, no frost (in Bohemia; in Eastern Slovakia winter was "as it should be" in January and February - freezing). Cold May ("No one remembers such cold weather in 60 years" - Litoměřice). A great drought started in the summer until the beginning of winter wheat sowing (Slaný). The average wheat price was exceptionally high. The grape harvest was average (grapes were not too ripe). 1st November a hard winter set in: heavy snow fall, the Elbe river froze over.

1595

Hard winter with snow until the second week in March, when the ice began to break and melt (on the Elbe river in Litoměřice on March 7th, "the ice was stronger than it has been for many years"). The wheat harvest was average. Due to frost, the grape harvest was low and of only mediocre quality. At Christmas all snow disappeared.

1596

The beginning of the year was relatively warm, people plowed. From 21st January the winter was variable. A terrible hot-spell in April and May. The beginning of the summer brought rainy weather for more than a month. In Bohemia a poor wheat crop, in Moravia a sufficient one. Wine was good (Litoměřice), in Slaný it was average.

1597

Winter 1596/97 very mild, warm, without snow; in January and February farm work could begin. It was getting cold at the end of Shrovetide and though it was not too harsh, the cold lasted until May. The grape harvest was small; the wine rather sour. Winter was harsh: November was cold with large amounts of snow, the Elbe river was already frozen by 12th November. By the end of the year it thawed considerably.

1598

Cruel winter. In Northern Bohemia the snow cover remained until the middle of March. In Moravia there was such a freeze "as has not been for 34 years" (Olomouc). On the Elbe the ice cover broke March 7th, then flooding began, during which the water-level was "about $3/_4$ of an ell =0,3 m = higher than in 1595" (Litoměřice). From 12th June until 6th July hot and dry. ("Such good weather for grapes hasn't been for a long time"). This weather alternated with a cold and rainy weather, which lasted about one month from the end of July. A number of times during the year there was flooding and wheat crop damage. A relatively early winter: 22nd September snow-storm in the area around Litoměřice. Windy, rainy and cold weather set in; people had to start heating. Bad vintage ("Great poverty and complaining because of the grape harvest"- grapes rotted and fell off the vines unripened).

3. Methodological notes

3.1 Style of dating

The dates are based on the Gregorian style. However, it must be noticed that in individual parts of today's Czechoslovakia style was not uniform. In Bohemia the last day of the Julian style was 6th January 1584 and the first day of the Gregorian style 17th January 1584, analogous to this in Moravia 3rd/14th October 1584, and in Slovakia 21st October/1st November 1587. The insecurity about the calendar lasted until the middle of 1604, because the new calendar was refused in a few places.

3.2 Data verification

An example of verifying the data of the Czech chroniclers can be seen in their weather reports on the 21st June 1588 when during a strong thunderstorm the town hall in the Western Bohemian town of Stříbro was hit by lightning and destroyed by fire. This agrees with the data of two strong thunderstorms on the afternoon of June 21st, reported in the neighbouring Bavaria according to the observations of Leonhard III Treuttwein in the town of Fürstenfeldbruck (Lenke, 1968).

Or according to the chronicler in the town of Litoměřice, the grape harvest on 30th October 1598 took place in rain, cold and snow. M. BORBONIUS describes this day as follows: "*dies nivosa, pluvia*", therefore there is good agreement.

3.3   Discrepancies between the chroniclers' reports

Sometimes chronicles comment on the question of how long a certain phenomenon had not taken place, e.g. "there has not been such a hard winter with snow like the one in 1590 for at least 40 years". However, statements like this should be handled with care, because from this evidence alone we are not able to ascertain the character of the winter in 1550. In another source the quality and quantity of vine harvested in 1590 is equalled to the harvest in 1540: in this case the comparison is accuraté, for in 1540 there really was a hot summer with abundant wine and low prices. The same holds true for the strong freeze in 1598, which they say had not been such for 34 years, because information about frost or any other kind of weather in 1564 is missing from that same chronicle. However, this could correspond to the winter of 1564/65 which was hard and long indeed.

Moreover, it is not always possible to infer the course of the weather in a given year from the price of wheat and foodstuff alone. For example, KNĚŽOVSKÝ noted in his Memories of 1590, "...the whole year was very dry... Prices were high as a result of the drought, but more so because of the dishonesty of the bakers, the prices were higher after the harvest than before...".

Finally, reports on the exceptionally dry year of 1589 are contradictory: in Litoměřice (Northern Czechoslovakia) an unbelievably poor vintage is reported. This does not match with the drought which is reported for that year. Either the weather was surprisingly different in a relatively small area, or the report of the Litoměřice chronicler does not belong to that year at all.

4. Conclusion

In Switzerland the peak of the "Little Ice Age" is considered to be at the end of the sixteenth century (PFISTER, 1980). In Czechoslovakia, however, an exceptional cooling of lasting character could not be observed. Therefore, concerning Czechoslovakia, the use of the term "Little Ice Age" is not accurate. It will, however, be necessary to verify this conclusion on the basis of longer time series than have been available up to now.

References

IPOLYI, A. (1887): Zierotin Károly Naplója. In: Alsó sztregovai és rimai Rimay János: Allámitarai és levelezése, A magyár tudományos Akadémia Kiadása, Budapest, 3-45

KATZEROWSKY, W. (1886): Die meteorologischen Aufzeichnungen des Leitmeritzer Stadtschreibers aus den Jahren 1564 bis 1607. Dominicus, Prag, 29 p.

KNĚŽOWSKÝ, V. : Paměti (Memories). Ms. University Library Prague, Sign. 54 A 61

LENKE, W. (1968): Das Klima des 16. und Anfang des 17. Jahrhunderts nach Beobachtungen von Tycho de Brahe auf Hven, Leonhard III. Treuttwein in Fürstenfeld und David Fabricius in Ostfriesland. Ber. Dtsch. Wetterdienst. 15, Nr. 110, Offenbach a.M., 49 p.

MUNZAR, J. (1984): A contribution to the reconstruction of weather in Central Europe at the end of 16th century. In: Mörner, N.-A. & Karlén, W. (eds.): Climatic changes on a yearly to millennial basis. D. Reidel Publ. Comp., Dordrecht, 339-342

MUNZAR, J. (1988): The climate in Central Europe in historical past and possibilities of its reconstruction. Historická geografie 27: Historical geography of environmental changes, Inst. of Czechoslovak and World History of the Czech. Acad. Sci., Prague, 109-122

MUNZAR, J. (1989): The beginnings of regular meteorological observations in the Czech lands from the 16th to the 18th centuries. Climatic changes in the historical and instrumental periods; Proc. Symp. held in Brno (Czechoslovakia), June 12th to 16th 1989 (in press)

PEJML, K. (1966): Příspěvek ke kolísání klimatu v severočeské vinařské a chmelařské oblasti od roku 1500-1900. Sb. Pr. H.M.Ú. Č.S.S.R. 7, Hydrometeorological Institute, Prague, 23-78

PEJML, K. & MUNZAR, J. (1968 a): Matyáš Borbonius z Borbenheimu a jeho meteorologická pozorování z let 1596-1598, 1622. Meteorol. Zpr. 21, 93-95

PEJML, K. & MUNZAR, J. (1968 b): Das Wetter in Basel in den Jahren 1596-1598 nach dem Tagebuch des Mathias Borbonius von Borbenheim. Vierteljahresschr. Naturf. Ges. Zürich 113, 407-416

PFISTER, C. (1980): Klimaschwankungen und Witterungsverhältnisse im Schweizerischen Mittelland und Alpenvorland zur Zeit des "Little Ice Age"; die Aussage der historischen Quellen. In: Oeschger, H.; Messerli, B. & Svilar, M. (eds.): Das Klima; Analysen und Modelle, Geschichte und Zukunft. Springer, Berlin, 175-190

RÉTHLY, A. (1962): Időjárási események és elemi csapások Magyárországon 1700-ig. Akadémiai Kiado, Budapest, 450 p.

Address of the author

Dr. J. Munzar, Geographical Institute of the C.A.S., Mendlovo nám. 1, 662 82 Brno, Czechoslovakia

Floods in the Ore Mountains (Krušné hory) and their foothills between 1784-1981

Jiří Kynčil

Summary

To solve the problem of flood control in the North Bohemian Coal Basin it was necessary to collect data on historical floods in that region. We therefore carried out historical research and the results were summarized in a paper "Floods in the Ore Mountains (Krušné hory) and their foothills between 1784-1981". Our contribution here presents information about this work and, as an example, describes floods which occurred in 1881 and 1909.

Zusammenfassung

Zur Lösung einiger Probleme des Hochwasserschutzes im Nordböhmischen Braunkohlebecken war es notwendig, Angaben über historische Überschwemmungen in diesem Gebiet zu sammeln. Darum haben wir historische Quellenforschung betrieben, deren Ergebnisse in der Arbeit "Überschwemmungen im Erzgebirge und seinem Vorland in den Jahren 1784-1981" zusammengefaßt wurden. Unser Beitrag hier bringt Informationen über dieses Buch und beschreibt als Beispiel die Hochwasser der Jahre 1881 und 1909.

1. Introduction

In the year 1978 I wrote a paper "Historical floods in water courses of the Ore Mountains". This was my first attempt to describe the floods in the North Bohemian Coal Basin of the years 1881-1955 on the basis of archive studies. Already in the following year 1979 was published the volume "Historical floods in the region of the Biela (Bílina) and Eger (Ohře)" containing my "Index of floods in the region of Biela and Eger in the years 1501-1940", as the area of the Ore Mountains and their foothills (the coal basins of Eger, Falkenau, and Brüx, the Kaiserwald and the Tepler uplands) reaches from the town Eger (Cheb) to Aussig on the Elbe (Ústí n. Labem). The collecting and the studying of records and descriptions of flood occurrences within our research area was continued. Through the times new and valuable written records were discovered in the North Bohemian district archives. The same applies for written sources from the University Library of Prague. These materials basically broadened my mind and some "white spots" in the existing index of floods could be added to, explained, or defined. Finally in 1983 the "Floods in the Ore Mountains and their foothills in the years 1784-1981" were published. This small volume consists of three chapters:

(1) An extended index of 88 floods (1784-1981) in the region of Eger and Biela;
(2) eleven selected descriptions of floods (1881-1981) in the region of Eger and Biela;
(3) reflections on how to use historical flood records by O. VITHA, Prague.[1]

As mentioned above, my contribution will, besides the information concerning the publication, bring two descriptions of major floods from the years 1881 and 1909 as examples.

2. The Brüx Flood of 1881

On March 9th and 10th the continuous - lasting almost thirty hours - heavy snowfall of Saturday 5th and Sunday 6th of March, which on Monday 7th of March afternoon was followed by intensive thawing together with rain, caused extensive floods in many places throughout Bohemia. In the evening of March 7th a dispatch from Karlsbad (Karlovy Vary) arrived at Brüx (Most) which noted an unusual rise in the water-level of the Eger river.[2]

On the following day it reached 45 Wiener Zoll (Viennese inches) at Kaaden (Kadaň), where the water flooded several houses. On March 9th the flood inundated the hop gardens at Postelberg (Postoloprty) and below Saaz (Žatec), and formed lakes further down the valley. At Micholop (Měcholupy) the Goldbach stream (Blšanka) damaged, among other things, the railway embankment. On March 8th at low water-level the ice in the Eger and Elbe rivers at Leitmeritz (Litoměřice) melted, on March 9th the water rose by 4.5 m and flooded the Schützeninsel (Schützen island), flowed into Fischern (Rybáře), flooded the Elbe restauration as well as the basin of Theresienstadt (Terezín), and cut off Mlikojed (Mlékojedy). For the same day Aussig on the Elbe reported that the town quarter at the river was inundated. Here the water mark reached 5.06 m, at Tetschen(Děčín) even 6.0 m.

---

[1] Amongst hydrologists there is a general consensus that one can calculate the culmination flow on the basis of hydraulic calculations of the known water-level mathematically. VITHA is basically negating this and declares that on the basis of the description of the course of the high flood and the resulting damages one can estimate the size of the culmination flow by way of the comparative method. And this estimation is in several cases nearer to the truth than the mathematical method.

[2] Eger - left-sided tributary of the river Elbe, springs from the Fichtelgebirge, flows through the land of Eger and the Sazer basin rich in hops, reaches the Elbe at Theresienstadt; tributaries from left side Zwodau, Rollau, Assigbach, from right side Rösslau, Odrau, Tepl, Aubach, Goldbach; length 316 (291,3) km; basin 5620 km^2 (5613 km^2); average flow 37,9 m^3/s.

Extensive floods also occurred in the region of lake Kommern, within and around Brüx.[3] The town was considerably damaged by the Weissbach (Bílý potok) and the Biela both of which overflowed their beds.[4]

On Wednesday 9th of March, due to continuous rainfall and thaw, the water-level of the Weissbach rose so much that the newly vaulted canal in Wenzel alley could not hold the amounts of water. The water flooded into the lower part of the alley and took the direction of the stone mill (Steinmühle) which already was in bad condition and collapsed. Numerous lower alleys were flooded, the ground floor living quarters of the afflicted Wenzel alley had to be cleared. Many courtyards and the threshing floors of the old barns, where supplies were stocked, were submerged. Also flooded was the Flecknerwiese (Fleckner Green) on which the meeting of the Gau athletes (Gau-Turner Treffen) had taken place the year before.

While in the Weissbach stream the water fell on Thursday March 10th, it rose in the Biela much more than anyone had ever experienced for many years. The vaulted dam in the Wassergasse (water alley) was completely submerged, likewise the gardens and courtyards along the ditch at the bridge in the Bischofsstraße (bishop street) whose pavement was washed away by the floods. Most of the Biela promenade was flooded, the meadow at the sugar refinery resembled a small lake with waters extending to the warehouses of which some already had to be cleared the evening before. The so-called bleaching-meadow, too, was inundated and this up to the tavern "Zum Kaiser von Österreich" (Emperor of Austria). The water also flooded into the open work mines of the Müllerschacht and of Strienitz, therefore not permitting any further work.

Looking down from the castle hill one could observe a large lake between Brüx and Görkau (Jirkow) which had completely submerged several villages and many meadows, fields, and thoroughways.

On many roads traffic had to be closed down. The road to Lindau (Lipětín) was seriously damaged. The railway embankments also suffered severe damages. The train to Teplitz (Teplice) had to cross streams of water in several places.

---

[3] Lake Kommern - a basin lake, once situated NW of the town Brüx in the former waters and swamps below the Ore Mountains. In the seventeenth century it had an extent of about 56 km² (caused by the continuous silting up), but the proper water surface was much smaller, ca. 6 km². In 1831 it only measured two km² and soon afterwards it was drained.

[4] Biela - river in NW Bohemia, left-sided tributary to the Elbe; length 80,1 km; basin 216,19 km²; average flow 5,51 m³/s.

On Friday March 11th the water fell. But still on Tuesday March 15th the traffic between Brüx and Oberleutensdorf (Horní Livínov) was only possible via Johnsdorf (Janov) and not until March 18th the road was clear again for carts. Footpassengers were advised not to use the road as the surface was covered by a thick layer of mud.

Of further places which were affected by the floods one was Görkau where the roads had suffered much. The river walls alongside the weirs were hollowed out and threatened to collapse. In low situated Prahn (Brány) ten houses were submerged by two metres of water. There also was loss of live-stock (drowned sheep, pigs, bee-hives) etc. At Ulbersdorf (Albrechtice) and Eisenberg (Jezeří), too, damage was done. The road to Kommern (Komořany) was impassable. At Kommern on March 9th the schools had to be closed because of the floods. In the room of one house the water stood one ell (0.591 m) high.

On Friday March 18th everywhere the waters fell and pleasant weather accompanied by wind helped to dry the flooded spots. Also most of the thoroughways which had been damaged by the floods and therefore had been impassable were already back into use, although one estimated it to take weeks before they could be restored to their former condition.

The damages caused by the floods in Brüx, Kommern, Görkau, Prahn, Ulbersdorf, and elsewhere, that is in a part of the lake Kommern of an estimated extent of ca. 70 km^2, have been unusually severe, likewise in private and in public property. At a maximum water-level of 229,6 m an area of 14,25 km^2 was flooded and the amount of water comprised of a minimum 20 million m^3.

In the time from 5th to 13th of March 1981 the following daily values were read at the stations for precipitation measurements:

Table 1 Amounts of precipitation (mm) from 05-13 March 1981

					Dates				
Station	5.3.	6.3.	7.3.	8.3.	9.3.	10.3.	11.3	12.3	13.3.
Eisenberg	8.3	10.6	20.3	2.3	.5	20.4	17.8	10.6	.0
Reitzenhain	.0	.0	26.2	3.0	3.0	27.7	42.1	37.0	.0
Türmitz	1.7	5.8	13.7	5.5	.4	20.7	2.9	10.3	.2
Zinnwald	.0	.0	.0	8.0	10.2	14.3	.0	.0	.0

3. The floods in the Ore Mountains and their foothills in February 1909

In the first half of the month January there had been heavy snowfall all over the country, forming a continuous cover. On February 3rd suddenly thaw occurred which was accompanied by daily heavy rainfalls up to February 6th. In the lowlands and at middle lies these were just rain or snowy rain, in the mountains mostly snow. In the region of the Eger and its tributaries the thaw was extremely quick. The masses of snow in the Ore Mountains completely melted. The following table gives the thickness of snow:

Table 2   The precipitation (mm) of 01-07 February 1909 at selected ombrometric stations

Station	1.2.	2.2.	3.2.	4.2.	5.2.	6.2.	7.2.
				Dates			
Kupferberg	-	-	46.3	52.6	-		
Wernsdorf	-	-	-	39.5	-		
Sosau	5.7	6.2	?	33.5	-		
Seestadtl	-	-	28.4	41.1	-		
Weipert			38.4	46.5			
Goldene Höhe	-	-	97.4	22.8	-		
Platten-Petsch	10.4	11.4	49.4	68.0	9.7	6.0	1.2
Glieden	5.6	16.9	53.1	61.1	12.7	4.2	.9
Sebastianberg	23.3	22.2	21.9	59.0	16.1	4.1	2.2

On almost all of the Bohemian rivers the ice congested. The ice-drift led to jams which resulted in major flooding of the surrounding country.

On the Eger river ice-drift was only very rarely connected with water-levels reaching the usual flood-levels of today or even more. A large amount of reports exist which register damages of bridges, foot-bridges, roads, and paths; many buildings were endangered, there was also damage of houses and implements etc.

The course of the flooding of the Eger was devastating. With continuous stagnation and jamming the ice in the Eger started to move on February 5th. The ice-drift reached Eger town on February 5th at 22.00 at +230 cm (the highest water-level in February 1897 was +200 cm) and Mostau (Mostov) on February 5th at 10.00 at +208 cm (the highest water-level in December 1902 was +180 cm). In Laun (Louny) the ice started to move in the morning of February 5th; here the water-level on February 6th at 8.00 was +445 cm (the maximum in 1890 was +400, in 1897 +300 cm).

The culmination flow of the Eger river in m^3 per s, the duration of the floods in hours, and the complete floodwave volume in million cubic metres, calculated from the annual flood, as shown in the Eger profiles:

Table 3   Eger floods in February 1909

Watercourse and place	Annual flood (m^3/s)	Date of flood	Culminated rate of flow (m^3/s)	Duration of flood (hrs)	floodwave volume (mio m^3)
Eger - Eger	70	03.-09.2.	250	46	3.6
Eger - Kaaden	187	03.-09.2.	635	58	46.7

The Biela river, too, overflowed its bed. On February 4th at 24.00 at Seestadtl (Ervenice) the level of +196 cm was reached, at Staditz (Stadice) the same day at 7.00 +138 cm. This flood which in the Biela lasted from February 3rd to 15th, reached a culmination flow of 48,0 m^3/s at Türmitz (Trmice) (where the annual flood is 17 m^3/s) and lasted 36 hours. The volume of the floodwave was 0.60 million m^3 and it culminated from 4th to 5th of February.

On February 7th it began to freeze, the weather was dry and the rivers therefore did not receive any new water, and a general lowering of water-levels commenced.

On February 9th heavy snowfall set in and the drifting snow reached a height of 70-80 cm. Equally unexpected all of February was very cold. On February 10th thaw started and caused an ice-drift in the Aussig stream (Chomutovka). Because no precautions had been taken, e.g. digging a ditch underneath the bridge, massive ice-floats heaped up at the stone bridge and the flood inundated the Grundtal road. Also on the military training range and along the Gärtner alleyway a proper stream flowed which passed through the Schneuer alley. To allow children to pass it crossings had to be erected. The rescue corps was working day and night to save the houses. The Aussig stream floods regularily in spring and children have been drowned.

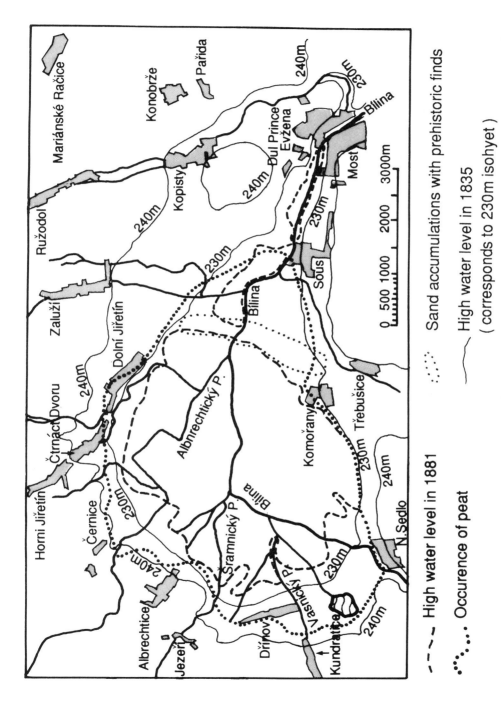

Fig. 1 Lake Kommern, according to a map by LOSERT (1940)

The flood in 1909 mainly flooded houses at Eidlitz (Údlice), as well as the district road in Pritschapl (Přečáply), it caused the breakage of the dam at Neusablitz (Nezabylice), tore away the mill at Bilenz (Bílence), and covered many meadows with sand.

Like at Komotau (Chomutov) the Hatschka stream (Hačka) was afflicted by floods. The inundation caused a lot of damage at Sporitz (Spořice), houses were flooded, the bed of the stream was completely drowned in rubble, and the waters ran through the village. At Trauschkowitz (Droužkovice) as well the flood had damaged many buildings. The same happened at Horschenitz (Hořenice).

The swelled Pöhlau (Pöhl stream, Polava) caused damage in parts of Weipert town (Vejprty), at Neugeschrei (Nové Zvolání), and at Böhmisch Hammern (České Hamry) even three people were drowned.

The floods also occurred in the Kleischer stream (Klíšsky potok) in the area of Aussig, even within the town of Aussig on the Elbe itself.

References

Archiv der Stadt Brüx, Akten aus den Jahren 1881-1883, Kreisarchiv Brüx

BRAUNER, J. M. (1904): Brüxer Gedenkbuch I. Hrsg. von der Stadtgemeinde Brüx

BRAUNER, J. M. (1905): Brüxer Gedenkbuch II. Hrsg. von der Stadtgemeinde Brüx

Brüxer Anzeiger 1881, 1897, 1927

Brüxer Zeitung 1881, 1927, 1932

Chronik der Stadt Eidlitz 1870-1935, Kreisarchiv Kaaden (Kadan)

Gedenkbuch der Gemeinde Oberdorf 1880-1930, Kreisarchiv Kaaden (Kadan)

KOŠLER, J. (1977): Kommerner See, Rekonstruktion der Überflutung aus dem Jahre 1881. Nicht veröffentlichte Handschrift des Autors, Prag

LOSERT, M. (1940): Vegetationsgeschichte Innerböhmens I: Der Kommerner See. Dresden

RICHTER, J. (1909): Der Eisgang auf den Flüssen Böhmens im Laufe der ersten Woche des Februar 1909. Österr. Wochenschrift für den öffentlichen Baudienst 15, Wien

Teplitz-Schönauer Anzeiger 1881, 1897, 1927

Wasserwirtschaftlicher Plan der Republik Č.S.S.R. (1954), Prag

WILD, J. (1926): Geschichte der Stadt Weipert. Franz Toms, Weipert (Vejprty)

Address of the author:

Dr. J. Kynčil, Ruska 298, CS-431 51 Klasterec nad Ohri, Czechoslovakia

Critical analysis of archive sources for historical climatology of Northern Italy

Dario Camuffo & Silvia Enzi

Summary

A large collection of data and a critical analysis of the existing archive sources in Northern Italy is under way. The aims are: to create a data bank of meteorological events and climatic hazards and to show the different cultural approach which characterized each period, the progress of historiography, and the critical editing of old manuscripts. The problem of dating is very complex, as several styles were used among the various cities and often more than one type was simultaneously used in the same place; finally, they were not always clearly declared in the manuscripts. A cross correlation between different chronicles and other historical sources is necessary in order to verify the actual dates. The climatic data are validated when the reliability of the event has also been established. To this end, some criteria are discussed. The main historico-philological ones are: self-consistency of the data, connected information, and cross checking of the sources; control of all the formal historical and philological aspects of the documents; considering texts written by direct witnesses as more reliable; checking the capability of the authors in reporting information; ascertaining whether events have been duplicated. The physical criteria: scientific consistency of the information either in itself or in relationship with other meteorological data; evaluating the particular importance of each information; stating a severity scale based on effects.

Zusammenfassung

In Norditalien werden gegenwärtig historische Klimadaten in größerem Umfang zusammengestellt; gleichzeitig wird das vorhandene Archivmaterial kritisch gesichtet. Angestrebt wird die Einrichtung einer Datenbank, in der meteorologische Ereignisse und Witterungsanomalien festgehalten werden. Darüber hinaus sollen die kulturelle Prägung der verschiedenen Epochen, die Fortschritte in der Historiographie und die Schwierigkeiten bei der Neufassung alter Manuskripte erfaßt werden. Als sehr komplex stellte sich das Problem der Datierung heraus, da in den verschiedenen Städten verschiedene Kalender in Gebrauch waren und mitunter auch nebeneinander verwendet wurden, was aus den alten Manuskripten nicht immer klar hervorgeht. Um die genannten Daten auf ihre Genauigkeit hin zu überprüfen, müssen die vorhandenen Chroniken mit anderen sicher datierbaren historischen Ereignissen korreliert werden. Um dieses Ziel zu erreichen, sollten folgende historiographische und philologische Kriterien berücksichtigt werden: (1) innerer Zusammenhang der Daten, (2) begleitende Informationen, (3) Vergleich der verschiedenen Quellen, (4) Überprüfung aller formalen und philologischen Aspekte eines Dokumentes auf Stimmigkeit, größere Vertrauenswürdigkeit von Augenzeugenberichten, (6) Überprüfung der Fähigkeit des Autors, Informationen unverfälscht wiederzugeben, (7) Sicherstellung der Authentizität der Berichterstattung. Darüber hinaus von Wichtigkeit sind die folgenden naturwissenschaftlichen Kriterien: (1) innerer wissenschaftlicher Zusammenhang der Information bzw. Übereinstimmung mit anderen meteorologischen Daten, (2) Bewertung der spezifischen Bedeutung jeder Information, (3) Gruppierung der meteorologischen Ereignisse nach der Intensität ihrer Auswirkungen.

1. Introduction

The Italian historical archives supply a large quantity of the Medieval Optimum, the Little Ice Age, and the Present Day Little Optimum, and a smaller amount of data for almost another millennium and a half.

The data gathering is underway in order to create a data bank of meteorological events and climatic hazards. The programme runs in five steps:

(1) searching the documentary sources;
(2) critical analysis of the source;
(3) evaluation of the author's reliability;
(4) collecting and filing data into the computer;
(5) critical analysis of each data information.

At present, the first four steps are carried out by routine, and only the data useful for specific research programmes are fully validated and analyzed (e.g. CAMUFFO, 1987; CAMUFFO & ENZI, 1990).

2. The problem of dating the archive sources and their possible validation

The modern Gregorian style substituted the old Julian one in 1582. Italy, at that time, was divided into a number of small states and dukedoms, each of which had their own method, and sometimes more than one, of dating events. The change in the calendar was only sometimes noted in the documents, as, for example, by SCHIAVINA ("*Annales Alexandrini*", seventeenth century). The correct interpretation of the date often becomes a serious problem. The dating styles were different (table 1) and not always clearly expressed. Therefore, it is necessary to search out, in the document, the day (e.g. 25 December, 1 January, 1 March) the official year began. However, the date cannot easily be recognized when the chronicle was not written in a strict chronological order. Sometimes, the year is indicated only by "ditto <anno>" i.e. "in the above mentioned year" without specifying the year and there is a continuous leap backwards and forwards between the past and the months ahead. Sometimes it is not clear when the changeover from one calendar to another occurred, or when the town changed the dating style. The worst case is when no explicit mention of the type of dating system is made and more than one calendar is used.

Table 1 Dating styles in use in ancient chronicles in comparison to the modern dating style

- Circumcision or Roman (i.e. "More Romano") or Numa: from the 1st January, as the Gregorian and Julian Calendars
- Incarnation, in use in Florence: from the 25th March postponed by 84 days
- Incarnation in use in Pisa: ended the 24th March, anticipated by 281 days
- "More Veneto" or "Romolo": from the 1st March, postponed by 2 months
- Easter: from the Easter Day
- Nativity: from the 25th December, occurring 6 days earlier
- Byzantine: from the 1st September, anticipated by 4 months
- Agiographic: it did not establish the year, but the day and month of the Patron Saint, and varied from town to town over the years
- Greek or Constantinople Indiction: from the 1st September, anticipated by 4 months
- Constantine or Caesar Indiction: from the 24th September, anticipated by 99 days
- Roman or Pontifical Indiction: from 25th December, anticipated by 6 days or more often from 1st July
- Indiction of Senna: starting from the 8th September, anticipated by 115 days
- From the rise to power of the Governor (Pope, Emperor, Prince, Podestà, Captains, Regents etc.)
- From the foundation of Rome

Note: There are also various other forms of dating in legal acts such as "A Nativitate", "Ab Incarna-tione", "Ab Incarnatione D.N.J.C.", "Anno D.N.J.C.", "Anno di nostra salute", or "Anno Millesimo", (this latter obviously after 1000) which appear to be synonyms used traditionally with the Circonci-sione calendar as well as literally, "Era Volgare".

Some authors used more than one calendar at a time, citing each clearly, for example BARONIO ("*Annales Ecclesiastici*", sixteenth century) who used three versions: the Year of Our Lord ("*Jesus Christi annus*"), the pontifical year of the elected Pope, the year of the Emperor's reign and the years of both the Eastern or Western Emperors, after the division of the Roman Empire. This means that there is no possible room for misunderstanding, although this does not mean that the particular author can be implicitly trusted to have correctly interpreted the dates given by the chroniclers whom he has used as references.

During the same period and in the same city different dating systems could be used and the type of calendar adopted was not always stated, thus causing a great deal of confusion, as illustrated by the various dating styles used in Venice (table 2). GALLICCIOLLI (1795) for example, who collected old documents, did not specify when dating was in "more Veneto" or "more Romano", and used the two styles haphazardly, so that it is not always easy to ascertain the exact date of any event.

Table 2   Dating styles in use at Venice

- calendar More Veneto, the most ancient and used; it was officially replaced by the "more Romano" which occurred in Venice with the fall of the Serenissima Republic (1797)
- calendar "More Romano"
- calendar "della Circoncisione"
- calendar *dei Magistrati*" or "Civil Collegiale", starting from St. Michele (29th September), originating from the "Indizione Cesarea" or "Constantiniana"
- "Indizione Constantinopolitana" during the more ancient times, simply indicated "Indizione"
- "Indizione Romana" at the end of the Republic, simply indicated "Indizione"
- Agiografic calendar, in common use

In absence of sufficient indications about the dating style, arriving at the correct date has only been possible by subjecting all the events that have been quoted to comparison with others which occurred that year the dates of which can be verified, e.g. historical events such as coronations, or the deaths of Popes or natural calamities such as earthquakes, or other phenomena such as eclipses or the passage of comets.

Also the internal consistency of the date has to be checked: day of the week and date must agree with the perpetual calendar. These criteria have been applied whenever possible, even in dealing with reliable authors who, in any case, sometimes used oral or written sources from different places or previous periods.

3. Problems in data validation

Verifying the data is as important as the data itself. In the last ten years, after the publication of LAMB's book (1977) on historical climatology, other milestone papers have appeared on the critical evaluation of the data, above all from a historical point of view (BELL & OGILVIE, 1978; INGRAM et al., 1978, 1981a, b; PFISTER 1984a, b, 1988; ALEXANDRE, 1987).

When only the prevalent climatic conditions over a fairly long period need to be discussed (for example, number of droughts or floods in a given century), exact dates are unnecessary. However, if the type of atmospheric circulation related to certain situations is to be analysed, then it becomes necessary to compare documents which refer to simultaneous events and exact dating is essential.

The need for correct dating also exists when comparing contemporary writings to verify the reliability of the text and the real severity of the event. For example, intense cold is referred to by different authors, but though living in the same area, in different years: this would suggest subjective opinions or more continent reasons on the intensity of the weather. Universal agreement in defining how cold a particular year was leaves no doubt about the objectivity of the statement.

On the other hand, finding the same information in more than one type does not necessarily mean that the date is correct, even though the event has been well documented. It could, in fact, be a collection (or repetition) of information from different origins with different degrees of authenticity. Finding the same event in many different texts, but each dependent on the other, should not automatically mean that the date can be considered reliable. It is not always easy to ascertain the dependence or independence of the sources, especially in the case of recurring literary formulae in ancient texts. Sometimes expressions appear which have a more formal than substantial value, such as: "Such event has not occurred within living memory, nor has it occurred before or since", stressing the importance of the event, which does not exclude its occurrence on other occasions.

Typical examples of the chain of transmission of dates can be shown some of which were particularly important because of their diffusion. In the first example, the chain of transmission begins with GALLICCIOLLI (1795), who carefully collected a certain quantity of original archives documenting climatological events of particular importance happening at Venice. According to the customs of his day, GALLICCIOLLI reported the sense rather than the literal quotation, only summarily citing the original. Some of the bibliographical notes were inexact while others did not even exist. This collection was faithfully reproduced by successive authors such as LEVI (1845), SEGARIZZI (1910), ZANON (1929), who cite, not GALLICCIOLLI, but the sources mentioned, without having checked them. This leads to series of real events consistently described and cited, which sometimes are formally inexact, especially in terms of the dates.

The case of TOALDO is particularly interesting, in that he was, without doubt, scrupulous when recording meteorological events of his time, but acritical in recounting exceptional events of the past, whether taken from chronicles, catalogues or other compilations. Unfortunately, TOALDO did not reproduce the original texts and the sources were rarely quoted, or summarily at the beginning of the chapter, and without specifying which particular event was being referred to. Reading the documents of the time has shown that many of the events cited by TOALDO (1770) are not to be relied upon. Moreover, the book published by TOALDO was most successful, and was translated into French and German, and quoted by PILGRAM (1788), ARAGO & BARRAL (1858), EASTON (1928). Such uncritical use has further perpetuated erroneus reports.

Modern scholars are correct in favouring first hand observations. However, this does not necessarily guarantee the competence, interests or emotions of the chroniclers nor that they may have exaggerated. The real causes of some climatic disasters may thus remain uncertain. As an example, ancient texts do not always indicate whether floods occurred due to heavy rains or due to the poor state of maintenance of the banks or the state of vegetation in relation with the run-off.

In practice, it was also found that data were not easy to classify into two categories only, i.e. as "good" or "bad". Not only are exact data needed, but the researcher must always be aware of all other related information and limits which exist when considering second hand information or information which contains formal inexactitudes. Sometimes descriptions can be found of events really happening, but they may be incorrectly or vaguely dated. Other examples exist of climatic events whose reliability is not totally verified. Therefore, it should be evaluated within which limits they can be soundly considered for particular purposes.

Not always an incompletely documented information must be rejected: it should be considered a climatic hypothesis which must be carefully investigated. The data should be verified by using different criteria, each of which establishes the relative limit of the data's reliability, as follows:

(1) A historico-philological validation should be based on the self-consistency of the data, on the border information and cross-checking of the sources; it leads to discarding from the subsequent analysis all the data which are in doubt. Even though data may be definitely incorrect because they may, for example, have been duplicated or falsified, they should, however, be mentioned together with the reasons why they have been discarded, in order to have a complete documentation of that period and make the work of other investigators easier. In data validating the following criteria were used:

(a) control all the formal historical and philological aspects (e.g. in type of document, language used, references to personages, places and facta, external witnesses etc.). Official acts of State recording calamities with an on-the-spot inspection and statement by a public notary, those pertaining to tax reductions or the awarding of subsidies or statements on shipping and merchandise losses after a meteorological calamity are extremely reliable. The data reliability also depends on the condition of the manuscript, whether it has been damaged, whether it is dirty, bound or legible;

(b) consider texts written by authors alive at the time of the events as generally more reliable. It is also important to note whether the writer was local, both in order to avoid distortions and to have reasonably accurate information about any antecedential sources which may later have been lost, in order to understand the local calendar;

(c) check whether the author was a scholar, whether he had free access to original or state documents when reporting preceding events, and whether he had any reason to alter them. The psychological conditioning of the time must also be considered e.g. when a comet passed overhead, it boded ill and so all past and future events were seen pessimistically. When an author, or a compiler, has been recognized to be highly accurate, it is possible to temporarily accept also the part of his news that cannot be compared with other chronicles;

(d) check the internal consistency of the data and above all compare the event in question with other events which can easily be verified;

(e) check whether other, similar events occurred in nearby places in the case of floods, drought, severe cold, etc. On the other hand, events described by independent sources, whose original was lost, may be considered acceptable;

(f) great care must be taken in ascertaining whether an event has been duplicated or whether such duplication refers to two separate events.

(2) A physical validation is based on the scientific consistency of the information, especially when it gives details which could not have been invented. The main criteria are:

(a) the text should be physically consistent with the facts reported, even though the author may have wrongly interpreted them;

(b) the data should be consistent with other meteorological information gleaned and reported over a wider scale, so that the event forms part of a coherent physical mosaic;

(c) a physical point of view is required in evaluating the peculiar importance of each piece of information, whose ensemble defines a climatic scenario. In some cases, a quantitative evaluation of the severity of the event is possible by judging its consequences.

(3) A few considerations should also be made from the mathematical point of view. The excessive severity which leads to certain data being discarded because of doubts concerning their validity can also cause uncertainties and errors in the analysis of the series. In fact, data missing should be considered an error comparable with the inclusion of wrong data. Long-term changes of climate may be evidenced by making harmonic analyses on unbroken, long series. It is, therefore, necessary to determine whether it is better to renounce the advantage of having a very long series to study secular changes and to divide the original series into two or more short sub-series in order to discard certain periods of lesser reliability. Besides, for the uncertain period substitute random data could be generated, using programmes designed to integrate the series without introducing spurious harmonics. Sometimes it might seem wiser to use data with fewer

guarantees, but which are, however, reasonably reliable. The choice, obviously, is sometimes highly subjective and should be made with extreme caution.

4. Conclusions

The archive sources existing in Italy cover the last millennium abundantly. The large quantity of manuscripts generally makes cross comparison of the sources possible, thus verifying the reliability of the data and the accuracy of each author. Each age should be considered individually, since the historical and scientific interests and aims changed with time. The number of chronicles is impressive: to give an idea, 35% of all documents available for the Middle Ages in Central Europe are from Northern and Central Italy, according to ALEXANDRE. Gathering climatic documentations is not particularly difficult in terms of data due to their abundance. What is difficult, is making an exact critical evaluation of their reliability especially in terms of the data itself.

Dating styles are not homogeneous and often very complex, but usually there are no problems in recognizing the correct date. Sometimes local chronicles may leave doubts, especially when dealing with winters and choosing the date between two contiguous years.

The validation of data is very important and requires an accurate analysis, based both on a historico-philological and a physical point of view.

It would be better not to divide the events into historically acceptable and not acceptable, in the absolute sense, but to look for the type of information that can be extracted from each text and its degree of reliability. The threshold of acceptable reliability depends on the kind of analysis which should be carried out, e.g. historic reconstruction, climatic scenario, and psychologic impact.

The rejection of data due to excessive severity may introduce uncertainty into the system. In fact, in the mathematical analysis of a climate time series, the lack of data due to their rejection for excessive severity, should be considered an error comparable with the inclusion of wrong data.

Once the historico-philological analysis has been carried out, the physical problem of how representative a report may be arises with different weight given to descriptions which may have been conditioned by the culture, the state of the land, the interactions between the ecosystem and human activity, or by the technology of the time.

A critical examination and comparison of the chronicles should help in recognizing any eventual exaggeration, especially when individual events may appear somewhat doubtful. Sometimes, the sequence of daily information which in itself may appear insignificant, such as "today rain" or "today drizzle" can, if taken together, supply a wider general picture, so that a comparison can be made between the monthly precipitation of that time and the present day. In this sense, daily news such as that given by SANUDO (sixteenth century) or GENNARI (eighteenth century) have a rather different meaning, in that they supply an exhaustive picture typifying a certain period.

Non-climatic factors, such as abandoning the land in time of war, enemy raids, systematic cutting of trees during a siege or for the construction of fleets, reduction in manual labour during or after an epidemic, indiscriminate pasturing or invasion of locusts can interfere in ways which can not easily be checked. All of these events may, however, contribute to the process of rendering an area desert when its hydrological balance is delicate, or when the type of cultivation is unsuitable for the ecosystem.

The frequency of the events described seems, at times, to be an indication of the climate, at others the psychological conditioning of a society severely tried. That climate greatly affected man is witnessed by the copious documentation regarding events which were not severe but, all the same, difficult to endure. In the case of events not influenced by anthropogenic factors, it is also possible to evaluate the intensity of the forcing climatic factors on the basis of their effects and these may be classified on a scale of severity.

Acknowledgements

This work was carried out under the Climatology and Natural Hazards Programme of the Commission of the European Communities DG XII (contract EV4C-0082-I-A) in cooperation with the National Research Council (C.N.R.) Strategic Project Climate, Environment and Territory of Southern Italy.

References

ALEXANDRE, P. (1987): Le climat en Europe au Moyen-Age. Contribution à l'histoire des variations climatiques de 1000 à 1425, d'après les sources narratives de l'Europe occidentale. Ecole des Hautes Etudes en Sciences Sociales, Paris, 827 p.

ARAGO, F. & BARRAL, J. A. (1858): Sur l'état thermometrique du globe terrestre. Oeuvres de F. Arago, Tome 8, Notices scientifiques 5, Paris

BELL, W. & OGILVIE, A. E. (1978): Weather compilations as a source of data for the reconstruction of European climate during the Medieval period. Climatic Change 1, 331-348

CAMUFFO, D. (1987): Freezing of the Venetian Lagoon since the 9th century A.D., in comparison to the climate of Western Europe and England. Climatic Change 10, 43-66

CAMUFFO, D. & ENZI, S. (1990): Reconstructing the climate of Northern Italy from archive sources. In: Jones, Ph. & Bradley, R. (eds.): Climate since 1500 A.D. Unwin Hyman, London

EASTON, C. (1928): Les hivers dans l'Europe occidentale. Brill, Leyden

Galicciolli, G. B. (1795): Memorie Veneziane antiche profane ed ecclesiastiche. Fracasso, Venice

Hennig, R. (1904): Katalog bemerkenswerter Witterungsereignisse von den ältesten Zeiten bis zum Jahre 1800. Abh. Königl. Preuß. Meteorol. Inst. II/4, Berlin

Ingram, M. J.; Underhill, D. J. & Wigley, T. M. L. (1978): Historical Climatology. Nature 276, 329-334

Ingram, M. J.; Farmer, G. & Wigley, T. M. L. (1981a): Past climates and their impact on Man: a review. In: Climate and history. Cambridge Univ. Press, Cambridge

Ingram, M. J.; Underhill, D. J. & Farmer, G. (1981b): The use of documentary sources for the study of past climates. In: Wigley, T. M. L.; Ingram, M. J. & Farmer, G. (eds.): Climate and history. Cambridge Univ. Press, Cambridge, 180-213

Lamb, H. H. (1977): Climate: present, past and future, Vol. 2, Methuen, London

Levi, M. G. (1845): Dell'inverno e di alcuni suoi effetti. Cecchini e Naratovich, Venezia

Pfister, C. (1984a): The potential of documentary data for the reconstruction of past climates, early 16th to 19th century, Switzerland as a case study. In: Mörner, N. A. & Karlén, W. (eds.): Climatic changes on a yearly to millennial basis. Reidel, Dordrecht, 331-337

Pfister, C. (1984b): Klimageschichte der Schweiz 1525-1869: Das Klima der Schweiz von 1525-1860 und seine Bedeutung in der Geschichte von Bevölkerung und Landwirtschaft. Vol. 1, Haupt, Bern

Pfister, C. (1988): Variations in the spring-summer climate of Central Europe from the High Middle Ages to 1850. In: Wanner, H. & Siegenthaler, U. (eds.): Long and short term variability of climate. Springer, Berlin, Heidelberg, 57-82

Pilgram, A. (1788): Untersuchungen über das Wahrscheinliche der Wetterkunde. Wien

Segarizzi, A. (1910): Iconografie della Laguna Veneta agghiacciata. Emporium 31, 59-69

Toaldo, G. (1770): Della vera influenza degli astri sulle stagioni e mutazioni del tempo. Saggio meteorologico, 1st and 2nd ed., Stamperia del Seminario, Padova

Zanon, F. S. (1933): Fattori meteorologici straordinari in Venezia e nei dintorni ricordati dai cronisti. In: Magrini, G. (ed.): La Laguna di Venezia. Vol. 2, Tome 3, Ferrari, Venice, 287-305

Addresses of the authors

Dr. D. Camuffo, Consiglio Nazionale delle Ricerche, I.C.T.R., Padova, Italy
Dr. Silvia Enzi, Consiglio Nazionale delle Ricerche, I.C.T.R., Padova, Italy

Reconstruction of the climate of Bohemia and Moravia in the last millennium - problems of data and methodology

Rudolf Brázdil

Summary

The contribution evaluates some methodological and data problems arising when utilizing written sources concerning the weather and indirect indicators for reconstructing the climate of Bohemia and Moravia in the last millennium.

Zusammenfassung

In dem vorliegenden Beitrag sollen neben methodischen Problemen auch die Schwierigkeiten, die mit der Interpretation der Daten aus historischen Wetteraufzeichnungen zusammenhängen, bewertet werden. Ebenfalls kritisch beleuchtet wird die Aussagekraft der indirekten Indikatoren, die für eine Rekonstruktion des Klimas von Böhmen und Mähren während des letzten Jahrtausends herangezogen werden können.

1. Introduction

The need for a qualified estimate of future scenarios of the climate and its impact on the environment and the human society produces considerable pressure on a thorough knowledge of the history of climate. An important key to the knowledge of the climate in the historical period (mostly the last millennium) are written sources containing either a direct description of weather and climate (as a rule data about extreme meteorological phenomena) or indirect data about phenomena, processes, and events dependent on weather and climate to a different extent. A detailed typology of historical climatic data and their sources is given, among others, by PFISTER (1988).

2. Written sources concerning weather and climate in Bohemia and Moravia

In Bohemia, the first written record on weather can be found in "KOSMAS Czech Chronicle" from 1092: "And just in the Easter week, the 1st of April, a large quantity of snow fell and such frost set in as seldom occurs in the middle of winter". Data relating to an earlier period, such as the report "on an extraordinarily dry year, 761, when in Bohemia it did not rain at all for 8 months" (HÁJEK's Chronicle) cannot be considered reliable according to HŘIBOVÁ (1956). In the twelfth to fourteenth centuries short reports on weather appear in annals written or dictated by high clerical dignitaries in monasteries usually only as a complement or background to political events or biographies of saints. They are very rare and usually concentrated in official collections of ancient texts. In connection with the penetration of Renaissance the interest in the study of weather as a factor affecting the agricultural production and, accordingly, even the financial results increased for practical reasons. Between the mid-fifteenth century and about the mid-seventeenth century, the chronicles were written mainly by wealthy citizens with properties in the country (fields, orchards, vineyards) and municipal clerks financially interested in the development of agriculture. The majority of these weather records is concentrated in the procès-verbal of the meetings of the local board or in "*Libri memorabilium*". On the pages of favoured almanacs, astrometeorological forecasts appeared often in connection with observations of people professionally interested in weather phenomena.

As the first systematic observations on weather in this country can be considered records carried out in Moravia in the years 1533-1545 by some of the ancestors of KAREL SENIOR FROM ŽEROTÍN, a representative of a well-known Moravian noble family who himself left observations of 1588-1589 and 1591 (KLEMM, 1983). In Bohemia the first known meteorological observations are the records of the physician MATHIAS BORBONIUS FROM BORBENHEIM in the years 1596-1598 and 1622 (PEJML & MUNZAR, 1968). The so far longest known series of the earliest continuous observations (1603-1612) are marginals of an unknown author in astronomical ephemerides compiled by DAVID ORIGANUS (DUBEC & PEJML, 1985).

Such regular daily weather records were, of course, rather an exception since mainly annalists' records of extreme weather phenomena predominated. From the seventeenth century, characterized by the Thirty Years' War with the ensuing penury affecting even the next generations, there exist few weather records, most of them of low value. A distinct increase of weather records occurred in the latter half of the eighteenth and the first half of the nineteenth centuries when they were carried out by provincial teachers, parsons, peasants, less often by the nobility clerks and citizens. But the quality of such records mostly did not exceed the level of the records from the second half of the sixteenth century (PEJML, 1968).

It is possible to state that the Czech weather records of meteorological character from the past centuries are characterized, contrary to those from other countries, by considerable splitting in place and time which makes the reconstruction of climatic fluctuations difficult. In addition many weather records were destroyed during frequent fires and inconsiderable reorganizations of municipal archives (PEJML, 1968).

3. Methodological problems of the analysis of written sources on weather and climate

Records of weather relating to the territory of Bohemia and Moravia are included in several major compendiums. Thus, to the period of 633-1700 is related a chronological overview of natural phenomena by STRNAD (1790), including, according to different sources, about 800 records from the whole of Bohemia on comets and meteors, eclipses, optical phenomena, severe winters and hot summers, rains, floods, etc. The occurrence of dry periods in Bohemia in the years 962-1893 was assessed by AUGUSTIN (1894). KROLMUS (1845) describes in his paper the occurrence of floods, dry and wet periods. Important are the papers by KATZEROWSKY (e.g. 1886), who compiled a list of reports for Litoměřice based on the archival material on the one hand, and on his own observations on the other. In all the above papers critical evaluations of the given reports are lacking. Thus, HŘIBOVÁ (1956) does not consider reliable data before the beginning of the twelfth century and those from KROLMUS' compilation. A critical approach towards data quality is not lacking in the paper by PEJML (1966) including written records on weather of the period 1500-1900 for the so-called North Bohemian vine and hop growing region (i.e. the region of the lower reaches of the Ohře between the towns of Žatec and Litoměřice) - further just called North Bohemian region - on the basis of which he then carried out the reconstruction of climatic conditions in that region. This study of PEJML's is the most important Czechoslovakian paper serving as a basis for the reconstruction of climatic conditions in Bohemia from the beginning of the sixteenth century.

Besides papers originating in this country there are weather records relating to the territory of Bohemia and Moravia included in papers of authors from abroad, such as HENNIG (1904) or BORISENKOW & PASETSKIY (1988). Many items of information on hydrometeorological phenomena included in the compendium by WEIKINN (1958-1963) are also related to the weather in Bohemia and Moravia. In further utilization and processing of the published and unpublished records the following facts are to be borne in mind:

(a)   Record density

The variable temporal density of records follows on the one hand from the natural temporal variability of weather and climate phenomena, on the other hand from the effects of the civilization factor. The growth of information is positively affected by the number of possible authors recording the events, the number of preserved records and chronicles, the state of social communication, recording and printing possibilities (such as the development of printing), negatively particularly by prolonged war events (KŘIVSKÝ & PEJML, 1988). An example of the unequal density of records of hydrometeorological events in Bohemia and Moravia is given in Fig. 1. Their frequencies correspond to the statement by PEJML (1965), that the normal frequency of records in our region only exists for the period 1550-1630. The quantitative rate of annual record density H_z, adapted according to the paper of PEJML (1968), can be written in the form:

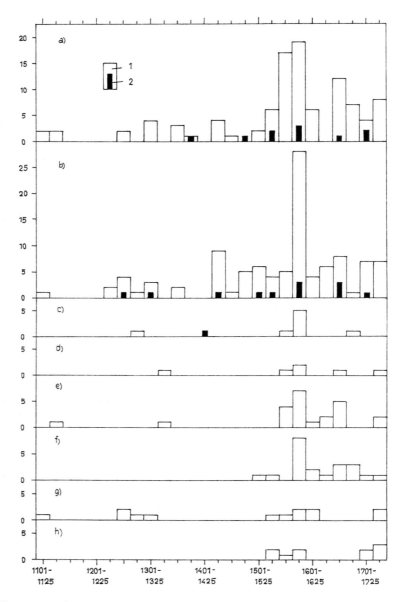

Fig. 1 Frequency of records of the occurrence of extreme hydrometeorological phenomena in Bohemia (1) and Moravia (2) in twenty-five-year periods in the time from 1100 to 1750. Explanations: (a) floods (cause of flood not indicated and cannot unequivocally be decided upon); (b) floods due to heavy or continuous rains; (c) floods due to the melting of the snow cover; (d) floods due to the melting of the snow cover and rain; (e) floods due to the movement of ice; (f) ice movement with possible damage; (g) strong frosts (freezing of streams, bottom ice); (h) drought (drying up of streams, low water-levels). Source: WEIKINN (1958-1963)

$$H_z = k_1 \frac{P_1}{365} + k_2 \frac{P_2}{52} + k_3 \frac{P_3}{12} + k_4 \frac{P_4}{4} + k_5 \frac{P_5}{1}$$

where P_i is the real number of observations, and k_i stands for the transfer coefficients ($k_1 = 84.1$; $k_2 = 12.0$; $k_3 = 2.8$; $k_4 = 0.9$; $k_5 = 0.2$). Indices i denote whether they are daily (1), weekly (2), monthly (3), seasonal (4) or annual (5) records. The value H_z moves within the limits 0-100%. H_z does not inform about the rate of information.

(b)   Record reliability

Record reliability is a reflection on the subject by the observer, depending on his cultural and education standards, observing and comparing ability, memory, carefulness, etc. In general it holds that the value of the weather record increases with the approach towards the time in which the author of the record lived. An essential prerequisite for good data quality is the comparing analysis not only with domestic, but also foreign sources (e.g. the whole region of Central Europe).

(c)   Spatial and temporal coordination of records

Some written weather records are related to major territorial units, which reduces their statement ability (i.e. the statement "dry weather in Bohemia"). In this case, with regard to interpretation, it is necessary to evaluate the spatial variability of the phenomenon studied. As for the regions of Bohemia and Moravia, this means that it is possible to neglect the spatial variability of temperature extremes (e.g. severe or mild winters) but, however, spatial differences in precipitation (e.g. dry or wet summers) can be much more substantial. Considerable regional differences will appear in the occurrence of floods due to heavy rains, as well as in the occurrence of some further meteorological phenomena (such as thunderstorms, hailstorms, windstorms). From the point of view of temporal coordination of records it is necessary to take into consideration changes in dating style (replacement of the Julian style by the Gregorian one) as well as the possibility of erroneous temporal coordination (e.g. in winters). A number of records also appear without a particular time specification in the course of the year, season or month.

(d)   Time specification

Time specification must be considered when evaluating meteorological causes of the phenomena and events described, especially if a meteorological phenomenon of the same intensity can have quite different effects (i.e. inundations due to precipitation, wind effects, broken dams). It is also necessary to take into consideration a possible different character of the environment (e.g. the extent of areas covered with forests or ponds).

(e)   Intensity of the phenomena described

The intensity of the phenomena described depends to a great extent on the personality of the observer (cp. paragraph b). The qualitative ambiguity of the description supports a certain standard of subjectivity in further processing of the records which depends on the knowledge and experience of the observer. A device in the classification of the intensity of phenomena is the introduction of some degrees, if the classification fulfills certain criteria. Thus, DUBEC (1985) recommends introducing the so-called seasonal index I for the individual seasons. Zero denotes a phenomenon of normal intensity, 1-5 is the increasing intensity with positive anomaly and (-1) - (-5) with negative anomaly. An example of this type of processing which, of course, involves a certain rate of subjectivity (DUBEC estimates it to 20-25%), is given in Fig. 2. An undoubted advantage of such an approach is, however, the compatibility of records within the given series.

(f)   Quantitative interpretation of written records

Quantitative interpretation of written qualitative records can be negatively affected above all by the following factors: incompleteness of records, subjectivity of the observer, variability of the weather, and a small number of long and homogeneous instrumental observations. The proper quantitative reconstruction is based on the comparison of frequencies of the series of weather extremes with the series of instrumental observations. The above facts can be illustrated by the example of the North Bohemian region, for which, based on written sources, frequencies of severe and mild winters were calculated according to individual decades in the period of 1501-1910 (PEJML, 1966). As reference the series of temperature observations from the station Prague-Klementinum was used, starting with measurements in 1775 which were extended down to 1771 by HLAVÁČ (1966) and on the basis of regression with Basel to 1755 by SVOBODA (1988). The station is situated about 50 km from the centre of the region, so that the spatial variability of air temperature in the temporal sense can be neglected, because temperature extremes affect only large territorial units. Thus, the correlation coefficient for winter temperatures between Prague-Klementinum and Litoměřice in the above region was as much as 0.99 in the period 1907/08-1936/37. The Prague temperature series can be considered to be homogeneous. However, the question of the possible increase of the effect of the temperature island of the city could be problematic. For reconstruction, again the methodology described by LYAKHOV (1984) was used. The limits of normal winter temperatures were given by the relation:

$$(t_{min} + t) / 2 = t = (t_{max} + t) / 2$$

where t is the long-term average, t_{min} and t_{max} the corresponding extremes of the mean winter temperatures. In the case of Prague-Klementinum the corresponding limiting values are -3.0 and 2.1°C, respectively. With regard to these limits all mild and severe winters were selected, divided by decades (1760/61-1769/70, ..., 1979/80-1980/89) and by periods of thirty years (1755/56-1784/85, 1779/80-1808/09, ..., 1959/60-1988/89). The differences of the corresponding frequencies of mild and severe winters were then correlated with mean winter temperatures of the corresponding decades and/or periods of 30 years (Fig. 3). From the thus obtained regression lines of the Prague series, on the basis of the different frequencies of mild and severe winter stated by PEJML, mean winter temperatures of the North Bohemian region were calculated, which were then reduced by the mean temperature difference of winters between Prague-Klementinum and stations in the centre of the region studied (the difference according to the mean values in the period of 1901-1950 was 0.9°C; cp. Fig. 4). In an analogous way it would be possible to reconstruct the precipitation conditions according to the number of extremely dry and wet summers as well.

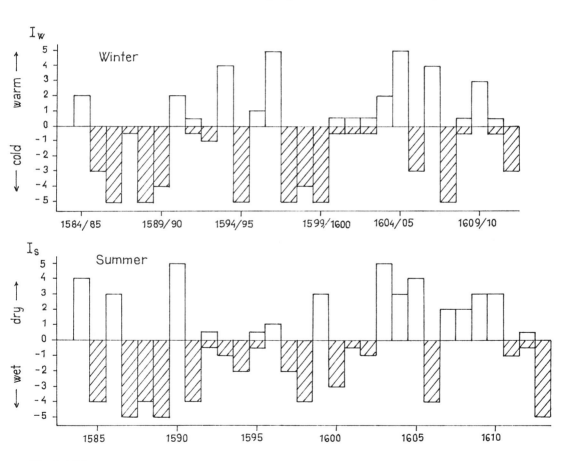

Fig. 2   Values of the seasonal indices of the temperature character of winters (Iw) in the period of 1584/85-1611/12 and the humidity character of summers (Is) in the period of 1584-1613 in Central Bohemia (according to DUBEC & PEJML, 1985)

4. Indirect written records of weather and climate

This group includes written sources which, although not mentioning the weather directly, can serve its reconstruction from the description of phenomena, processes and activities depending on it. Many of them are included in papers quoted in the preceding section. They can be divided into two groups, geophysical (such as data about floods, solar activity) and biological sources (such as data about the phenophases of plants, doing farm work, vintage, attacks of grasshoppers).

From the data about floods (e.g. WEIKINN, 1958-1963) it is possible to obtain direct or indirect information about their meteorological causes (cp. Fig. 1), i.e. the occurrence of heavy rains (they can be judged also in the case of floods of the summer half-year, where the cause is not explicitly stated), warming (the movement of ice, floods due to the thawing of the snow cover), long periods of drought (a conspicuous lowering of the water-levels, drying up of brooks and rivers), periods of strong frosts (freezing of rivers, bottom ice), the depth and melting of the snow cover (floods due to snow melting). However, the fact must not be forgotten that the conditions for run-off were different in the past from those met today in a cultural landscape strongly affected by man.

The occurrence of floods of the Elbe in the last millennium was related to changes in sun activity, characterized by the occurrence of large sunspots (in parallel there were also stated polar lights and the occurrence of ^{14}C-oscillations in tree-rings, corresponding very well with solar activity) described in a paper by KŘIVSKÝ & PEJML (1988). Linking up with former conclusions by KŘIVSKÝ (1953), who found that in Bohemia the secular period of increased precipitation was connected with secular minima of solar activity, an analogous dependence is also stated for the occurrence of floods and solar activity. As follows from a number of papers, the evaluation of the relations between solar activity and hydrometeorological phenomena is very contradictory.

Also in the case of the group of biological records there remains the problem of the relation between the phenomenon studied and the weather and a possibility of ambiguous interpretation. Particularly historical data concerning vine growing are much in demand. Decisive are not only the yields or the area of vine growing, but particularly the quality of the wine. Wine of excellent quality signalizes a dry, hot summer, whereas a cold, rainy summer is reflected in a worse quality or in prolonged vintage. Data in ledgers about work in the vineyards or wages for that work in January or February document a mild course of winters. In the same way, an early beginning of the harvest is caused by a dry and warm weather. Analogous dependencies can also be formulated for the hop yields, but bad harvest can be due to both dry weather and unfavourable temperature conditions in the decisive months. The interpretation of the above records reflects, as a rule, data obtained in the present century. That is why it is necessary to take into consideration also fundamental differences in agricultural production methods.

Historical biological climate indicators were employed in the above climate reconstruction, particularly in the North Bohemian region by PEJML (1966, 1968). Data of analogous character of the latter half of the fifteenth century in the Louny district were processed by VANIŠ (1982). According to the book of accounts of 1450-1472, he states that the climate in the Louny district was warm at that time, the winters being relatively mild.

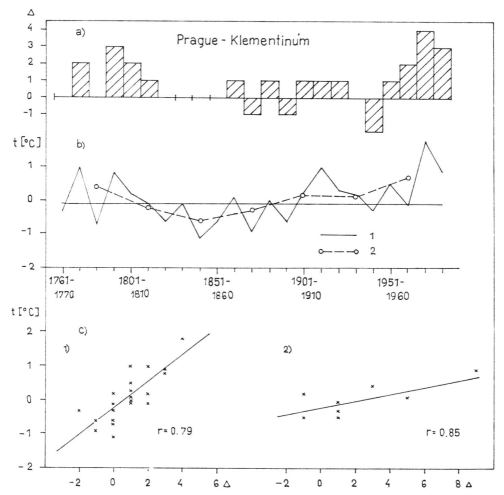

Fig. 3 (a) Differences (Δ) in the number of mild and severe winters according to decades for Prague-Klementinum according to the LYAKHOV (1984) criteria in the period of 1761-1989; (b) the variation of mean winter air temperatures in periods of 10 (1) and 30 (2) years in Prague-Klementinum in the period of 1760/61-1988/89 (the first period of 30 years 1770/71-1799/1800, the last decade 1979/80-1988/89); (c) the correlation of mean winter temperatures (t) and differences in the number of mild and severe winters (Δ) in Prague-Klementinum for decades (1) and for periods of 30 years (2); r - correlation coefficient. Equations of regression lines: (1) t = -0.26 + 0.40Δ; (2) t = -0.21 + 0.11Δ

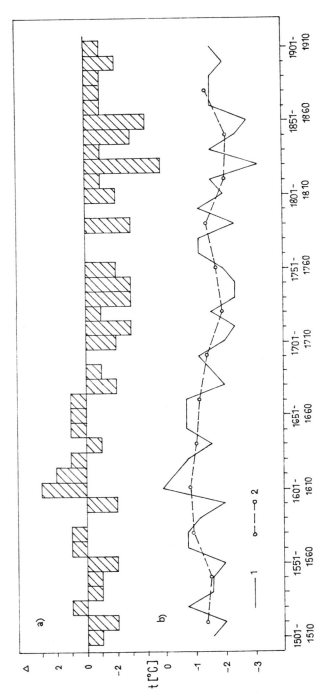

Fig. 4 Fluctuation of the temperature character of winters in the North Bohemian region in the period of 1500/01-1909/10: (a) differences (D) in the number of mild and severe winters in decades according to data by Pejml (1966); (b) mean temperatures of decades (1) and periods of 30 years (2) of winters reconstructed with respect to the differences D in part (a) of the figure according to regression relations found for Prague-Klementinum in Fig. 3 c

4. Conclusion

The hitherto development of historical climatology in Czechoslovakia, documented by problems of written materials on weather, shows a certain lag in comparison with the neighbouring countries. The historical records were systematically evaluated and employed for the reconstruction of the fluctuations of the climate starting with the sixteenth century only for the North Bohemian vine and hop growing region, data from other places being of rather accidental character. Essentially fewer written records on weather are related to the territory of Moravia than to the territory of Bohemia. But with few exceptions active cooperation of historians is missing. Missing are also papers utilizing other indirect methods for the reconstruction of the climate of the last millennium. The solution of this unsatisfying state should proceed in the following directions:

(a) consistent inventarization of accessible sources, both domestic and from abroad, on weather relating to the present territory of Czechoslovakia, evaluation of their credibility, and the formation of the corresponding data base;
(b) fundamental processing of those data fitting the needs of climate reconstruction on the territory of Czechoslovakia in the historical period;
(c) publication of the revised source material, thus making it accessible also to research workers from other countries;
(d) utilization of indirect biological or geophysical indicators and methods for climate reconstruction (such as tree-ring analysis, pollen analysis);
(e) climate reconstruction for the territory of Czechoslovakia in the historical period in the context of the Central European region to be utilized to check the credibility of the European scenarios of future climatic changes.

References

AUGUSTIN, F. (1894): Sucha v Čechách v době od roku 962-1893. A. Reinwart, Praha, 27 p.

BORISENKOV, Ye. P. & PASETSKIY, V. M. (1988): Tysyatcheletnyaya letopis neobytchaynykh yavleniy prirody. Mysl, Moskva, 524 p.

DUBEC, K. (1985): Několik poznámek o historických pramenech ke kolísání klimatu v Česku a o jejich základním zpracování. Klimatické změny, 120-132

DUBEC, K. & PEJML, K. (1985): Příspěvek k poznání klimatu ve středních a severozápadních Čechách v období 1584 až 1647. Klimatické změny, 195-203

HENNIG, R. (1904): Katalog bemerkenswerter Witterungsereignisse von den ältesten Zeiten bis zum Jahre 1800. Abh. Königl. Preuß. Meteorol. Inst. 2, 1-93

HLAVÁČ, V. (1966): Jak se jeví kolísání klimatu za posledních dvě stě roků v pražské teplotní řadě. Meteorol. Zpr. 19, 33-42

HŘIBOVÁ, B. (1956): Význam historických meteorologických zpráv pro dnešní klimatologii. Meteorol. Zpr. 9, 159-162

Katzerowsky, W. (1886): Die meteorologischen Aufzeichnungen der Leitmeritzer Stadtschreiber aus den Jahren 1564-1607. H. Dominikus, Prag

Klemm, F. (1983): Die Entwicklung der meteorologischen Beobachtungen in Österreich einschließlich Böhmen und Mähren bis zum Jahr 1700. Ann. Meteorol. (N.F.) 21, 1-48

Krolmus, W. (1845): Kronyka čili děgepis wssech powodnj poslaupných let, suchých i mokrých, aurodných a neaurodných na obilj, owoce a wjna, hladů, morů a giných pohrom w králowstwi Českém. Tiskem Karla Wetterla w Žitnobranské ulici, Praha, 261 p.

Křivský, L. (1953): The long-range variability of annual precipitation in Prague-Klementinum in the period 1805-1951 and in relation to the solar activity. Publ. Astr. Obs. ČSAV 23, 37-72

Křivský, L. & Pejml, K. (1988): Solar activity, aurorae and climate in Central Europe in the last 1000 years. Trav. Géophys. 33, 77-151

Lyakhov, M. Ye. (1984): Klimatitcheskiye ekstremumy v tsentralnoy tchasti yevropeyskoy territorii SSSR v XIII-XX vv. Izv. A.N. S.S.S.R., Ser. Geogr. 6, 68-74

Pejml, K. (1965): Kolísání klimatu v 16. a v 17. stol. v české vinařské a chmelařské oblasti. Meteorol. Zpr. 18, 164-167

Pejml, K. (1966): Příspěvek ke kolísání klimatu v severočeské vinařské a chmelařské oblasti od r. 1500-1900. Sb. Pr. H.M.Ú. Č.S.R. 7, 23-78

Pejml, K. (1968): Poznámky ke kvantitativní interpretaci kronikářských záznamů z let 1770-1833. Meteorol. Zpr. 21, 56-63

Pejml, K. & Munzar, J. (1968): Matyáš Borbonius z Borbenheimu a jeho meteorologická pozorování z let 1596-1598, 1622. Meteorol. Zpr. 21, 93-95

Pfister, C. (1988): Klimageschichte der Schweiz 1525-1860: Das Klima der Schweiz von 1525-1860 und seine Bedeutung in der Geschichte von Bevölkerung und Landwirtschaft. Paul Haupt, Bern, Stuttgart

Strnad, A. (1790): Chronologisches Verzeichnis der Naturbegebenheiten im Königreiche Böhmen, vom Jahre Christi 633 bis 1700. Herrlische Buchhandlung, Prag, 123 p.

Svoboda, J. (1988): Pokus o rekonstrukci měsíčních teplot Prahy-Klementina zpětně do roku 1755. Manuscript, unpublished

Vaniš, J. (1982): Historická geografie Lounska v druhé polovině 15. století. Hist. Geogr. 20, 127-186

Weikinn, C. (1958-1963): Quellentexte zur Witterungsgeschichte Europas von der Zeitwende bis zum Jahre 1850 (Hydrographie). Teil 1 (Zeitwende-1500) 1958; Teil 2 (1501-1600) 1960; Teil 3 (1601-1700) 1961; Teil 4 (1701-1750) 1963, Akademie-Verlag Berlin

Address of the author

Prof. Dr. R. Brázdil, Department of Geography, Masaryk University, Kotlářská 2, 611 37 Brno, Czechoslovakia

Methodological aspects of climate reconstructions on the basis of dendrological data

Margarite Chernavskaya

Summary

The information needed for the verification of the historical climate reconstructions may be obtained from dendrological data. In normal conditions with no factors limiting tree growth (for example in the central part of the Russian plain) it is a rather complicated problem to extract the essential climatic signal. In this case it is necessary to use a response function in order to reveal the significant correlation between the tree growth indicators and individual elements of climate. Some promising results were obtained for Central and Eastern Europe.

Zusammenfassung

Die für die Überprüfung historischer Klimarekonstruktionen notwendigen Informationen können anhand von dendrologischen Daten gewonnen werden. Unter Normalbedingungen, wie sie beispielsweise im zentralen Teil des Russischen Tieflandes bestehen und sich durch uneingeschränkte Wachstumsbedingungen auszeichnen, ist es relativ problematisch, aus den Dendrodaten das entscheidende klimatische Signal abzuleiten. In diesem Fall muß die signifikante Korrelation zwischen Wachstumsindikatoren und individuellen Klimaelementen mit Hilfe einer "response function" ermittelt werden. Vielversprechende Ergebnisse konnten bereits für Mittel- und Osteuropa erzielt werden.

1. Introduction

The Department of Climatology and Hydrology of the Institute of Geography at the U.S.S.R. Academy of Sciences has recently been engaged in studying the variability of climate in Europe, especially in Eastern Europe (the Russian Plain), in the historical past. The work includes the collection and systematization of proxy data about climatic variations over the historical period, the analysis of proxy climatic indicators' series, the development of techniques for the reconstruction of climatic conditions, as well as the analysis of temporal and spatial climatic changes over the last millennium and earlier.

The sources of climatic information about the U.S.S.R. European territory can be divided into three groups: instrumental data, both systematic and episodic, with a 250-year record maximum; historical evidence, including annals, archives, diaries and other data covering the last millennium; and natural climate indicators, such as glaciological, palynological, limnological, and dendrological data covering the entire historical period. These sources differ in terms of the length of data series, accuracy of dating and in the nature of climatic information contained therein.

It should be stressed that reliable results on climatic reconstructions of the historical past can be obtained only by using different kinds of proxy indicators which allow a mutual cross checking of results obtained from independent data types.

2. Data, methods and results

The information value of various proxy indicators depends on the accuracy of time reference of proxy data and the degree of correlation between proxy indicators and instrumental series. Reliable reconstructions based on proxy indicators and on linear correlation relationships can be obtained if the value of the corresponding correlation coefficient is at least 0.7. In this case, the reconstructed series of climatic indicators contains no less than 50% of the data on the variability of climatic conditions (ZOLOTOKRYLIN et al., 1986).

The search for correlative connections between the indices of the growth of a tree and various meteorological elements is based on the known fact that trees growing at the treeline are very sensitive to changes in the factors limiting their growth. At the northern limit of forest growth, where the thermal regime of the growth period is the limiting factor, some researchers have demonstrated close correlative links with air temperature (POLOZOVA & SHIYATOV, 1979).

At the same time the effectiveness of reconstructing climatic conditions using dendrochronological series depends a great deal on the comparability of the level of spatial generalization of the data. At the local level it is essential to compare dendrological and climatological series derived under identical conditions. At a higher level of geographical generalization, for example at the zonal level, it is necessary to use climatological series derived appropriately from latitudinal belts. In Russia the smoothed three-year anomalies in the mean annual air temperature for the 57°30' N - 72°30' N latitudinal belt in relation to the mean for the period 1881-1975 and the generalized series from tree-rings from conifers along the northern treeline from Kola Peninsula to Chukotka for the period 1458-1975 form the basis of the reconstruction of thermal conditions of past centuries. The existence of a fairly close positive correlation (coefficient of correlation 0.8) provides grounds for climatic reconstruction (Fig. 1). In the seventeenth century when the culmination of the Little Ice Age occurred, the mean annual temperature in Northern Eurasia was lower than at present by approximately 1.2 ± 0.2°C (CHERNAVSKAYA, 1985).

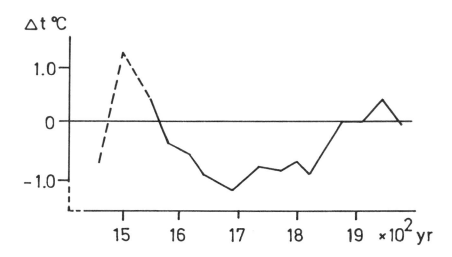

Fig. 1 Reconstructed mean annual temperature. Broken line indicates periods with insufficient data coverage

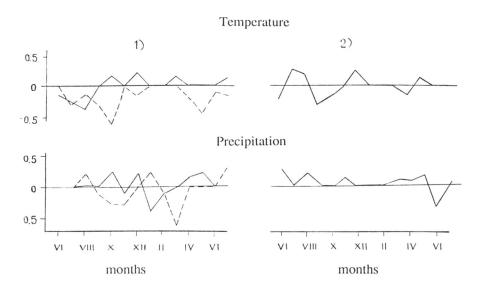

Fig. 2 Function of the response of early wood increment (1) and maximum density of late wood (2) to changes in temperature and precipitation

In close-to-normal conditions, without a clearly pronounced limiting factor, it is a rather complicated problem to extract the essential climatic signal. In this case analysis of the functions of the growth response of tree-rings to climatic variability is used to reveal significant correlations between tree growth indices and climatic parameters (FRITTS, 1976). We obtained response functions for a number of habitats of pine in Central and Eastern Europe. The collection of dendrological samples includes more than 300 cores from living trees, with their ages varying from 100 to 220 years. About 20 dendrological sites were examined on the territory between 50-60°N and 16-60°E.

In order to construct dendrological time-series the technique of principal components is very efficient since it allows one to sort out experimental data on the basis of contributions of individual trees into the overall growth variability component or in accordance with the place occupied by weight projections of individual trees on the plane of the first two components. Such methods allow one to identify, within the first habitat, certain individual trees or groups of trees which are made different by their phenotypical features and micro-environmental conditions and to select, for the purposes of chronological constructions, such trees which contain a substantial share of the overall growth variability component.

In the absence of the climatic factor inhibiting the growth and development of trees, edaphic and geomorphological conditions can become catalysts of trees' response to climatic variability. In the Southern Moravia region, a joint Soviet-Czechoslovakian expedition collected samples of pines growing in two areas lying close to each other, but having different soils and geomorphological conditions (KYNČIL & CHERNAVSKAYA, 1992). Two basic types of soil were formed in the region as a result of aeolian and denudation processes: magnesium rendzinas on serpentinites, which are fine-grained, stony, with good permeability and drying properties; and heavy, impermeable, sometimes water-logged pseudogley podzolic soils on serpentinite laterites. Scales of the width of early wood and maximum density of late wood were obtained for pines growing on those two types of soils. The relationships between these dendrological indices and climatic changes are different in the two habitats. Trees which grow on a steep slope with western exposure on well drained soils (broken line on Fig. 2) are more sensitive to changes in temperature and precipitation than those growing on a flat ground with a slightly swampy soil (solid line on Fig. 2).

A function describing the response of maximum density of old wood to climatic changes has been obtained for the studied territory, too. Maximum density depends on the temperature of the previous summer; it has a positive correlation with the temperature in September. Temperature conditions of the current year have no substantial effect on the magnitude of maximum density. As regards precipitation, the most significant correlation is a negative correlation with the month of July of the current year.

The above-said allows one to draw the conclusion that dendrological data can be used for climatic reconstructions in conditions of a moderately moist and warm climate. To do this, it is essential to select groups of trees which are under extreme conditions in terms of other natural factors, for instance, edaphic and geomorphological, which enhances the sensitivity of trees to climatic changes.

References

CHERNAVSKAYA, M. M. (1985): Reconstructions of temperature conditions during the Little Ice Age in Northern Eurasia; based on dendrological data. Polar Geography and Geology 9, 321-328

FRITTS, H. C. (1976): Tree-rings and climate. Academic Press, London, 576 p.

KYNČIL, J. & CHERNAVSKAYA, M. (1992): Dendroclimatology of the relict pine forests in the Middle Moravian region. Data of Meteorological Studies 15, Sov. Geophys. Com., Moskow, 96-100

POLOZOVA, L. G. & SHIYATOV, S. G. (1979): The influence of climatic factors on the radial growth of trees in the higher areas of the Ural Mountains. Trudy G.G.O. 403, Gidrometeoizdat, Leningrad, 114-119

ZOLOTOKRYLIN, A. N.; KRENKE, A. N.; ZYAKHOV, M. E.; POPOVA, V. B. & CHERNAVSKAYA, M. M. (1986): Climate fluctuations in the Russian Plain in the historical past. Izv. A.N. S.S.S.R., Ser. Geogr. 1, 26-36

Address of the author

Dr. M. Chernavskaya, Institute of Geography, Academy of Sciences, Staromonetny 29, Moskow 109017, U.S.S.R.

The combination of historical documents and biological data in the reconstruction of climate variations in space and time

Joël Guiot

Summary

The combination of documentary and tree-ring data, which are complementary, is useful to provide reliable climatic reconstructions. This involves appropriate statistical techniques. The solution is illustrated by the extrapolation of annual temperature series back to the end of the eleventh century at gridpoints separated by 5° latitude and 10° longitude in Western Europe and Northwestern Africa. The most important result is a warm period during the Middle Ages followed by a long cold period from the sixteenth to the nineteenth century and a continuous warming since the middle of the eighteenth century in the whole studied region except in the Southwest (Spain, Morocco). There is thus a disconnection between the Central and the Western Mediterranean basin.

Résumé

La combinaison de données d'archives historiques et de cernes d'arbres permet d'obtenir des reconstructions climatiques fiables grâce à leur complémentarité. Cela nécessite un ensemble de techniques statistiques appropriées. La solution de ce problème est illustrée par l'extrapolation jusque la fin du 11ième siècle des séries de température annuelle aux points de grilles espacés de 5° de latitude et 10° de longitude en Europe occidentale et Afrique du Nord. Le résultat marquant est la succession d'un Moyen-Age chaud, d'une longue période froide du 16ième au 19ième siècle, et d'un réchauffement continu depuis un siècle dans toute la région étudié à l'exception du Sud-Ouest (Espagne, Maroc). Il y a donc une déconnection nette entre la partie centrale et occidentale du bassin méditerranéen.

1. Introduction

The aim of this paper is to assemble the climate information available from historical and biological sources in order to obtain more powerful reconstructions. Proxy data originating from historical documents are usually accurate indicators of the past climate. There are archives, i.e. written records of environment clues very abundant from the eleventh century (ALEXANDRE, 1987), or phenonological records, i.e. data on the timing of recurrent biological phenomena, such as vintage, wheat harvest, blossoming of plants, animal migration. These data have the disadvantage to be discontinuous in time and space.

Biological proxy data have the advantage, particularly in Europe and North America, to be abundant and continuous. They are essentially tree-ring series and document the annual growth of some arboreal species. Mostly ring widths are considered, but ring densities are often better correlated with the climate of more specific periods of the year. Dense networks of such data exist at least since the beginning of the sixteenth century (BRADLEY & JONES, in press) and a great number of long series are available for the last millennia. Consequently problems in interpretation - less true for the density data (SCHWEINGRUBER et al., 1979) - consist in the difficulty to separate the various components (e.g. temperature and precipitation) of the climatic signal (SERRE-BACHET, 1989).

For regions where historical or tree-ring data are lacking, isotopic data derived from ice cores offer the advantage of an annual time resolution for the historical period (DANSGAARD et al., 1971).

All these records are generally qualitatively presented in the literature and sometimes converted into climatic scales. Statistical methods, which analyse these data and make them comparable by transferring them into quantitative climatic information, are well developed in many fields. A technique enabling to take advantage of the complementarity of these data is presented here.

2. The data

The meteorological data used are the annual series gridded by JONES et al. (1985) between latitudes 35°N and 55°N by steps of 5° and between longitudes 10°W and 20°E by steps of 10°. So 20 series could be obtained from 1851 to 1984 with missing data mainly before 1900 A.D. This gives a (134, 20)-matrix, which will be often referred to in the study as the set of the predictands.

The set of the proxy series used in this study is far from being exhaustive. A part of them is made up of tree-ring chronologies of various species from various sites. The trends of these series are modelled by negative exponents, polynominals or filtered curves as proposed by FRITTS (1976) and indexed series are obtained by dividing each ring width by its trend. The series used are the following: (1) GdR1: oak ring series from west of the Rhine, Germany, extending from 820 to 1964 A.D., collected and indexed by HOLLSTEIN (1965); (2) GdS2: oak ring series from Germany, extending from 840 to 1949 A.D., collected and indexed by HUBER & GIERTZ-SIEBENLIST (1969); (3) GBdB: oak ring series from Belfast, Northern Ireland, extending from 1001 to 1970 A.D., collected and indexed by BAILLIE (1977); (4) GBdE: oak ring series from Southwestern Scotland extending from 946 to 1975 A.D., collected and indexed by PILCHER and BAILLIE (1980); (5) I199: pine ring series from Southern Italy extending from 1148 to 1974 A.D., collected and indexed by SERRE-BACHET (1985); (6) F606: larch ring series from la Vallée des Merveilles, Southern French Alps, extending from 1100 to 1974 A.D., collected and indexed by SERRE (1978); (7) F884: Pine ring series from Mont Ventoux, Southern France, extending from 1660 to 1975 A.D., collected and indexed by SERRE-BACHET (pers. comm.); (8) I609: pine ring series from Northern Italy, extending from 925 to 1984 A.D., collected and indexed by BEBBER (pers. comm.); (9) F607: larch ring series from l'Orgère, northern French Alps, extending from 1353 to 1973 A.D., collected and indexed by TESSIER (1981) ; (10) F608: larch ring series from Mercantour, Southern French Alps, extending from 1701 to 1980 A.D., collected by GUIBAL (pers. comm.) and indexed for this study with 40-year cut-off digital filter; (11) F609: larch ring series also from Mercantour, extending from 1732 to 1981 A.D., collected by GUIBAL (pers. comm.) and indexed like F608.

Another group of proxy series is made up of data extracted from historical archives. These historical data have been compiled by various historians and/or climatologists: (12) IsBe: BERGTHORSSON's decennial estimates of temperature in Iceland, extending from 1050 to 1550 A.D.; these data are criticized by BELL & OGILVIE (1978) and reported as unreliable before 1170 A.D. and after 1450 A.D. (INGRAM et al., 1978); the unreliable decades are considered as missing; (13) BrTe: summer temperature index of BRAY (1982) based on German and French grape harvest data and Central England temperatures (MANLEY, 1974), extending from 1453 to 1973 A.D.; (14) PfTh: the PFISTER (1981) thermal index in Switzerland averaged on an annual basis from 1550 to 1829 A.D.; (15) VFrL: the average annual dates at the beginning of the vintage in Northeastern France, French Switzerland, and South Rhineland of LE ROY LADURIE & BAULANT (1981), extending from 1484 to 1879 A.D.; (16) VSwL: the average annual dates at the beginning of the grape harvest in Switzerland reported by LEGRAND (1979), extending from 1502 to 1979 A.D.; (17) LAsw: frequency of southwesterly surface winds in England, 1340-1978, from direct observations from 1669 to 1978 in the London area and from historical proxy data before; these data were reconstructed by LAMB (1982).

A third category of data is provided by ^{18}O data from the Arctic ice cores which are indicators of temperature: (18) CaCe, located in Camp Century, Greenland, ^{18}O quasi-decennial values extending from 1200 to 1970 A.D., collected and analysed by DANSGAARD et al. (1971); (19-20) aO^{18} and bO^{18} located in Central Greenland (WILLIAMS & WIGLEY, 1983), 30-year running means of annual maxima of δ^{18}O in ice cores, extending from 1180 to 1800 A.D.

To these data are added: (21-23) the first three principal components, Mcp1, Mcp2, and Mcp3 of the 17 longest cedar ring series in Morocco, sampled by MUNAUT and TILL and analysed by TILL (1985); these series, extending from 1068 to 1979 A.D., represent nearly 40% of the total variance of the 17 raw series.

The period 1068-1979 A.D. is retained as a period where sufficient information is available. The group of the proxy data is a matrix of 912 rows and 23 columns. These series are referred to as the predictors.

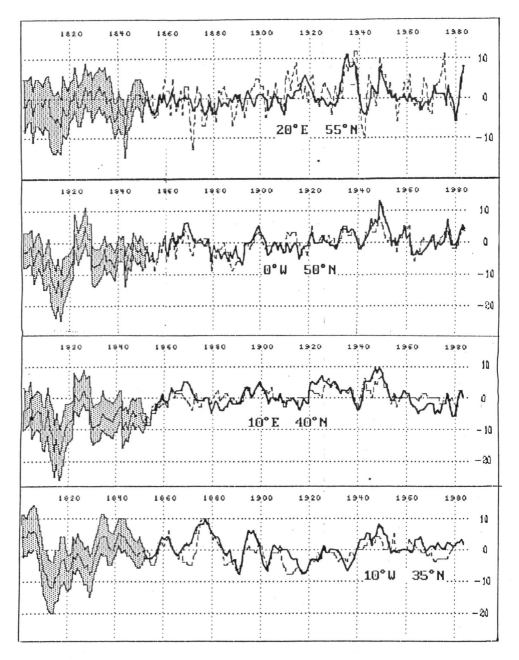

Fig. 1 Comparison of the reconstructed temperatures (heavy line) from 1851 - 1984 to the actual temperatures (dotted line) of four typical locations, from north to south. For the period before 1851, the actual data have been replaced by the 90% confidence interval

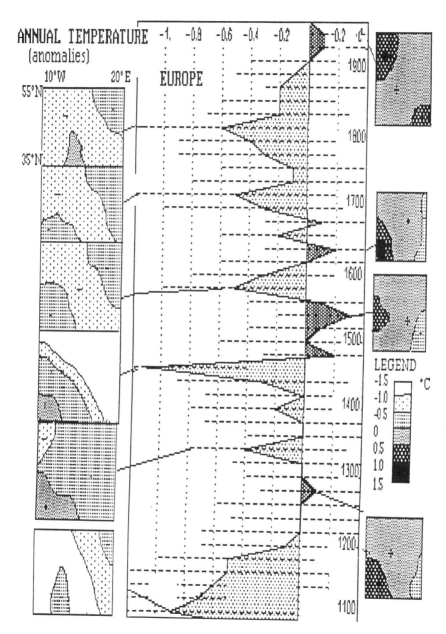

Fig. 2 The central curve represents the reconstructed annual temperature averaged over Europe on the basis of the series between 40°N and 55°N and between 10°W and 20°E (exclusive of the most southern series). The boxes to the left and right represent the spatial distribution of the temperature anomalies over the total region 35°N to 55°N; 10°W to 20°E) for the extreme periods

3. Data conditioning

The predictand and the predictor matrices contain missing data. For the proxy data, the gaps are estimated by a best analogues method. The major interest of this method is to avoid all assumptions on the linearity of the relationship between the variables. This is particularly recommended when, like here, the series are highly heterogeneous.

If the period of study is sufficiently diversified, each observation has its close analogues in the same period. The similarity between these analogues is measured here using an Euclidian distance. It is then natural to consider the mean of the analogues weighted by the inverse squared distance as good estimates of the missing data.

The estimates by analogues are compared to the actual values, where they are available, to measure their reliability. The corresponding correlations range from 0.45 (for F608 and F884) and 0.86 (LAsw, CaCe, I609) with a mean value of 0.73. According to the numbers of degrees of freedom and the diversity of the proxy series, the estimates can be considered as reliable.

For the meteorological data matrix (20 temperature series), the multiple regression is used, but it cannot be applied straightforwardly because the number of regressors is not constant on the total interval (1851-1984). In fact, for each observation, a particular regression has to be computed using all the available regressors. The verification correlations range between 0.62 (at 35°N) and 0.92 (British Islands) with a mean of 0.76. The results are also considered as significant.

4. Reconstruction of temperature

After the two matrices have been filled up, the proxy series can be calibrated on the annual temperature series on the basis of the common observations. The two data sets have been previously transformed into principal components (PCs). Indeed, a large proportion of the high order PCs represents extremely small proportions of variance so that they are presumably indistinguishable from the statistical noise. The first 10 PCs of the 20 temperature series explaining together around 90% of the variance and the first 19 PCs of the 23 proxy series explaining 95 % of the variance are kept.

4.1 Spectral decomposition

Since proxy series may record the climatic signal differently when the forcing is confined to a single year or when it is persistent over several years and because they have a specific time resolution (yearly to decennial), it has been suggested (GUIOT, 1981, 1985, 1989) that low and high frequency variations can be reconstructed separetely by a method called canonical spectral regression. Complementary symmetric digital filters are a simple and efficient tool for this task. A low-pass filter is used to isolate the variations greater than decennial of the series and the complementary high-pass filter is used to isolate their annual to decennial variations. Thus, the 10 PCs of the temperature series and the 19 PCs of the proxy series are divided into high and low components.

A calibration is performed in the low frequency and in the high frequency domain and tested separately. If the low-frequency relationships are not reliable, the reconstructions are impossible, but if only the high-frequency reconstructions are spurious, the low-frequency reconstructions are nevertheless useful in the knowledge of the long term variations of the climate.

4.2 Calibration

In the two frequency bands, bootstrap regressions based on the method of EFRON (1979), adapted by GUIOT (1989), are calibrated on the common period, 1851-1979 A.D. This bootstrap regression may be summarized as follows: from the 1851-1979 A.D. interval, 129 pseudo-random numbers are randomly taken with replacement using an uniform distribution protocol and used to resample the actual observations. We should insist here on the fact that an observation is considered as a vector of 19 proxy data and 10 temperature data corresponding to the same year. The observations selected in this way become a pseudo data set. This is arbitrarily repeated 50 times. For each replication, the regression coefficients are computed and applied to proxy series to obtain the corresponding reconstruction. The reconstruction is compared to the actual climatic series both on the retained observations set and on the others (verification statistics are so calculated 50 times). The mean and standard deviations of the verification statistics may be obtained dependently on the calibration and independently. The final reconstruction is given by the median of the 50 replicated reconstructions and a 90%-confidence interval is given by the 5th and 95th percentiles.

The bootstrap method permits an independent verification without losing observations in the calibration. For each of the 50 simulations, the estimated mean standard deviations are compared to the actual ones, both on the randomly drawn observations and on the others. The correlations between estimated and actual observations are lower for the high frequency PCs, but this must be appreciated as regards the reduced number of degrees of freedom for autocorrelated time series. The most important feature is the lack of reliability of the high frequencies for components 3 to 6 and 8 to 10, while the low frequency PC estimates are reliable.

Table 1   Verification of the reconstructions

		a	b-	b	b+	c	d	e	f
1	0W55	-1.18	-3.69	0.11	4.52	4.93	5.63	0.73	129
2	0W50	-0.33	-3.51	0.07	4.14	5.30	5.38	0.70	129
3	0W45	-0.75	-3.38	0.21	4.32	5.67	5.18	0.66	129
4	0W40	-0.81	-3.74	0.33	5.06	5.90	4.48	0.53	125
5	0W35	-2.96	-4.66	-0.44	4.57	5.97	5.58	0.66	118
6	1E55	-2.06	-3.67	0.12	4.50	7.03	4.88	0.65	129
7	1E50	-0.88	-3.43	0.22	4.36	6.28	4.36	0.60	129
8	1E45	1.40	-3.37	0.33	4.60	4.92	4.88	0.68	129
9	1E40	0.38	-3.92	0.07	4.71	3.85	4.84	0.60	119
10	1E35	-2.47	-3.45	0.50	5.12	4.60	3.88	0.54	121
11	2E55	1.17	-3.75	0.09	4.52	8.10	4.39	0.53	129
12	2E50	1.29	-3.77	0.13	4.65	6.96	3.91	0.54	129
13	2E45	-1.49	-3.55	0.45	5.06	5.90	3.57	0.46	129
14	2E40	-0.92	-3.57	0.75	5.76	5.09	4.43	0.58	122
15	2E35	-2.00	-3.26	0.74	5.38	5.02	4.35	0.67	78
16	1W55	0.72	-3.40	0.45	4.87	3.68	6.05	0.66	95
17	1W50	0.71	-3.23	0.48	4.77	4.07	6.29	0.76	111
18	1W45	-0.34	-3.17	1.14	6.38	3.22	3.66	0.57	29
19	1W40	-6.85	-3.65	0.12	4.58	6.07	5.58	0.72	116
20	1W35	-1.24	-3.63	0.43	5.09	4.89	5.00	0.64	127

(a) actual means, (b) estimated mean, (b-) mean lower estimates, (b+) mean upper esti-mates, (c) actual standard deviations, (d) estimated standard deviations, (e) correlation between actual and reconstructed temperature series, (f) number of degrees of freedom, given by the number of non-missing data in the original array. Columns a to d are given in tenth of degrees C.

4.3   Extrapolation and final verification

The 10 temperature PCs are extrapolated from the proxy PCs in the low-frequency domain as in the high-frequency domain. The entire spectra are recomposed by adding the reconstructed high frequency PC series to the low frequency ones. The reconstructed series are correlated to the actual ones with an average coefficient of 0.59 on the 1901-1979 A.D. period and 0.64 on the 1851-1900 A.D. period. The reconstruction of the raw temperature series is obtained by postmultiplying the 10 PC series matrix by the eigenvector matrix. The mean correlation between estimated and actual values is 0.63 (table 1), with a maximum of more than 0.70 in the northwest. These reconstructed series are obtained with a mean 0.90-level confidence interval of about 0.3°C, which is about 80% of the average standard deviation of the actual temperature series. Fig. 1 shows that the reconstructions are less good in the northeast, i.e. in Eastern Germany and Poland, where precisely no proxy series were used.

5. Discussion

An indicator of the reliability of the reconstructions is obtained from the comparison with independent reconstructions. BRIFFA et al. (1988) reconstructed the summer (April to September) temperature in Western Europe. In particular, it appears from both works that the year 1816 was one of the coldest years in the millennium, mainly on the Atlantic coast, France, and Corsica.

Fig. 2 presents the trend of the annual temperature in Europe, north of 40°N, and its spatial distribution from 35°N to 55°N and from 10°W to 20°E for the extreme periods. For cold periods a clear disconnection (SERRE-BACHET et al., 1990), between the Western Mediterranean coast (particularly Morocco) and the central one (Italy, Greece) can be observed. The Central Mediterranean region is connected more closely with Western Europe than with Morocco and Spain.

After the very cold twelfth century, the period from 1200 to 1400 A.D. was warm mainly in the southwest. This warm period, often called the "Little Optimum", is confirmed by ALEXANDRE (1987) who computed a mean index of winter severity of -1 (for regions north of the Alps as well as for those to the south), which must be opposed to a mean index of - 1.7 for 1000-1200 A.D. In the so-called "Little Ice Age", we remark two cold periods: 1550-1620 A.D. and 1750-1880 A.D. From 1820 A.D. up to now, we can observe a clear trend towards warming. The southwest has apparently not experienced these cold periods and consequently there is no significant warming during the twentieth century. The precipitation reconstructions in Morocco (TILL & GUIOT, 1990) indicate that the previous centuries were dry, although extreme years, as 1816, knew an important moisture.

Time series analysis is applied to the actual and reconstructed temperature series to estimate the percentage of temperature variance explained by the own past of the series (Fig. 3). The higher this percentage is, the higher is the persistence of the temperature (i.e. the trend of the series including the human impact which has been stronger and stronger). Fig. 3 shows that this persistence has a geographical distribution. Southern series, and mainly southwestern series, are persistent, whereas northeastern series are white noises. The distribution of the percentage of variance explained by the same models is also given in Fig. 3 for the reconstructed series of the same period (1851-1979 A.D.) and of the total period (1068-1979 A.D.). There is a great coherency. It is understandable that the persistence is higher in the series reconstructed from proxy series, which are themself often smoothed. The actual gradient (northeast-southwest) is a little biased as the reconstructed gradient is north-south. This is due to the lack of proxy series in the northwest and the southeast. Nevertheless this shows the coherency of the 20 reconstructions, which is also a clue to reliability.

This study shows how to make a synthesis of the various proxy series available for a better knowledge of the climatic changes. Additional records must be used to obtain a maximum reliability of the gridded temperature reconstructions. This study also shows that the Western Mediterranean climate has known an evolution different from the North European. Information originating from the north of Europe cannot be directly transferred to Southern Europe. More proxy series must be collected concerning the Mediterranean climate so as to get the most reliable reconstructions.

Even if a small part of the data used are obsolete, this work proves that the combination of tree-ring series and data from historical archives provide reconstructions with an increased reliability. The precision obtained (about 0.3°C) - which can be improved by using more data and such of better quality - is suffiently accurate to analyse climatic changes as such which occurred during the last millennium and particularly the recent human impact on climate.

	10°W			0			10°E			20°E		
55°N	0	18	29	25	14	30	6	32	26	5	19	22
50°N	15	24	27	6	14	27	0	23	35	0	25	25
45°N	17	22	42	19	26	43	12	38	36	0	40	42
40°N	56	48	72	23	29	53	12	42	40	12	48	55
35°N	33	47	72	34	70	78	15	39	61	28	66	74
	a	b	c	a	b	c	a	b	c	a	b	c

Fig. 3 Percentage of variance explained by the autocorrelations of the temperature series (persistence) in function of the location: (a) actual series on 1851-1979; (b) reconstructed series on 1851-1979 ; (c) reconstructed series on the total period 1068-1979

References

ALEXANDRE, P. (1987): Le climat en Europe au Moyen-Age. Contribution à l'histore des variations climatiques de 100 à 1425, d'après les sources narratives de l'Europe occidentale. Ecole des Hautes Etudes en Sciences Sociales, Paris, 825 p.

BAILLIE, M. G. L. (1977): The Belfast oak chronology to 1001 A.D. Tree-Ring Bulletin 37, 1-12

BELL, W. T. & OLGIVIE, A. E. J. (1978): Weather compilation as a source of data for the reconstruction of Europan climate during the Medieval period. Climatic Change 1, 331-348

BERGTHORSSON, P. (1969): An estimate of drift ice and temperature in 1000 years. Jökull 19, 94

BRADLEY, R. & JONES, P. D. (in press): The climate since A.D. 1500. Harper and Collins, Academic Press, London

BRAY, J. R. (1982): Alpine glacial advance in relation to a proxy summer temperature index based mainly on wine harvest dates, 1453-1973 A.D. Boreas 11, 1-10

BRIFFA, K. R.; JONES, P. D. & SCHWEINGRUBER, F. H. (1988): Summer temperature patterns over Europe: a reconstruction from 1750 A.D. based on maximum latewood density indices of conifers. Quat. Res. 30, 36-52

DANSGAARD, W.; JOHNSEN, S. J.; CLAUSEN, H. B. & LANGWAY, C. C. (1971): Climatic record revealed by the Camp Century ice core. In: Turekian, K. K. (ed.): The Late Cenozoïc Glacial Ages. Yale Univ. Press, New Haven

FRITTS, H. C. (1976): Tree-Rings and Climate. Academic Press, London, 567 p.

GUIOT, J. (1981): Analyse mathématique de données géophysiques, application à la dendro-climatologie. Ph.D. Thesis, Institut d'Astronomie et Géophysique, Louvain-la-Neuve

GUIOT, J. (1985): The extrapolation of recent climatological series with spectral canonical regression. J. Climatol. 5, 325-335

GUIOT, J. (1989): Method of calibration and comparison of methods. In: Cook, E. R. and Kairiukstis, L. A. (eds): Methods of Dendrochronology. Kluwer Academic Press and IIASA, Dordrecht, 165-178 and 185-193

HOLLSTEIN, E. (1965): Jahrringchronologische Datierung von Eichenhölzern ohne Waldkante. Bonner Jahrb. 165, 12-27

HUBER, B. & GIERTZ-SIEBENLIST, V. (1969): Unsere tausendjährige Eichen-Jahrringchronologie durchschnittlich 57-fach (10-150) belegt. Sitzungsberichte I: Biol.-, Mineral.-, Erdkunde & Verwandte Wiss. 178 (1-4), Österr. Akad. Wiss., Vienna, 37-42

INGRAM, M. J., UNDERHILL, D.J. & WIGLEY, T. M. L. (1978): Historical climatology. Nature 276, 329-334

JONES, P. D.; RAPER, S. C. B.; SANTER, B.; CHERRY, B. S. G.; GOODESS, C.; KELLY, P. M.; WIGLEY,T. M. L.; BRADLEY, R. S. & DIAZ, H. F. (1985): A grid point surface air temperature data set for the northern hemisphere. U.S. Dept. of Energy, Washington, TR022

LE ROY LADURIE, E. & BAULANT, M. (1981): Grape harvests from the 15th through the 19th century. In: Rotberg, R. I. & Rabb, T. K. (eds): Studies in Interdisciplinary History. Princeton Univ. Press, 259-269

LAMB, H. H. (1977): Climate: Present, past and future. Methuen, London, 825 p.

LAMB, H. H. (1982). Climate history and the Modern World. Methuen, London, 387 p.

LEGRAND, J. P. (1979): Les fluctuations météorologiques exceptionnelles durant les saisons printanières et estivales depuis le Moyen-Age. La Météorologie VI 13, 131-141

MANLEY, G. (1974): Central England temperatures: monthly means 1659-1973. Q.J.R. Meteorol. Soc. 100, 389-405

PFISTER, C. (1981): An analysis of the Little Ice Age climate in Switzerland and its consequences for agricultural production. In: Wigley, T. M. L.; Ingram, M. & Farmer, G. (eds.): Climate and History, 214-248

PILCHER, J. R. & BAILLIE, M. G. L. (1980): Eight modern oak chronologies from England and Scotland. Tree-Ring Bull. 40, 23-34

SCHWEINGRUBER, F. H.; BRÄKER, O. U. & SCHÄR, E. (1979): Dendroclimatic studies on conifers from Central Europe and Great Britain. Boreas 8, 427-452

SERRE, F. (1978): The dendroclimatological value of the European larch (*Larix decidua* Mill.) in the French Maritime Alps. Tree-Ring Bull. 38, 25-33

SERRE-BACHET, F. (1985): Une chronologie pluriséculaire du Sud de l'Italie. Dendrochronologia 3, 45-66

SERRE-BACHET, F.; GUIOT, J. & TESSIER, L. (in press): Dendroclimatic records in SW Europe and N. Africa. In: Bradley, R. & Jones, P. D. (eds.): Climate since 1500 A.D., Harper and Collins, Academic Press, London

SERRE-BACHET, F. (1989): Tree-rings in the Mediterranean area. Evolution of climate proxy data in relation to the European Holocene. Paläoklimaforschung 6, Akad. Lit. Wiss., Mainz

TESSIER, L. (1981): Contribution dendroclimatique à la connaissance écologique du peuplement forestier des environs des chalets de l'Orgère (Parc National de la Vanoise). Travaux Scientifiques du Parc de la Vanoise 11, 29-61

TILL, C. (1985): Recherches dendrochronologiques sur le cèdre de l'Atlas au Maroc. Unpubl. Ph.D. thesis. U.C.L., Louvain-la-Neuve

TILL, C. & GUIOT, J. (1990): Reconstruction of precipitation in Morocco since 1100 A.D. based on Cedrus Atlantica tree-ring widths. Quat. Res. 31, 225-235

WILLIAMS, L. D. & WIGLEY, T. M. L. (1983): A comparison of evidence for Late Holocene summer temperature variations in the Northern Hemisphere. Quat. Res. 20, 286-307

Address of the author:

Dr. J. Guiot, Laboratoire de Botanique Historique et Palynologie, C.N.R.S UA 1152, Faculté de St-Jérôme, F-13397 Marseille Cédex 13, France

Climatic changes and biological structure of the human populations in Poland in the Middle Ages

Janusz Piontek

Summary

This investigation aims at determining the impact of climatic changes in the Middle Ages on the biological structure of skeletal populations in the area of Poland. These studies may contribute to the verification of the statements expressed by other biological and anthropological sciences. Biological features strongly susceptible to the influence of economic and ecological conditions are useful for the analysis of climatic change. Body height may also be included as it shows a strong relationship to changes in annual temperatures in the last millennium. The data on the body structure of skeletal populations from various prehistoric and historic periods may contribute to the verification of studies of climatic changes in historical periods.

Zusammenfassung

Diese Untersuchung zielt darauf ab, den Einfluß klimatischer Veränderungen im Mittelalter auf die Skelettstruktur damaliger Bevölkerungsgruppen im Gebiet des heutigen Polen aufzuzeigen. Möglicherweise können die Untersuchungen dazu beitragen, die Ergebnisse von weiteren biologischen bzw. humanbiologischen Disziplinen zu verifizieren. Diejenigen biologischen Merkmale, die in starkem Maße von ökonomischen und ökologischen Bedingungen geprägt werden, sind für die Analyse klimatischer Veränderungen geeignet. Zu diesen ökonomisch/ökologisch sensitiven Merkmalen gehört die Körpergröße, da hier für das letzte Jahrtausend eine starke Abhängigkeit von den Schwankungen der jährlichen Temperaturen nachgewiesen werden konnte. Daten über die Körperstruktur und den Skelettaufbau unterschiedlicher Populationen aus verschiedenen prähistorischen und historischen Perioden können dazu beitragen, die Untersuchungen über Klimaveränderungen in historischer Zeit zu überprüfen.

1. Introduction

The influence of climatic changes on the biological structure of population may be considered from two points of view: (1) as an adaptive process comprising transformations of the gene pool of the population caused by natural selection, (2) as an adaptability process consisting of adaptation of features of organisms to environmental conditions in the process of ontogenetic development within the plasticity of morphological features.

The first (adaptive) process led in the past to a strong morphological differentiation of kind because of the fact that human groups, when migrating, settled (in historical times) new ecological niches. The relationship between climatic conditions and morphological differentiation were shown on very varied anthropological material (cp. CROGNIER, 1981). Some of the most typical examples of features showing this type of dependence are: the face shape of Asiatic Mongoloids, the shape of nose among various peoples, occurrence of Mongoloid fold among Asiatic peoples, the magnitude and proportions of body among Eskimos and Massais etc. The list of features differentiating human races which are supposedly of great adaptive importance in certain climatic zones were compiled by various authors (cp. BIELICKI, 1975).

The second (adaptability) process shows that in the ontogenetic development the level of formation of a morphological feature depends on the character of the environmental conditions in which the process of development takes place. This process does not lead to a change in the genetic structure of the population. Only the phenotypic characterization of morphological features undergoes changes.

Therefore, two kinds of features may be distinguished: (1) features formed strongly by the individual's genotype - highly inheritable features, (2) features strongly modified in the development of an individual by environmental conditions - low inheritable features.

Climatic factors, if they show high changeability in certain geographic areas, may strongly modify environmental conditions and thus influence the course of adaptive and adaptability processes. In historical periods human populations did not undergo strong adaptative processes. It is thought that racial differentiation of man was formed during the Palaeolithic period. After the Neolithic revolution new ecological behaviours considerably limited the opportunity of influence of natural selection in human populations (PIONTEK, 1989).

This work aims at determining the impact of climatic change in the Middle Ages on the biological structure of skeletal populations in the area of Poland. These studies may contribute to the verification of the statements expressed by other biological and anthropological sciences.

It is difficult to expect that in the Middle Ages climatic changes might induce adaptive processes of transformations of the gene pool of the population. That is why an attempt was made to answer the following question: did climatic changes in the Middle Ages influence the formation of phenotypic features, strongly dependent on environmental conditions?

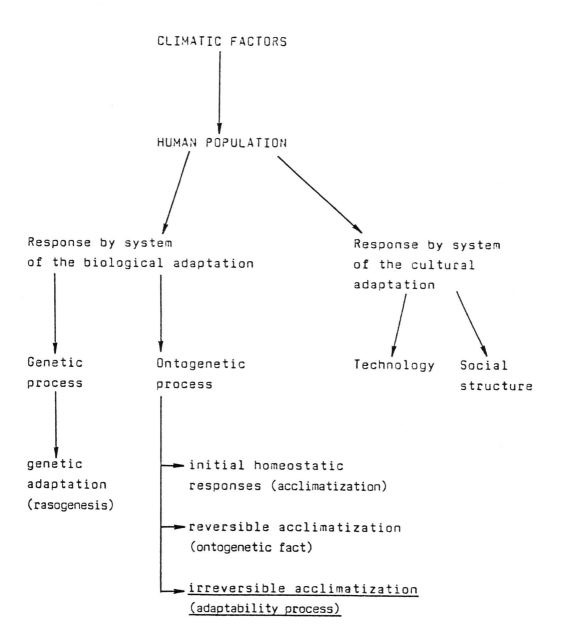

Fig. 1   Model showing the influence of climatic changes on the biological structure of the population and ways of the population's adaptation to these changes

2. The influence of climatic changes on biological structure of populations: a research model

The human system consists of at least five elements, such as ecological niche, human population (in biological dimension), economic structure, social structure, and ideological control subsystem which are interrelated. The feedback mechanisms between the elements determine the structure of the system. Fig. 1 shows a model of the structure of the human system and the relation between the system and climatic factors. In this model it is assumed that climatic factors may mainly change the structure of the system's ecological niche (natural environment). In this situation a new characterization of ecological niche may bring about changes in the biological and economic structure of the population. We think that the social structure and the ideological control subsystem may also be submitted to changes, but only through the influence of other elements of the system on these factors.

Fig. 2 shows a model interpretation of the influence of environmental (climatic) factors on the biological structure of human populations. This model assumes that a population may react to the change of environmental conditions through changes in the intensity of the influence of cultural (technological, social, etc.) and of biological (adaptive and/or adaptability) factors. What is interesting in our studies are the biological processes, and in particular the irreversible acclimatization changes (adaptability processes).

3. Analysis of examples

It was shown in physical anthropology that the body height is a particularly sensitive feature which reacts to the change of conditions of individual development of man (BIELICKI, 1986). A relation was shown between the interpopulational differentiation of body height and climatic conditions (adaptive process), economic conditions, and social structure (adaptability process).

In order to show the influence of climatic changes on the biological structure of the population, the following data has been collected: data on body height in the recent millennium in three regions of Poland. This data comes from studies on skeletal populations. In particular regions materials were elaborated using similar research methods. Table 1 presents body height of eleven skeletal populations from the area of Silesia. Table 2 lists data for four populations from the area of Wiślica (Małopolska), whereas table 3 gives the data for four populations from the area of Lubiń (Wielkopolska).

The data on annual temperature changes, according to fifty-year averages observed in the recent centuries, were taken from the literature (LAMB, 1972). The dependency between changes in annual temperatures in the last millennium and changes in body height in particular regions is shown in Fig. 3-5. A strong relation between these two features is presented. Periods of higher annual temperatures correspond to higher values of body height.

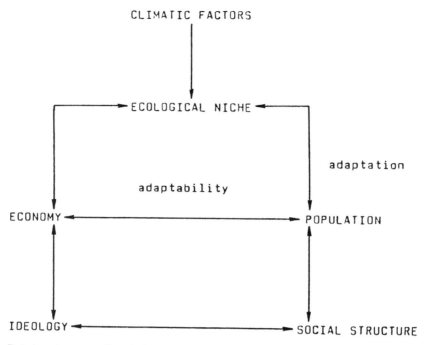

Fig. 2   Relations between climatic factors and elements of the biocultural system

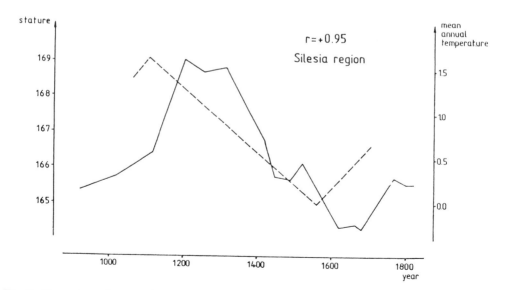

Fig. 3   Dependency between body height (stature; broken line) and the average annual temperature during the last millennium. Region of Silesia

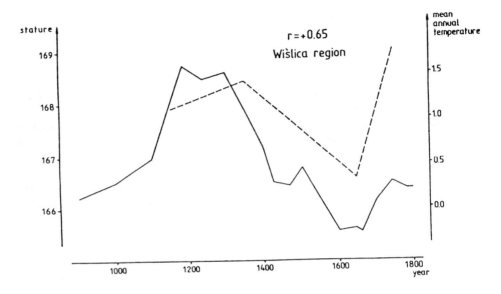

Fig. 4 Dependency between body height (stature; broken line) and the average annual temperature during the last millennium. Region of Wiślica

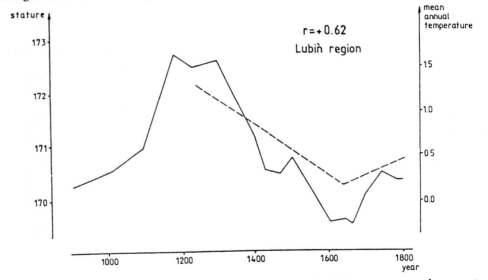

Fig. 5 Dependency between body height (stature; broken line) and the average annual temperature during the last millennium. Region of Lubiń

Whereas the periods of lower annual temperatures correspond on average to lower values of body height in skeletal populations, the correlation coefficients between the studied features oscillate between +0.95 and +0.62.

4. Conclusions

(1) Climatic changes which change environmental conditions influence the biological structure of human populations;
(2) Biological features strongly susceptible to the influence of economic and ecological conditions are useful for the analysis of climatic changes. Body height may be included within this type of features as it shows a strong relationship with changes in annual temperatures in the last millennium;
(3) The data on the body structure of skeletal populations from various prehistoric and historic periods may contribute to the verification of studies on climatic changes in historical periods.

Table 1   The time series in stature of the populations from the Silesia region (in cm)

Population, chronology	Males		Females	
	N	x	N	x
Groszowice, X-XI centuries	8	169.0	3	160.6
Milicz, XI-XII	104	166.2	89	154.2
Niemcza, X-XII	14	169.3	5	160.4
Tomice, IX-XII	13	167.6	14	159.0
Brzeg Głogowski, X-XI	20	168.2	5	161.8
Opole, XIV	17	166.8	8	159.1
Wrocław, XIII-XV	30	167.6	21	157.8
Wrocław, XVI-XVII	20	166.6	20	157.8
Wrocław, XV-XVI	19	165.7	22	155.8
Wrocław, XIV-XVI	5	164.1	2	154.8
Pawłów, XV-XVI	32	164.5	25	152.7

N = number of individuals, x = average body height

Table 2 The time series in stature of the populations from the Wiślica region (in cm) (Wiercińska, 1978)

Chronology	Males	Females
X-XIII centuries	167.8	158.1
XII-XIV	168.4	158.4
XIV-XVIII	166.6	154.6
XVIII-XIX	168.9	159.3

Table 3 The time series in stature of the populations from the Lubiń region (in cm) (Henneberg et. al., 1986)

Chronology	Males		Females	
	N	x	N	x
XIII-XIV centuries	6	172.1	4	159.3
XV-XVI	32	170.0	26	160.8
XVII	27	171.4	6	160.3
XVIII-XIX	40	170.8	30	157.6

N = number of individuals, x = average body height

References

Bielicki, T. (1975): Natural selection and human morphology. In: Salzano, F. M. (ed.): The role of natural selection in human evolution. North-Holland Publ. Comp., 203-216

Bielicki, T. (1986): Physical growth as measure of the economic well-being of populations. In: Falkner, F. & Tanner, S. M. (eds.): Human growth. Plenum Press, New York, 283-305

Crognier, E. (1981): Climate and anthropometric variations in Europe and the Mediterranean area. Ann. Hum. Biol. 8, 99-107

HENNEBERG, M.; WRZESIŃSKA, A. & BRODNICKA, J. (1986): Materiały szkieletowe z cmentarzyska (XIII-XVIII w.) przy kościele św. Leonarda w Lubiniu, gmina Krzywiń. Opracowanie wstępne. Prz. Antropol. 50, 365-379

LAMB, H. H. (1972): Climate: present, past and future. Methuen, London

PIONTEK, J. (1989): Biological consequences of the "Neolithic Revolution": The case of the Middle European populations. In: Hershkovitz, I. (ed.): People and culture in change. B.A.R. Int. Ser. 508 (i), 367-374

PIONTEK, J. (1990): Comparative statistical analysis of the Late Medieval populations from Poland. Glasn. Antropol. Društ. Jug. 5-17

WIERCIŃSKA, A. (1978): Postcranial skeleton and natural selection. Proc. Symp. Natur. Select., Liblice, C.S.A.V., Praha, 337-346

WIERCINSKI, A. (1978): The meaning and scope of anthropology. Coll. Antropol. 2, 10-16

Address of the author:

Prof. Dr. J. Piontek, Department of Human Evolutionary Biology, Adam Mickiewicz University, Fredry 10, PL-61-701 Poznań, Poland.

The temperatures of Southwest Germany since 1500 - The examples of Lower Franconia and Northern Württemberg

Rüdiger Glaser

Summary

The present article summarizes some methodological and research results of an investigation carried out by the palaeoclimatological working group of the Geographic Institute of the University of Würzburg in 1983-1990. This investigation was performed within the "Paläoklimaprogramm der Bundesregierung". The aim was a seasonal scale reconstruction of the historical climate of Lower Franconia and Northern Württemberg in Southwest Germany using instrumental data, narrative sources, and harvest records for vine, grain and hay, as well as dendrological proxy data. The possibilities of the method and the usefulness of the proxy data are discussed and evaluated. Regional differences between Franconia and Northern Württemberg are registered.

Zusammenfassung

Die vorliegende Arbeit faßt die wesentlichen Untersuchungsergebnisse der Arbeitsgruppe "Paläoklimatologie" am Geographischen Institut der Universität Würzburg zusammen. Die Untersuchung wurde im Rahmen des Paläoklimaprogramms der Bundesregierung durchgeführt. Ziel war eine Klimarekonstruktion von Unterfranken und Nordwürttemberg auf jahreszeitlicher Ebene mit Hilfe von Instrumentenmeßdaten, Schriftquellen und Ernteergebnissen von Getreide, Heu, und Wein, sowie von Dendrodaten. Die methodischen Möglichkeiten sollten ebenso wie die Tauglichkeit der Proxydaten diskutiert und abgeschätzt werden. Regionale Unterschiede zwischen den beiden Arbeitsgebieten sollten ebenfalls untersucht werden.

1. The natural setting of the study areas

The study areas are part of the Southwest-German cuesta landscape. The areas are rather similar. Lower Franconia is an embayment area underlain by the Muschelkalk limestone. The major part is covered with loess, which has enabled an intense agriculture at present as during the past. In the natural landscape there is a contrast between the gently rolling plains of the "Gäuland" and the deeply dissected Main valley and its tributaries. The basin is surrounded by mountain regions of the uplands ("Mittelgebirge"). To the west lies the Spessart, a forest covered variegated sandstone landscape ("Buntsandstein-Landschaft"); to the north lies the volcanic landscape of the Rhön; and to the east the escarpment of the Steigerwald. In the south there is a gentle transition from Mainfranken to the Bauland, an undulating landscape dominated by elongated elevations (Riedel), which in the west is bounded by the Odenwald. To the south the region adjoins the Kraichgau. Both regions likewise form part of the South German "Gäuflächen". Administratively they form part of Württemberg. The "Gäuflächen" extend southwards. To the south and southeast of these regions of very similar landscape rise the Löwensteiner Mountains. The latter form part of the "Keuperwaldberge". The "Gäuflächen" and Keuperwald Mountains together form what is known as the Neckarland.

2. Climatic pattern - regionalisation

It has been repeatedly demonstrated that the regional palaeoclimate has to be taken into account (HAGEDORN & GLASER, 1990). In the context of this investigation the important question is whether both regions are climatically significantly different or not. Should present-day data indicate a difference, this would tend to suggest that regional differences also existed in historical times.

For this reason product-moment correlations of monthly mean temperature and precipitation at several climatic stations in the study area were calculated. The results clearly showed that the regions do exhibit differences in climate. The differences are not fundamental, but do justify separate consideration of the two regions, Unterfranken and Württemberg.

3. The method

A comprehensive evaluation of the proxy data has to include all relevant non-climatological natural and human influences (GLASER, 1991). This objective was reached by an ecological-anthropogenic analysis of the different and complex interactions between climate and the human and natural environment (PFISTER, 1985). In the ideal case it is possible to quantify the influences in an operational manner.

The historical instrumental data from the years 1781-1788 and 1804-1889 had to be homogenized because of varying measurement techniques, likewise recent data because of the increasing influence of urbanization and station displacement. The narrative sources were subjected to a critical analysis because of the subjectivity of the writer (Fig. 1; ALEXANDRE, 1987). Most of the data consisted of harvest reports. On account of the influence of anthropogenic as well as natural factors upon harvest, it was necessary to develop a procedure to eliminate the non-climatological influences. A procedure was worked out in which the time-series were separated into their low and high frequencies (binomial filtering and residuals). Remaining errors required a descriptive corrective. For this anthropogenic data, such as population growth, prices, etc. were collected and included (see also GLASER & WALSH, 1991).

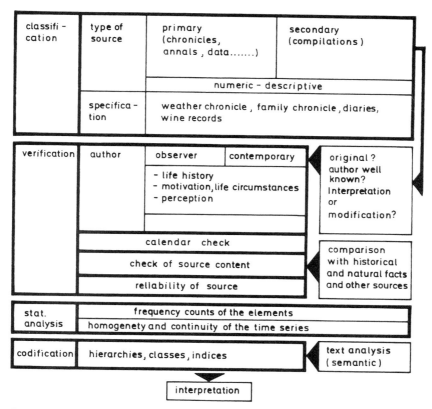

Fig. 1   Procedure of source analysis

A subsequent codification enabled the integration of the descriptive harvest reports and the deduction of standard curves. Tree-rings already existed as regional standardized time series. Besides the standardized chronologies of the tree-rings, we also investigated the "Wuchswerte" (growth values of the trees) and the so-called "Weiserjahre" (years of regionally significant change in growth rate; cp. BECKER & GLASER, 1991).

The climatological calibration of the numerical historical data was worked out using the principles of actualism (as usual in palaeoclimatology), which means by interpretation of stochastic models of their recent relations. Factor analysis as a means of reducing the complexity of the data structure was found to be unsuitable. The appropriate calibration method was found to be multiple linear regression on different temporal calibration levels. The proxy data were entered in the calculations as the dependent and the climatological data as the independent quantity over the number of years (cases). The resultant statistical relations

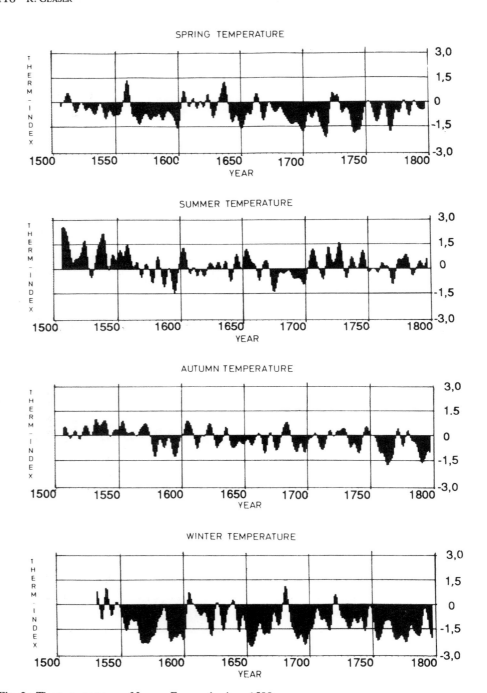

Fig. 2a The temperatures of Lower Franconia since 1500

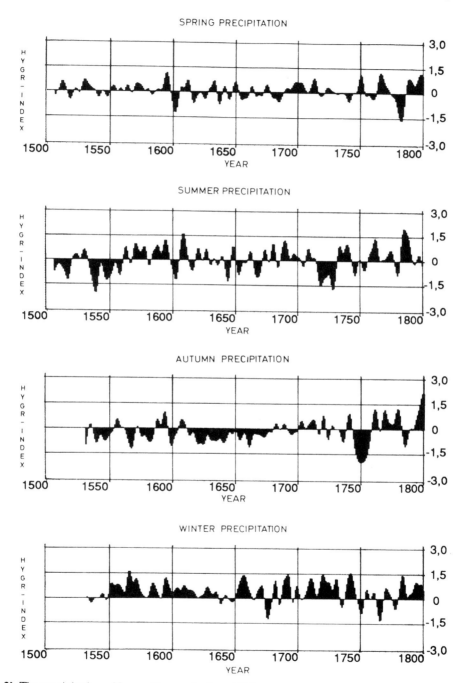

Fig. 2b The precipitation of Lower Franconia since 1500

could be very well explained by ecological factors. By inversion it was possible to derive from these statistical results equations with which one could transpose the filtered data into climatological data. The investigations with different methods showed that certain results had to be interpreted as "methodological results". To compensate for methodological errors, the derived climatological data were converted to indices.

This evaluation corresponds essentially with the method we used for the narrative sources. Because of the favourable temporal overlapping of the proxy data and the narrative sources, both could be linked with the instrumental data. Furthermore, we ascertained that the use of a single indicator leads to a high rate of error. Only the synthesis of several different indicators and additional checking against historical narrative sources provided reliable results. The regional character of each of the indicators meant that generalisations about the relations between plants and their environment could not be made. These findings underline the importance of regionalisation in palaeoclimatology whenever biological indicators are used.

4. The climate pattern since 1500

The climatological chronologies obtained were compared with the climate of a base period 1901-1960. The value "0" represents the average of the precipitation and temperature for this period.

4.1 The climate of Lower Franconia

The strongest deviations from the period 1901-1960 appeared in winter and spring temperatures and winter precipitation (Fig. 2). Both seasons were almost always cooler than in the base period. The colder winters were accompanied by higher precipitation, but precipitation in spring was similar to 1901-1960. Generally autumn temperature shows a downward trend between 1500 and 1800. Precipitation in the sixteenth and seventeenth centuries was mostly below average, but was followed by a rapid increase. Summer temperatures were mostly higher than during the base period.

Summarizing changes in temperature since 1500 it is possible to recognize a period between 1550 and 1890 in which the temperatures were below average compared to the current century and these low temperatures correspond with what some climatologists call a "Little Ice Age" (LAMB, 1977; LAUER & FRANKENBERG, 1986; LIEBSCHER et al., 1988). The greatest differences are in winter and springtime. Since 1500 we have had from time to time very considerable fluctuations, in which sine shaped trends as well as abrupt events occur. Until the end of the seventeenth century there is a higher regularity of the seasons than during the eighteenth century, in which fluctuations are obvious. The differences are to be interpreted as an accentuation and not as a fundamental climatic change.

4.2 The climate of Northern Württemberg

The results for Northern Württemberg (Fig. 3) are basically similar to those for Main-franken: much cooler than at present in the winter and spring months, with smaller deviations in summer and autumn (see also GLASER, 1990). The similarity in timing was checked by a PEARSON correlation analysis which proved to be significant at the 99% level. The significant phases are also present. The accentuation of seasons is almost identical. Despite these far reaching similarities, differences in timing are also identifiable. These will be described in the next chapter.

4.3 Differences in climate history

A significant difference between the climate time series presented here is the less marked drop in Württemberg winter temperatures around 1650, according to literature the height of the Little Ice Age. In the Württemberg series, the decline in temperature is only hinted at. In the spring temperatures too, the drop in temperature is of a much smaller order than in the Mainfranken series. Also there are differences at least in the timing of the peaks of the maximum and minimum summer temperature series. Autumn temperatures showed similar phenomena to the winter and spring temperature series. Using the same method suggests that there do exist real regional peculiarities of both climatic regions. They underline the importance of regionalisation in historical palaeoclimatology. For more far reaching conclusions as regards large-scale climatic history the examples presented are not sufficient.

5. Conclusions

The investigated areas exhibit significant long-term as well as short-term fluctuations. Those appear to be phases which correspond to well-known phenomena of the Little Ice Age. As well as these long-term fluctuations, there are also extreme years, often occurring in groups.

Methodologically the selected approach of synthesizing different indicators, descriptive sources, and instumental data has been tested. Use of indicators must include the reconstruction of all the main influences. Finally this leads to a system-oriented treatment of the reconstruction of past environments. Examinations of recent data have shown that the use of single indicators does not yield really reliable results.

Calibration procedures should render results which are easily interpretable. Nevertheless it can occur that the statistical procedures used may influence the results. This investigation clearly demonstrated that a regional approach is essential. Only from a dense regional climatic pattern conclusions about a past European climatic system can be deduced.

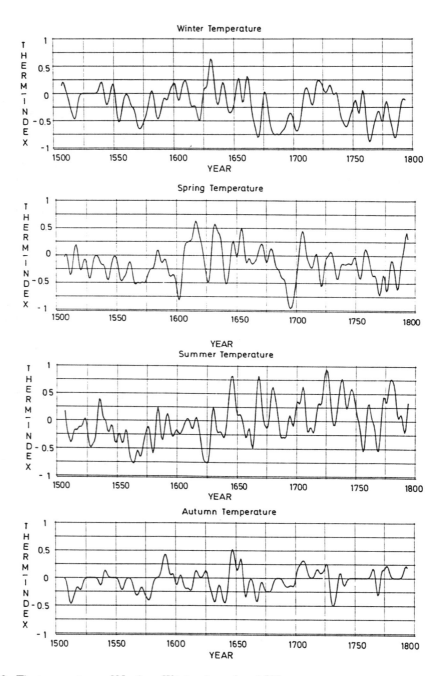

Fig. 3   The temperatures of Northern Württemberg since 1500

References

ALEXANDRE, P. (1987): Le Climat en Europe au Moyen-Age. Contribution à l'histoire des variations climatiques de 1000 à 1425, d'après les sources narratives de l'Europe occidentale. Ecole des Hautes Etudes en Sciences Sociales, Paris, 827 p.

BECKER, B. & GLASER, R. (1991): Baumringsignaturen und Wetteranomalien (Eichenbestand Guttenberger Forst, Klimastation Würzburg). Forstwiss. Centralblatt 110, 66-83

GLASER, R. (1990): Die Temperaturverhältnisse in Württemberg in der frühen Neuzeit. Z. Agrargesch. Agrarsoz. 38/2, 129-144

GLASER, R. (1991): Klimarekonstruktion für Mainfranken, Bauland und Odenwald anhand direkter und indirekter Witterungsdaten seit 1500. Paläoklimaforschung 5, Akad. Wiss. Lit., Mainz

HAGEDORN, H. & GLASER, R. (1990): Zur methodischen Konzeption und Regionalisierung in der Paläoklimatologie. Berl. Geogr. Abh. 53, 251-260

GLASER, R. & WALSH, R. P. D. (eds.) (1991): Historical climatology in different climatic zones - Historische Klimatologie in verschiedenen Klimazonen. Würzburger Geogr. Arb. 80, 251 p.

LAMB, H. H. (1977): Climate: present, past and future. Methuen, London, 835 p.

LAUER, W. & FRANKENBERG, P. (1986): Zur Rekonstruktion des Klimas im Bereich der Rheinpfalz seit Mitte des 16. Jahrhunderts mit Hilfe von Zeitreihen der Weinqualität und Weinquantität. Paläoklimaforschung 2, Fischer Verlag, Stuttgart, 54 p.

LIEBSCHER, H.-J.; KRAHE, P. & WITTE, W. (1988): Rekonstruktion der Witterungsverhältnisse im Mittelrheingebiet von 1000 n.Chr. bis heute anhand historischer hydrologischer Ereignisse. Abschlußbericht zum BMFT-Forschungsvorhaben LOF 10/85, 62 p.

PFISTER, C. (1985): Klimageschichte der Schweiz 1525-1860. Paul Haupt, Bern, 184 p.

Address of the author:

Dr. R. Glaser, Geographisches Institut der Universität Würzburg, Am Hubland, D-8700 Würzburg, F.R.G.

Variations of climate in Hungary (1540-1779)

Lajos Rácz

Summary

The best treatise on meteorological phenomena which was published in Hungary is the treatise of RÉTHLY (1962, 1970). He summarized the climatic observations he found in annals and chronicles of Hungarian history, dealing with the period from Roman times to the year 1800. Indirect observations of climatic phenomena, for example reports on floods, harvests, vintages etc., were also taken into account. In the scientific investigation presented here the climatic changes of the period from 1540 to 1779 have been analyzed, using the compilation published by RÉTHLY. The so-called "third generation" of treatises about the history of climate (HENNIG, 1904; EASTON, 1928; WEIKINN, 1958), to which RÉTHLY's treatise also belongs, were accused of negligence concerning a sound criticism of the sources used, cp. for instance the historians ALEXANDRE (1987) and FARMER (INGRAM et al., 1981). Therefore only contemporary sources have been used for climatic analysis in order to avoid possible pitfalls in RÉTHLY's treatise.

Résumé

Le meilleur recueil des événements météorologiques qui a été publié en Hongrie est l'oeuvre de RÉTHLY (1962, 1970). Il a repris les observations climatiques des annales et des chroniques relatives à l'histoire de Hongrie, et cela pour une période qui s'étend de l'époque romaine jusqu'à l'année 1800. Les observations concernant les phénomènes climatiques ont été également relevées, comme par exemple les inondations, les récoltes, les vendanges etc. Dans le traité présent j'ai analysé les variations climatiques pour la période 1540-1779 en utilisant le recueil édité par RÉTHLY. La "troisième génération" des recueils de l'histoire du climat (HENNIG, 1904; EASTON, 1928; WEIKINN, 1958), dont fait partie l'ouvrage de RÉTHLY, a été accusée par certains historiens comme ALEXANDRE (1987) et FARMER (INGRAM et al., 1981) parce que les auteurs de ces compilations manquent de critique des sources. Pour éviter les pièges éventuels des sources du recueil de RÉTHLY, et ensuite, pour les analyses climatiques je n'ai utilisé que les données des sources contemporaines.

1. Introduction

The means available for us to trace the climatic changes in Medieval and modern Hungary are limited and modest. The dendrochronological results obtained from an analysis of long tree-ring sequences are confined to the nineteenth and twentieth century.

As for palynological analysis, we have to consider that this method does not provide results which are exact and differentiated enough. Certainly the "rat thermometer" of KORDOS (1977) gives us a starting point, but with regard to our combined efforts to reconstruct the history of climate during the whole Holocene, this method is neither exact enough to reconstruct the climate of the last two centuries nor can we rely on its dating accuracy.

Under these circumstances there was no other possibility than to obtain the necessary information with the help of historical sources referring to climatic phenomena.

Since the beginning of the nineteenth century reports exist on climate but generally they deal with extraordinary events in the past. Scientific editions did not start to appear before the last third of the nineteenth century. Since that time research on climate in Hungary has not been interrupted. The most detailed editions are the compilations by RÉTHLY (1962, 1970), entitled : "Les événements climatiques et les sinistres causés par eux en Hongrie". This fundamental work was used as a basis for our analysis of changes in Hungarian climate.

The time our reconstruction of the Carpathian Basin's climate dates back to may be considered as the beginning of a new era, respecting many things. Thus, for example, the number of sources which were obtained due to RÉTHLY's research work increased considerably after 1540. Moreover, the conquest of Buda, the capital of Hungary, by the Turks in 1541 and the Turkish occupation with the subsequent presence of various armies for more than 150 years were decisive for the history of Hungary with regard to the "classical" chronology. And finally in the middle of the sixteenth century a new period in the history of climate started, the "Little Ice Age".

On the other hand our investigations end in the year 1799 because of two reasons: firstly, the introduction of instrumental measurements in Hungary in the year 1780 caused the onset of a new era of research work. Secondly the year 1780 is an important date in view of the political history of the region. It was the year of empress Marie-Thérèse's death. She achieved the consolidation of the Habsburg's Europe. It must be said that the time in question brought along dramatical changes for Hungary: it remained surrounded by two world powers, it lost its independence and a considerable number of its population. But in spite of this it was re-united at the end of this epoch, given a special statute, although remaining a part of the European Empire of the Habsburgs. At the end of the eighteenth century Hungary was an exhausted country with a reduced population and had to take in many colonists belonging to different ethnic groups.

It should be stressed that RÉTHLY was stimulated for his research work by the famous German Palaeoclimate School. The Hungarian specialist used the German sources on the history of the Carpathian Basin from HENNIG (1904) and WEIKINN (1958). From a critical point of view there seems to be one inevitable question: are the doubts, advanced by ALEXANDRE (1987) and other specialists regarding the reliability of the results obtained by this German School also justified for RÉTHLY's treatise? This was a fundamental question for us: we had to consider the reliability, authenticity and importance of the scientific documentation before we could start with our own reconstruction.

Those specialists of climatic history who have had a philological education too, such as ALEXANDRE and LE ROY LADURIE, reproach the German School and the authors of the climatic treatises belonging to the "third generation" (VANDERLINDEN, BRITTON, EASTON) as having made many chronological errors and mistakes in the interpretation of sources. This reproach seems to be justified.

Perhaps there are some doubts regarding RÉTHLY's treatise, but his philological competence and his scientific thoroughness should not be questioned: to edit the sources he completed hard research work in the archives over more than 50 years. He also subjected the sources to serious criticism. It should be noted in this context that RÉTHLY published his first paper on this subject in the year 1914. In spite of this some compilations of the "first generation", which must be handled carefully, can be found in his documentation. To exclude inherent risks we had to examine the documents a second time, which made the selection of the sources much easier.

To effect this "second examination" we had to check the contents of RÉTHLY's treatise. For this work we adopted the principles of INGRAM and PFISTER (INGRAM et al., 1981; Pfister, 1984).

It must also be stressed that the 240 years we have investigated document a much more favourable period than the Middle Ages: the quantity and the quality of the sources greatly improved. Also the different Medieval dating styles, rendering the use of the documents more difficult, were abandoned at the beginning of the sixteenth century.

The sources of our research work are subdivided as follows:

(a)   Chronicles and annals

Chronicles and annals constitute the most important group and were supplemented by information from diaries and the "Historia Domus", a chronicle of monasteries. Of course, phenological data was most important. The first group amounts to about 35% of our documents and forms the basis of our research work.

(b)   Documents on the administration and management of domains

We used this information very seldom.

(c)   *Personal documents and notes*

Within this group we mostly used personal diaries and letters. The notes concerning the exploitation of large properties, mostly belonging to the nobility, and the letters of journeys gave us most important information on changes in climate in the whole region and the whole country. The common correspondence showed us the political, economic, familiar and agricultural situation from region to region. This information amounts to about 45% of our sources.

(d)   *Non-instrumental diaries*

In Hungary the interest in meteorological observations and systematic investigations was made public by several doctors of medicine and by scientific teachers at the end of the seventeenth century. The journal entitled: "Sammlung von Natur- und Medicin Geschichten", edited in Breslau, today Wroclaw, rapidly became the most important forum of climatic observations made in Hungary during the early eighteenth century. It includes a lot of valuable evidence on the economic history of the region. The information amounts to about 15% of our sources.

(e)   *Instrumental diaries*

Instrumental diaries exactly document the results of instrumental measuring. Instrumental observations started in the year 1755, preceded by some individual, more or less serious attempts. The introduction of these instrumental measurements is connected to the name of WEISS, who was professor for mathematics at the University of Nagyszombat. Instrumental data represents 3-4% of the entire evidence. We know that our sources have to be completed by information from other documents such as notes on large agricultural estates, registers of land property and taxes or systematic and serial reports concerning vintages.

2. Chronological and spatial distribution of historical sources on climate

Two remarks have to be made as to the chronological distribution:

(1) the number of sources increased markedly during the time in question;
(2) the number of notes concerning extreme meteorological deviations also increased during the time in question.

Thus, in the middle of the sixteenth century we could rely on sufficient information from the Kingdom of Hungary and Transylvania. But we had no information about the regions which were occupied by the Turks for a long time. Above all, most of the information did not concern the entire year but concentrated on summers and winters mainly.

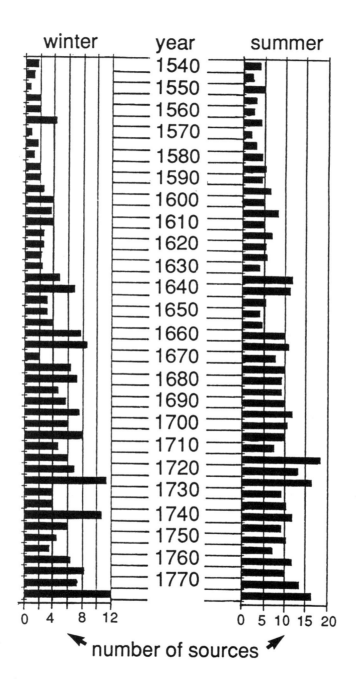

Fig. 1 Chronological distribution of historical sources

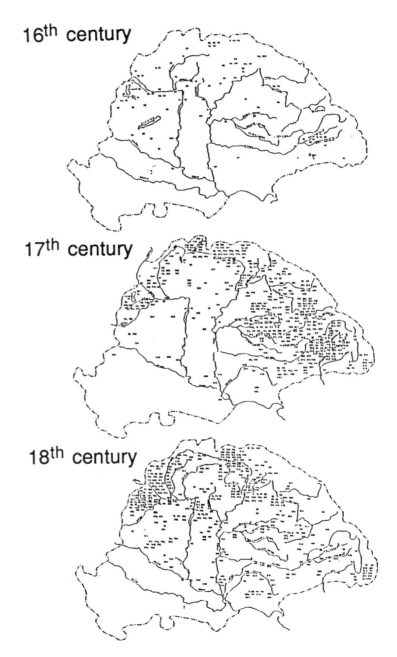

Fig. 2 Chronological and spatial distribution of climatic observations in Hungary

In the seventeenth century the situation changed with regard to the richness of the documents because of changes in the political and military frontiers. The importance of the Transylvanian and the Partium archives increased in an extraordinary way, whereas those of the Hungarian Kingdom ameliorated only slightly. The only important sources from the occupied regions were the reports on military movements.

The regional distribution of the sources changed radically in the eighteenth century. The northwestern part of Hungary dominated, the importance of Transylvania decreased. At the same time more and more frequently documents from the regions formerly occupied by the Turks were passed on.

3. The analysis of the sources

To analyse our sources we adopted two procedures in order to obtain a sensible differentiation and a convenient quantification of our information of the 240 years in question. We regret that the insufficiencies of our sources only permitted a sytematical comparison of the two opposed seasons with the methods mentioned above. Therefore we examined and coded the years from 1540 to 1700, which are represented by irregular sources, with the help of an unprecise dissection.

We subdivided the winters into:	strong winters	(-1)
	cold winters	(0)
	mild winters	(1)
We subdivided the summers into:	very hot summers	(-1)
	warm summers	(0)
	cool summers	(1)

To examine the climate of the eighteenth century we used the method developed by PFISTER (1984). Therefore we differentiated between regular or non-remarkable months (0); months which were very dry or very rainy and very cold or very warm (-3 and +3), and intermediate stages.

4. Long-term changes in the climate of Hungary

4.1 The winters

The winters of the second half of the sixteenth century were colder than average. The peak of the series of very hard winters during the period beginning with the year 1550 was between 1595 and 1602. At the turn of the century the river Danube froze three times: in 1595/96, 1601/02 and 1607/08. This phenomenon also points to the general cooling of the climate.

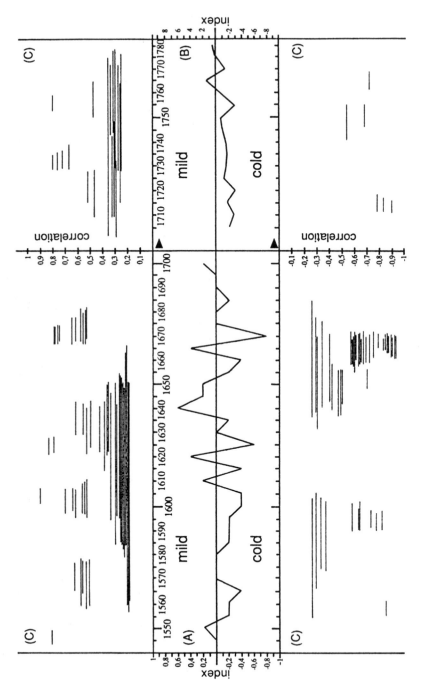

Fig. 3   Winter temperatures in Hungary, 1540-1779. Diagrams A and B are based on the average 5-year temperature index of winter coldness. Diagram C reflects the results of trend calculations. Periods with warmer tendencies appear above, those with colder tendencies below the zero line (cp. diagrams A and B)

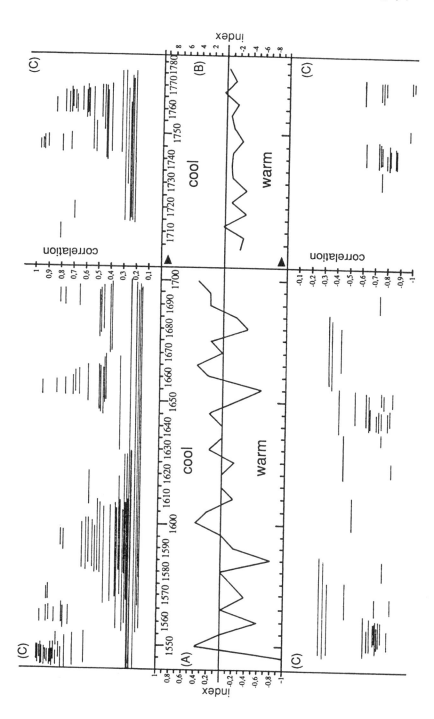

Fig. 4   Summer temperatures in Hungary, 1540-1779. Diagrams A and B are based on the average 5-year summer temperature index. Diagram C reflects the results of trend calculations. Periods with cooler tendencies appear above, those with warmer tendencies below the zero line (cp. diagrams A and B)

A repeated change between hard and mild winters took place after the year 1610. The cooling of the years between 1621 and 1624 was less than the cooling at the turn of the century.

A warm peak can be traced between 1636 and 1643, giving way to a period of mild winters, only interrupted twice by a strong cold interval between 1652 and 1658 (the river Danube froze in 1656/57) and between 1667 and 1671.

The winters in the eighteenth century were a little colder than the average but we have no proof of really hard winters. The two "negative" exceptions (the winters between 1714 and 1718 and those between 1729 and 1733) in the first third of the eighteenth century cannot be regarded as conclusive. Besides, they are not comparable to the severe winters in the sixteenth and seventeenth century. On the other hand, the winters were particularly mild during the warm peak in the eighteenth century between 1761 and 1768.

4.2 The summers

From the beginning of our period of examination until the end of the sixteenth century very warm and dry summers followed each other. The warming reached the highest peaks between 1540 and 1545, 1557 and 1561 and between 1580 and 1585. It must be stressed that this period of warming favoured intensively the extension of Mediterranean garden culture into the Carpathian Basin. This is demonstrated by investigations of PENTEK and SZABO concerning the history of plants.

The meteorological conditions changed completely at the end of the sixteenth and the beginning of the seventeenth century. From the middle of 1590s until the end of the first decennium of the seventeenth century there was an important period of cool and rainy summers. The main cooling took place between 1597 and 1606. During the whole seventeenth century neither warm nor cool summers predominated for a longer time. The character of the summers changed from year to year. But a slight warming followed the cool summers at the beginning of the seventeenth century. It reached its maximum with the heat-waves in the summers between 1635 and 1637 and was balanced by the strong cooling between 1638 and 1641.

This alternation between cool and very warm summers lasted until the end of the seventeenth century with a relatively warming maximum between the years 1652 and 1654 and a relatively cooling maximum at the end of the seventeenth century.

The general warming in the eighteenth century was interrupted by a cool spell between 1713 and 1716. This was followed by a period of very warm summers lasting for more than 10 years with maxima between 1717 and 1722, later between 1726 and 1729.

In the eighteenth century the Hungarian people believed that climatic variations were caused by the Devil. The last witch burnt in Szeged in 1728 was, among other things, accused of having sold the summer rains to the Devil. She was sentenced to death and burnt on the Isle of the Sorceresses.

Since the end of the seventeenthirties the warming began to decrease and the character of the summers approached the temperatures of present-day seasonal means.

References

ALEXANDRE, P. (1987): Le climat en Europe au Moyen Age. Contribution à l'histoire des variations climatiques de 1000 à 1425, d'après les sources narratives de l'Europe occidentale. Ecole des Hautes Etudes en Sciences Sociales, Paris, 827 p.

EASTON, C. (1928): Les hivers dans l'Europe occidentale. Brill, Leyden

HENNIG, R. (1904): Katalog bemerkenswerter Witterungsereignisse von den ältesten Zeiten bis zum Jahre 1800. Abh. Königl. Preuß. Meteorol. Inst. 2/4, Berlin

INGRAM, M. J.; UNDERHILL, D. J. & FARMER, G. (1981): The use of documentary sources for the study of past climates. In: Wigley, T. M. L.; Ingram, M. J. & Farmer, G. (eds.): Climate and history. Cambridge Univ. Press, Cambridge, 180-213

KORDOS, L. (1977): Changes in the Holocene climate of Hungary reflected by the "vole-thermometer" method. Földrajzi Közlemények 1-3, 25-68

PAPP, Z. (1984): A vulkáni tevékenység klimatikus hatásainak vizsgálata Magyarországon az évgyürüanalízis tükrében. Botanikai Közlemények 2, 109-121

PFISTER, C. (1984): Klimageschichte der Schweiz 1525-1860. Das Klima der Schweiz von 1525-1860 und seine Bedeutung in der Geschichte von Bevölkerung und Landwirtschaft. 2 Vols., Bern, 3rd ed. 1988

RÉTHLY, A. (1962): Idöjárási események és elemi csapások Magyarországon 1700-ig. Budapest

RÉTHLY, A. (1970): Idöjárási események és elemi csapások Magyarországon 1701-1800-ig. Budapest

SAMMLUNG von Natur und Medicin Geschichten ... so sich Anno ... in Schlesien und anderen Ländern begeben. Academie Naturae Curies in Breslau, Leipzig, Budissin, Erfurt, 1719-1730

WEIKINN, C. (1958): Quellentexte zur Witterungsgeschichte Europas von der Zeitwende bis zum Jahre 1859. Berlin

Address of the author:

Dr. L. Rácz, Centre for Regional Studies of the Hungarian Academy of Sciences, Rákóczi ut. 3, Pf. 261, H-6001 Kecskemét, Hungary

The mathematical handling and analysis of non-homogeneous and incomplete multivariate historical data series

Viva Banzon, Giorgiana de Franceschi & Giovanni P. Gregori

Summary

Two methodological approaches for analyzing both continuous and discrete data series are discussed. (1) Regarding the search for periodicities, mathematical refinements of the ARP and CETRA filter technique (GREGORI, 1990) are presented, as well as a procedure for the systematic search for period families, forefathers, and family relations within an ARP. (2) The second procedure allows to distinguish between "quiet" and "perturbed" periods in a multivariate data series, using an objective search for outliers, and providing a quantitative estimate of a multidimensional "activity" or "anomaly" index. The example presented here is an application to an ionospheric data series. This procedure can be very useful either for assessing quantitatively and objectively the climatically anomalous periods within a given area, or for performing the "pre-scanning" of a given data set (namely, selecting within the data base situations that may refer or respond to completely different and independent physical mechanisms).

Zusammenfassung

Zwei methodische Näherungen zur Analyse von stetigen und diskreten Datenreihen werden diskutiert. (1) Was die Suche nach Periodizitäten betrifft, werden die mathematische Filtertechniken ARP und CETRA (GREGORI, 1990) und ein Verfahren zum systematischen Aufsuchen von Periodenreihen und deren Bezügen innerhalb von ARP vorgestellt. (2) Das zweite Verfahren erlaubt, in einem multivariaten Datensatz zwischen Grundperioden und deren Störungen zu unterscheiden. Dabei wird ein objektives Verfahren zum Aufsuchen von Ausreißern benützt und eine quantitative Abschätzung eines multi-dimensionalen "Aktivitäts-" oder "Anomalie-Index" bereitgestellt. Das hier verwendete Beispiel ist eine Anwendung dieses Verfahrens auf eine ionosphärische Datenreihe. Das kann sowohl für die quantitative und objektive Abschätzung klimatischer Perioden als auch für die verläßliche Beurteilung des betrachteten Datensatzes sehr nützlich sein, insbesondere dann, wenn das Datenkollektiv Vorgänge wiedergibt, die sich auf unterschiedliche physikalische Mechanismen beziehen.

1. Introduction

The type of problems to be tackled in data handling of non-homogeneous and incomplete historical series requires two preliminary considerations:

(1) the non-repetitivity of the physical experiment "evolution of the environment", and
(2) the need to develop procedures appropriately akin to reality.

The first point is basically the very concept of HERACLITUS OF EPHESUS (ca. 500 B.C.): "Upon those who step into the same rivers, different and different waters flow down."

That is, we will never be able to measure a phenomenon that has already occurred. Hence, we can only speculate and attempt to interpret what is within our own reach and at our disposal, and are therefore constrained to accept all kinds of information, no matter how scanty or poor. This is an unusual situation from the viewpoint of the professional mathematical statistician who customarily requires some given confidence limits before accepting any conclusion. This requirement is correct, for example, in laboratory investigations, i.e. whenever it is presumably possible to repeat as many times as needed a given experiment in order to get a suitable data base. In the case of environmental research, however, a good investigator cannot ignore any hint, no matter how seemingly irrelevant; yet, at the same time, he must be selective in accepting any given evidence.

The second problem, in the ultimate analysis, has much deeper roots related to the methodological consciousness of Man in front of reality[1]. Concerning the choice of methodology, one should first decide what, and then how, to search within a given data base: one should try to get as much information as possible from the observational evidence, albeit one

---

[1] The methodological consciousness of man in front of natural reality is still a largely unexplored topic *per se*, although it is certainly a fundamental aspect for the advancement of natural sciences. Few facets have been investigated: NEUMANN (1949) has examined the psycho-analytical aspects, while KOYRÉ (1967) has discussed the conflict between philosophy and technology in the ancient world. At the end of the nineteenth century, a hard debate arose on whether history should be conceived from the traditional humanistic viewpoint, or rather only as the history of the evolution of the concept of science and of scientific knowledge (e.g. KRAGH, 1987). The same concept of historiography underwent a substantial evolution all along the history of mankind (cp. COLACINO et al., 1988, also for additional comments on the other items here above). The best known such debate is concerned with such fundamental items as empirism, positivism, pragmatism, ...But, other aspects do not seem to have been adequately investigated. E.g., it may appear hard to believe that, provided that the theoretical and scientific background was "at hand", the radio was invented by a young man, with a degree from a technical high school but no university degree, and not by one of the outstanding scientists of the most famous universities of his time. GUGLIELMO MARCONI in fact stated: "My chief trouble was that the idea was so elementary, so simple in logic, that it seemed difficult for me to believe that no one else had thought of putting it into practice" (from a poster hanging on the wall of a room of the Italian National Research Council). The point is that the mistakes of the past ought not to be repeated at present. Essentially, the ultimate target of such a methodological consciousness is the relation between pure and applied science, and the government policy on how to promote the development of science for the advantage of society.

should also be careful not to attempt to get more than what is objectively contained in the available experimental data. Moreover, the tendency towards hyperspecialization of different disciplines, including professional statistics, results in the increasing dependence of the climatologist on methods contributed by increasingly specialized mathematicians. This implies that, as opposed to the late nineteenth century and early twentieth century, the mathematical tools are no longer developed by the geophysicists to fit specifically the requirements of the application to a given data series. Rather, a geophysical data set is assumed to fit some suitable mathematical requirements in order that some given mathematical tools can be used. Incomplete and non-homogeneous data series require the development of *ad hoc*, intuitive, common-sense methods, able to extract from the available data set "all" possible information (both the highly reliable and the least reliable one, from the viewpoint of statistics), while also satisfying suitable robustness requirements.

It is from this general viewpoint that the two methodologies discussed in this paper were developed. The first involves methods for the search for periodicities. Since a detailed presentation has been previously published in GREGORI (1990), here in section 2 we only discuss some improvements. The operators ARP and CETRA are mentioned with a few minor changes to ameliorate their practical efficiency by noise reduction. It also contains some short comments on the best way to search for period families, forefathers, and family relations utilizing the output of CETRA.

The second part of the present paper focuses on a different procedure which here is briefly called the "pre-scanning". Given any historical data series (either one- or multi-variate, more or less homogeneous and complete), one must first recognize the eventual existence of different kinds of processes. For example, in a geomagnetic data series one clearly recognizes magnetic storms and quiet days, and therefore it makes no sense to take an uncritical average over all days. The physical system is manifestly quite different on different occasions: in fact, from time to time it is so different that the two situations cannot even be compared with each other. Similarly to this, a naturalist divides living beings into kingdoms, e.g. all animals into mammals, fishes, etc., before investigating common features, averages, etc. Such pre-scanning is customary in some fields of geophysics, like in geomagnetism (as above) where several "geomagnetic indices" have been envisaged and extensively debated in great details. The approach holds for phenomena varying either in time or space, or both. This is in fact the same logical problem that inspired the search for gravity anomalies or for geomagnetic anomalies (by means of the "regional residual analysis") in a data set which is not a historical data series, but rather an array of measurements performed in a given 2D area. Differently stated, the crucial point is to focus on what is statistically distinct from its nearby data (called either an "active" datum or an "anomalous" datum). The entire such process, however, is normally applied on an intuitive basis. Several drawbacks are usually encountered, related to the practical way of evaluating a quantitative indexing or labelling of the "anomalous" or "perturbed" data or conditions, or to the reason why one such index should be 1D and not some nD vector itself, etc. The availability of more and more powerful computers renders it possible to overcome several such caveats by means of some logical and practical improvements. This problem is discussed in section 3, while section 4 contains some short final conclusions.

2. Methods

2.1 The general rationale

The approach is to search for a strictly inductive data analysis in contrast to a deductive one. Logical induction searches for intrinsic evidence in the data base *per se*, independent from any speculations or more or less arbitrary assumptions. Logical deduction, in contrast, is a search for a model, where a few axioms lead to some logical frame or mathematical scheme, by which all experimental data can be fitted and "explained" within some given presumed chain of causes and effects.

For a given data series (either complete and homogeneous or not) one of the first tasks is to determine its eventual repetitivity in time (and/or space). The superimposed epoch approach is applied (in 1D series). For point-like processes this is accomplished by the operator[2] ARP by which, whenever a peak (or relative maximum) appears in its output histogram (named "arp"), an apparent periodicity occurs in the data set corresponding to a given period T. But, if the phenomenon has an apparent periodicity T, it will also show an apparent periodicity at kT (k=1,2,..). Moreover, if a phenomenon has a fundamental period T, it could also have some higher harmonics of T, i.e. say T/h (h=1,2,...). Therefore, every T could be associated to an entire period family, having forefather T and family members {Tk/h} (k,h=1,2,...). Therefore, three further problems arise: (1) how to recognize any simple periodicity T, (2) after having recognized several such T's, how to recognize a forefather and a period family, and (3) after having eventually recognized several such period families with their respective forefathers, how to recognize the family relations between different families (cp. Gregori, 1990, 1990a).

2.2 CETRA improvements

The first problem of finding the repetitivity of the peaks in the arp is solved by way of the operator CETRA[3] (by which a moving average is computed over a "movable window"

---

[2] For this and for several other details refer to Gregori (1990, 1990a). For practical applications refer to Banzon et al. (1990 and 1990a), Fiorentino et al. (1988), Gregori & Pavese (1985), Gregori et al. (1988), Pavese & Gregori (1984), and Pavese et al. (1992). ARP is an acronym for Automatic Research for Periodicities. Its basic idea is the superimposed epoch approach. It was first defined by Pavese & Gregori (1984).

[3] CETRA is an acronym for Computing Errors, Trends, and Associated parameters. Its basic idea is still the superimposed epoch criterion. It is explained, in addition to Gregori (1990, 1990a), by Alessandrini et al. (1987).

along the plot; see the references above). A minor drawback is that the CETRA output appears noisy for T close to zero owing to the border effect (the arp is defined only for T>0). To eliminate such an inconvenience we defined arp also for T<0 using a specular reflection of the former arp with respect to the vertical axis T=0. This re-definition of ARP actually coincides with the cross-bilateral-ARP (or xb-ARP) (cp. GREGORI, 1990, 1990a for additional specific details), an operator originally defined for a different application as follows. Consider two historical data series, related to two different phenomena A and B. One must decide whether any event of the kind A is apparently occurring either before or after some corresponding event of the kind B or vice versa. Hence, the operator xb-ARP assumes, on a trial basis, that the origin of time coincides with any given event of the class A and considers, statistically, the occurrence relative to it of any event of the class B. The mirroring of arp mentioned above is equivalent to apply xb-ARP to two historical data series being identical to each other and coinciding with the unique original data series. Such a procedure has been applied in several different cases (not shown here) and always was quite effective in reducing the statistical noise and in increasing the efficiency and sensitivity of CETRA for small values of T.

For all applications of CETRA to arp, a consistent and apparently invariant feature was a downward step of the output function vs. T, always occurring for a period T equal to ~3/20 of the total time interval spanned by the original historical data series. This value actually depends on the width of the moving window we chose. Several such examples can be found in the investigations described in the references quoted here above. The four examples shown in Fig. 1a represent a randomly simulated "historical" data series (the random data base ensures the existence of no eventual physical periodicity). After careful inspection and several trials we diagnosed the cause of the unwanted nuisance which can be envisaged as follows. Consider the case of a flood data series which contains a list of only the years, not the actual complete dates, of the occurrence of a flood (the date is seldom available for old events). Then, when a flood is treated by ARP and subsequently by CETRA its time coordinate is arbitrarily located at the middle of its respective year. This causes a concentration of points exactly at the middle of every year (and no points fall in any first or second halves of every year). In this way, it happens that the moving window of CETRA abruptly includes or excludes all points exactly located at the centre of a given year: hence, a step-like trend appears at some specific exact location.

Therefore, the obvious modification to be applied to the method is either to consider the complete date, or, without loss of generality and in a much simpler way, to locate the datum of a flood occurring at a given year at some random time instant along that year. This criterion was applied to the same four random data sets that were used for Fig. 1a. Fig. 1b shows that the unwanted step disappears. Fig. 1c plots the difference between the two figures and it very clearly shows that such a step is actually a repetitive feature that, on some unlucky circumstances, could even simulate some false apparent periodicity.

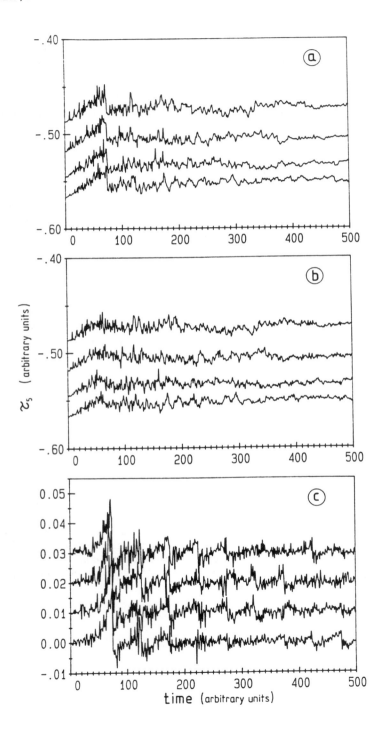

To sum up in general, when applying CETRA to any data set (being either an arp, or any time series to be analyzed) it is very important to relocate in any case the abscissas of the input data in some random way. This introduces no actual bias (since, in fact, one does not search for a time resolution finer than the minimum interval of definition of the datum itself; e.g. if this one is rounded off to 1 year, one cannot search for details of a month or of a day). Such a "trick" is essential to avoid unwanted mathematical bias and misleading false evidence.

2.3 Period families, forefathers, and family relations

When a set of different periodicities T's has been evidenced by CETRA an automatic procedure capable of recognizing families, forefathers, and family relations does not yet seem possible. We found that direct visual inspection cannot be easily substituted by computer. The output plot of CETRA promptly and clearly shows the presence of an eventual dominating period T_0. Assume that such T_0 is a forefather. Then, evaluate (with the aid of a computer) its family $\mathcal{F}(T_0)$ and reject from the original set of T's all $T \in \mathcal{F}(T_0)$. Then redraw the output plot of CETRA without the parts of the plot relative to $T \in \mathcal{F}(T_0)$ and, by visual inspection, proceed to search for a new period family etc. Therefore the best possible procedure seems to be a combined use of direct visual inspection and computer algorithms for rejecting the periods already assigned to a family: in fact, visual inspection takes into account also all the relative ordinate values of the CETRA plot and not simply the abscissas alone.

Fig. 1   Four random sequences were generated to simulate four different historical data series to which the operator CETRA was applied. The four outputs are shown in Fig. 1a (shifted on the vertical scale for clarity, units being arbitrary in every case). Note for all four cases the relative downward step at a period ~3/20 of the total time interval spanned by the original data series (= 500 units). To eliminate this nuisance, every datum of the original historical data series was randomly distributed within its respective discrete elementary time interval of definition (for example, the time of occurrence of a flood, or of an earthquake etc., was positioned randomly within the one year interval ignoring its actual exact date and time instant). The result of such modification, applied to the same data used in Fig. 1a, is shown in Fig. 1b. The advantages are even more evident in Fig. 1c, which shows the difference between the two previous figures: a regular recurrence of the step-like feature is found which eventually damps off, but clearly gives a misleading impression of a periodic pattern that is only a mathematical bias. See text for discussion

3. The pre-scanning

Here a general argument is presented, but for clarity purposes one specific example is discussed. This is a one-variate case, although the principal idea can be promptly generalized to any multi-variate case. The example gives an ionospheric datum, namely the critical frequency f_oF_2 of the F_2 layer, as it is measured every hour LT from the Rome station. The data sets for two months were considered: March 1989 (a geomagnetically perturbed month) and June 1989 (a geomagnetically quiet month). We know that the data base shows a prominent diurnal variation, by the fact that the ionosphere over the vertical of the sounding station is substantially different at different hours LT. Therefore it would be nonsense to statistically compare among themselves f_oF_2's measured at different hours LT. It was then decided to group the data for different days by hour and use a moving window of 31 days to examine every day within this group. That is, for every one of such 24 data series (every one referring to one specific hour LT), consider one given date (or time) t and one given $f_oF_2(t)$ datum at time t. Consider also the 15 data f_oF_2 of the 15 days preceding t, plus the 15 data f_oF_2 of the 15 days following t. In this way, a set is obtained composed of altogether 31 data f_oF_2 (such a procedure was applied by using also several data f_oF_2 of February, April, May and July 1989, whenever needed).

Fig. 2   Two examples of derivation of an "activity index" are shown by applying the pre-scanning procedure described in the text. The data base is the f_oF_2 (critical frequency of the F_2 layer of the ionosphere) measured in Rome. Because of a large diurnal modulation, only data measured at the same local time (i.e. one hourly value per day) were compared with each other. The outliers (with respect to a Gaussian distribution) were detected and rejected, using a moving average. By this, a mean, a standard deviation, and a 95% confidence limit were evaluated, which can be considered the expected values at any time instant for normal conditions. Finally, the index was defined as the deviation of the actual measured value at the given instant of time with respect to its expected mean, expressed as the percentage value evaluated with respect to the corresponding 95% confidence limit. In this way, an "activity index" was finally computed for every time instant. The final result, plotted in this figure, refers to March 1989, a geomagnetically perturbed month (and the large geomagnetic storm is clearly shown by the diagram of Fig. 2a), and to June 1989, a geomagnetically quiet month (but, the plot of Fig. 2b shows some activity on some occasions along the month; such episodes do not appear to be related to geomagnetic activity; a much more extensive physical discussion is needed). These examples show the efficiency of such an approach for pre-scanning any given (even multi-variate) data set, in order to detect intervals of anomalous behaviour of the physical system with respect to its own statistical trend. Notice that for some short periods of time (e.g. on June 27th and 28th) the ionosonde was down and the plot is not defined and here appears flat.

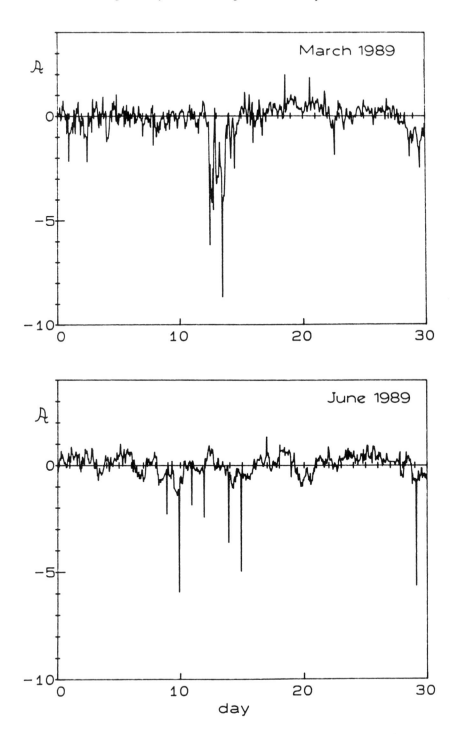

The distribution of every such set of 31 data f_oF_2 was then considered and a rejection procedure was applied as follows.

Step 1: The number of points is n=31. Evaluate the average μ (n), the rms deviation σ (n), the 95% confidence limit τ_5 (n), and its standard deviation σ (τ_5(n)). Moreover, evaluate the likelihood function L (n), which is the product of the probability densities computed, for every point by the Gaussian distribution of the n points, by means of the parameters μ (n) and σ (n) evaluated above. After evaluating L (n), take its n-th root B (n) = $[L(n)]^{1/n}$.

Step 2: Search for a datum among the n=31 points which is the farthest away from μ (31). Reject it and remain with n=30 points;

Step 3: Re-apply step 1 albeit with n=30;

Step 4: Re-apply step 2, thus remaining with n=29 data points. Etc.

In this way, the following sequences are computed τ_5 (31), τ_5 (30), ... and B (31), B (30), ..., with the error bar sequence σ (τ_5 (31)), σ (τ_5 (30)), ...

Plot either B (n) or $-\tau_5$ (n) vs. n. By definition, such quantities must be non-decreasing functions of n. The total number n is decreased iteratively. When both B (n) and $-\tau_5$ (n) increase step-wise, this indicates that we have rejected the exact number of points which are eventually not partaking into the Gaussian distribution. We applied this to several cases, and it was promptly and unambiguously observed that B (n) is definitely less robust than $-\tau_5$ (n) (by the fact that the B (n) vs. n plot appeared much more fluctuating and unstable than the $-\tau_5$ (n) plot). Therefore, it was decided that $-\tau_5$ (n) is more suitable for such an application than B (n).

Therefore, consider the sequences $-\tau_5$ (n) and σ ($-\tau_5$ (n)) (n=31,30,...). Consider all differences δ_h = $\{[-\tau_5$ (31-h)] - $[-\tau_5$ (31-h-1)]\}$ (h = 0,1,2,...) and their respective error bars $\sigma(\delta_h)$ = $\sqrt{\sigma^2$ (τ_5 (31-h)) + σ^2 (τ_5 (31-h-1))}. Consider three possible conditions (and one must decide which conditions ought to be used)

$$\delta_h \geq \sigma (\delta_h) \tag{1a}$$

$$-\tau_5 (31-h-1) \geq -\tau_5 (31-h) \cdot K \tag{1b}$$

$$\delta_h \quad \text{Max} \tag{1c}$$

where K is a constant to be suitably chosen depending on how strict one wants the rejection criterion to be. Sometimes it is sufficient to use only the first condition, while at other times it can be better to apply also the second one. On other occasions, one could use (1a) and (1c). In the example above only the condition (1a) was applied, provided that the sequence 31, 30, ... be interrupted at 15 (when interupted at 10 the scatter of $-\tau_5$(n) cuts off almost all points). The criterion for deciding by computer where the "step-like" variation is located (a decision that only a direct visual inspection could give in the best way) actually depends on the total number of points being considered (31 in the example above) and on how they behave statistically. Such arbitrariness is in fact related to the physics of the problem, and to the severity of the rejection criterion that the researcher wants to apply. In general, the rejected points should actually be very few, or sometimes the empty set. The largest h value for the rejected points (i.e. satisfying an appropriate subset of the conditions (1)) is the value to be chosen for the cut: that is, the final correct Gaussian distribution must be left with its 31-h-1 points, or h+1 points must be rejected. When this has been done, one is left with two parameters $\mu(31\text{-}h\text{-}1)$ and $\tau_5(31\text{-}h\text{-}1)$ for one specific value h fixed as above.

At last, define an index of activity or of anomaly (call it as you prefer) by means of the relation

$$\mathcal{A}(t) = \frac{f_o F_2(t) - \mu(31\text{-}h\text{-}1)}{\tau_5(31\text{-}h\text{-}1)} \tag{2}$$

Notice that $\mathcal{A}(t)$ can be either positive or negative.

In the case of our example, repeat the procedure for every one of the 24 data series and in all such cases get one sequence of $\mathcal{A}(t)$ for every t (expressed in hours LT). At last, plot the final result (Fig. 2). The large magnetic storm of March 1989 is clearly recognized but even the "quiet" June 1989 shows some activity which does not appear to be generally correlated with the standard geomagnetic activity indices. The physical discussion of such distinctions is not of concern to the present paper which is mainly oriented towards climatological problems. It should just emphasize the heuristic potentiality of such a general approach.

The entire procedure can be easily generalized to the case of a multi-variate data series, by which one evaluates a corresponding multi-variate $\vec{\mathcal{A}}(t)$ (one vector component for every one-variate data series at a time). Notice that every such vector component of $\vec{\mathcal{A}}(t)$ is an actual dimensionless number (owing to the definition (2)), hence there are no problems related to the units being chosen in every one-variate data series (see below).

An important point is the need for recognizing *a priori* the eventual astronomical modulation, in order to select, like in the example here above, data which are significantly comparable with each other (otherwise the physical system is so different that one must reason as if dealing with different physical systems).

The choice of 31 data for every Gaussian distribution was motivated in the example here above by the fact that such a value is close to the rotation period of the Sun (which is known to affect the ionosphere). Obviously, when dealing with some other application, one can choose even a different value (e.g. 21, or central value plus or minus 10 data). The unique requirement which has always to be considered is that there is need for some minimum total number of points entering into one given Gaussian distribution, otherwise the rejection analysis does not work.

The result of Fig. 2 appears interesting, especially when considering that the leading criterion in such an analysis is completely independent from any arbitrary choice, besides the 31 choice as above, plus the choice of the constant K entering into (1b). But, the 31 (or else) value is not very critical, as it appears very likely that the final result will be only very slightly affected by it, while the K choice is an important choice, depending on how strict we want our selection to be. That is, this physical (not mathematical) point depends on the "resolution" or detail we want to apply in defining different states of our physical system.

Therefore, such $\mathcal{A}(t)$ indices can be computed for several sets of data, referring to different physical outputs of the same physical system (e.g. different ionospheric parameters, geomagnetic field components, airglow records, etc., or, for climate research, temperature, humidity, precipitation, pressure data for the same site or for different sites in some given area, etc.). Then, all such indices can be considered as a unique multi-variate vector index $\vec{\mathcal{A}}(t)$ that can thus characterize in an expressive way the statistical and physical evolution of the entire system by considering altogether as many degrees of freedom as there are vector index components.

Concerning climatological applications, this is a way of giving a clearly stated and conceptually simple definition of the climate in a given area and at a given time, and on how much it deviates from its standard statistical behaviour. E.g., one can refer, in addition to $\vec{\mathcal{A}}(t)$ itself, also to its "modulus" or "norm", defined by

$$|\vec{\mathcal{A}}(t)| = \sqrt{\sum_j [\mathcal{A}_j(t)]^2} \qquad (3)$$

where the suffix $_j$ denotes one vector component of $\vec{\mathcal{A}}(t)$. Such a norm denotes the absolute value of the amount of the deviation (positive or negative for every component of the vector index) expressed in units of 95% confidence limits of every vector index component. Notice that the definition (3) is possible and meaningful just as every $\mathcal{A}_j(t)$ is a dimensionless number: otherwise, the choice of different units, say, for temperature and precipitation, would make the final result completely arbitrary and meaningless. We define such a property of such vector index components by stating that they are "homogeneous" among themselves with respect to a change of units.

4. Conclusion

Four results are given in this paper. Two are concerned with improvements of the operator CETRA in order to reduce some caveats related to the noise in its output. One such improvement is related to the border effect for the periodicities close to zero. The second such improvement is concerned with an unwanted calculational bias which produces a stepwise decrease (close to ~3/20 of the total time lag spanned by the historical data series being analyzed). This effect could sometimes play an important role, mostly in relation to its iterative (although damped) repetition, which could even simulate a false apparent periodicity. The third result is concerned with the best possible procedure to recognize period families, forefathers, and family relations. The conclusion (almost an obvious one) is that a combined application of direct visual inspection and computer aided selection is recommended, as it appears impossible or very cumbersome to substitute the potentialities of direct visual analysis by a computer program which can also take into account the value on the ordinate scale of the output of CETRA. The fourth result gives a way of defining in an objective way an index of "anomaly" or of "activity" $\vec{A}(t)$ for every one-variate data series, or one such vector index $\vec{A}(t)$ for a multi-variate data series. This is likely to be potentially very effective for defining in a quantitative and objective way the deviation of climate in a given area from its standard statistical behaviour by expressing such a deviation in units of 95% confidence limits for every vector component of $A(t)$. Such an index appears also very well suited for carrying out the pre-scanning of any given one-variate or multi-variate historical data series, i.e. for recognizing actual situations in which the physical system behaves in a completely different way (e.g. a geomagnetician recognizes quiet and storm time conditions, a zoologist distinguishes between reptiles and insects, etc. before applying his statistics etc.). The rejection criterion for selecting outliers appears to be a crucial aspect in such a derivation, and needs to be further developed before attaining the optimum final methodology for geophysical and environmentological applications (HAWKINS, 1980).

Acknowledgements

This research has been accomplished in partial fulfilment of a research grant from a CEE program on climatic research and from the Italian CNR (Strategic Project on Climate and Environment in Southern Italy). The research has been carried out within an ESF program on the history of climate in Europe. The authors gratefully acknowledge Silvia Pau for careful data handling and Enrico Lo Cascio for the preparation of the figures. Special thanks go to Prof. Dr. C. Schönwiese, Frankfurt, for translating the English summary.

References

ALESSANDRINI, B.; PAPI, G. M.; DE FRANCESCHI, G. & GREGORI, G. P. (1987): The secular variation of the geomagnetic field and the shape of the Earth. Phys. Earth Planet. Inter. 48, 84-114

BANZON, V.; COLACINO, M.; DE FRANCESCHI, G.; DIODATO, L.; GREGORI, G. P.; PAVESE, M. P. & SANTOLERI, R. (1990): Tiber floods, anomalous climatic events in the upper Po valley, and volcanic activity. In: Schröder, W. (ed.): Advances in Geosciences. Interdiv. Comm. on History of I.A.G.A., Bremen-Roennebeck, 73-79

BANZON, V.; COLACINO, M.; DE FRANCESCHI, G.; DIODATO, L.; GREGORI, G. P.; PAVESE, M. P.; & SANTOLERI, R. (1990a): A study on the Tiber floods, on the anomalous climatic events in the Tanaro valley (upper Po valley) and on their relations with volcanic activity (preprint).

COLACINO, M.; GREGORI, G. P.; VALENSISE, M. R.; CHIARINI, F. & MASTROGREGORI, M. (1988): Climate as a historiographical problem. In: Schröder, W. (ed.): Past, present and future trends in geophysical research. Interdiv. Comm. on History of I.A.G.A., Bremen-Roennebeck, 212-249

FIORENTINO, E.; GREGORI, G. P.; DE FRANCESCHI, G.; ALESSANDRINI, B.; COLACINO, M.; GUERRINI, A.; MELONI, A.; PURINI, R.; SANTOLERI, R.; SILVESTRI, M. & VALENTI, C. (1988): Multi-variate analysis of historical data series. In: Schröder, W. (ed.): Past, present and future trends in geophysical research. Interdiv. Comm. of I.A.G.A., Bremen-Roennebeck, 251-318

GREGORI, G. P. & PAVESE, M. P. (1985): Climatologia storica. Boll. Geofis. 9/1, 63-74

GREGORI, G. P.; SANTOLERI, R.; PAVESE, M. P.; COLACINO, M.; FIORENTINO, E. & DE FRANCESCHI, G. (1988): The analysis of point-like data series. In: Schröder, W. (ed.): Past, present and future trends in geophysical research. Interdiv. Comm. of I.A.G.A., Bremen-Roennebeck, 146-211

GREGORI, G. P. (1990): A few mathematical procedures for the analysis of incomplete historical data series. In: Schröder, W. (ed.): Advances in geosciences. Interdiv. Comm. on History of I.A.G.A., Bremen-Roennebeck, 80-127

GREGORI, G. P. (1990a): Multidimensional statistical analysis of incomplete point-like historical data series. Proc. First HEFEST Workshop, Erice, Feb 27 - March 3, 1989, ed. by S. Martellucci & G. P. Gregori, 65 p.

HAWKINS, D. M. (1980): Identification of outliers. Chapman and Hall, London and New York, 188 p.

KOYRÉ, A. (1967): Dal mondo del pressapoco all' universo della precisione. Nuovo Politecnico, 134 p.

KRAGH, H. (1987): An introduction to the historiography of science. Cambridge Univ. Press, Cambridge, Italian translation publ. 1990 by Zanichelli, Bologna, 256 p.

NEUMANN, E. (1949): Ursprungsgeschichte des Bewußtseins. Rascher Verlag, Zürich, Italian translation, Astrolabio, 1978, 416 p.

PAVESE, M. P. & GREGORI, G. P. (1984): An analysis of six centuries (XII through XVII A.D.) of climatic records from the upper Po valley. In: Schröder, W. (ed.): Historical events and people in geosciences. Selected papers from the symposia of the Interdiv. Comm. on History of I.A.G.A., during the IUGG General Assembly, held in Hamburg 1983, Verlag Peter Lang, Bern, 185-220

PAVESE, M. P.; BANZON, V.; COLACINO, M.; GREGORI, G. P. & PASQUA, M. (1992): Three historical data series on floods and anomalous climatic events in Italy. In: Bradley, R. S. & Jones, P. D. (eds.): Climate since A.D. 1500. Routledge, London, 155-170

Addresses of the authors:

Dr. V. Banzon, I.F.A. (Ist. di Fisica dell'Atmosfera), C.N.R., p. le L. Sturzo 31, I-00144 Roma, Italy
Dr. G. de Franceschi, I.N.G. (Ist. Nazionale di Geofisica) via di Villa Ricotti 42, I-00161 Roma, Italy
Prof. Dr. G. P. Gregori, I.F.A. (Ist. di Fisica dell'Atmosfera), C.N.R., p. le L. Sturzo 31, I-00144 Roma, Italy

Long-term fluctuation of hydroclimate elements in Poland

Małgorzata Gutry-Korycka & Jerzy Boryczka

Summary

Periodical fluctuations of the elements controlling the water balance of a given river basin (i.e. precipitation, run-off, and air temperature - elements affecting evaporation, storage capacity and lake level changes) were investigated with the help of BORYCKA's statistical model which has been developed on the basis of the FOURIER series analysis. It was assumed that the duration of long-term fluctuations of every element was average from year to year. On the basis of selected empirical series the optimal periods (T_j), the amplitude of their change (b_j) and the phase shifts (c_j) were calculated. For our investigation BORYCZKA's statistical model, which is able to detect and to statistically verify the optimum periods T_j of multi-periodical variations, has been used. The optimum periods (T_j) are specified as the local minima of the residual variance ε^2, the maximum values of the multiple correlation coefficient (R) and the minimum of the standard deviation (S); the results were verified by the FISHER-SNEDECOR statistical test F. The extrapolation of time trend function values of empirical series can be used for reconstructions ($t<0$) or forecasts ($t>0$). Statistical measures of changes due to human activity have been found, being the linear components of the time trend equation. The changes are separated from the natural secular changes. On analysis the empirical series proved a distinguishable relationship to solar activity. The trend of human activity is either increasing or decreasing, depending on local conditions.

Zusammenfassung

Die den Wasserhaushalt einer gegebenen Region bestimmenden Größen (z.B. Niederschlag, Abfluß, Temperatur und, hiervon abgeleitet, Evaporation, Speicherkapazität und Seespiegelstände) sind periodischen Schwankungen unterworfen, die mit Hilfe eines von BORYCZKA entwickelten statistischen Modells analysiert wurden. Hierbei wurde angenommen, daß die langfristigen Schwankungen gleichmäßig über die Jahre verteilt waren. Auf der Basis ausgewählter empirischer Datenreihen konnten die Optimumperioden (T_j), die Amplitude ihrer Schwankungen (b_j) und die Phasenverschiebungen (c_j) kalkuliert werden. Das Modell von BORYCZKA, das für diese Berechnungen verwendet wurden, basiert auf der von FOURIER entwickelten Reihenanalyse und ist in der Lage, die Perioden größter Schwankungen der einzelnen Steuerungsgrößen (T_j) zu erkennen und statistisch zu verifizieren. Die Optimumperioden (T_j) wurden spezifiziert als die lokalen Minimalwerte

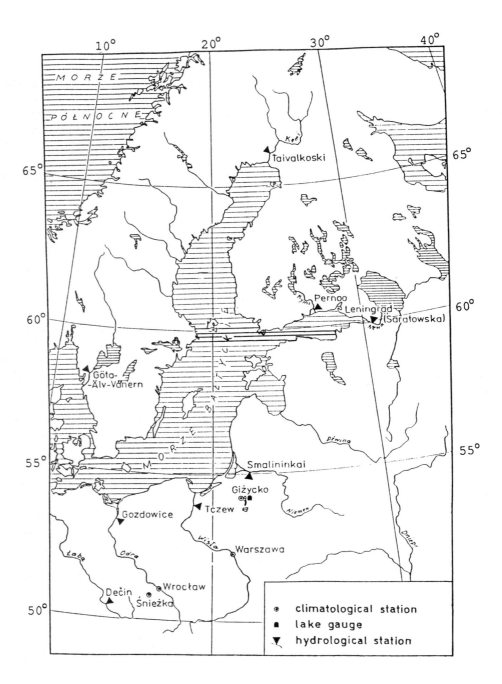

Fig. 1   Map of selected stations and gauges used in scientific investigations

der Summe der quadratischen Abweichungen ε^2, als Maximalwerte des multiplen Korrela-tionskoeffizierten (R) und als Minimalwerte der Standardabweichung (S). Die Ergebnisse wurden mit Hilfe des FISHER-SNEDECOR Tests F überprüft. Die Extrapolation zeitab-hängiger Funktionswerte aus den empirischen Datenreihen erlaubt sowohl Rekonstruktio-nen (t<0) als auch Voraussagen (t>0). Der anthropogene Einfluß auf die Schwankungs-breite der einzelnen hydroklimatischen Elemente findet seinen statistischen Ausdruck als lineare Komponente der zeitabhängigen Gleichung. Die anthropogenen Schwankungen werden deutlich von den natürlichen unterschieden. Die untersuchten, empirischen Daten-reihen zeigen einen erkennbaren Zusammenhang mit der Sonnenaktivität. Die Tendenz des menschlichen Einflusses ist in Abhängigkeit von den lokalen Verhältnissen entweder zu- oder abnehmend.

1. Introduction

Elements of the hydrological cycle, such as precipitation, evaporation, run-off and storage capacity are subject to natural periodical changes in the course of time. These can be daily, seasonal, annual or long-term fluctuations due to the rotation of the Earth, the circulation of the Earth around the Sun, and also due to century-long changes in the Sun's activity (HERMAN & GOLDBERG, 1978). Moreover, they are also liable to anthropogenic influence, i.e. a man-made increase in atmospheric dust leading to increasing rates of absorbed radia-tion, or to increasing amounts of condensation nuclei and CO_2 (Greenhouse effect) in the atmosphere. In addition, other kinds of human impact such as river regulation, land reclamation, urbanization etc. should also be taken into account.

The aim of such an attempt is to assess periodical changes in the hydroclimatic elements and to explain their causes. The anthropogenic components were also taken into considera-tion and predictions until the year 2040 have been made.

Instrumental measurements of hydrological elements in Poland and selected areas in Northeastern Europe have been analysed and were seen to reflect the climatic change from the seventeenth to the twentieth century (cp. Fig. 1, 2). The following records of in-strumental data, varying considerably in length, have been examined: data on sun activity in Zurich (1700-1978), lake level data of the Great Masurian Lakes (1846-1986), data on precipitation measured in Warsaw, Wrocław (1859-1979), Giżycko (1838-1986), and Śnieżka (Snow Hill, 1885-1979); temperature data from Warsaw (1779-1980) and Wrocław (1851-1979), and river discharge rates from selected Northeast European rivers, i.e. Elba (Łaba)-Dečin (-A=51,104 km²) (1856-1969), Niemen-Smalininkai (-A=81,200 km²) (1812-1979), Vistula-Tczew (-A=193,866 km²) (1901-1980), Oder-Gozdwice (-A=109,364 km²) (1901-1980), Neva-Saratovskaja-Leningrad (-A=281,000 km²) (1858-1984), Göta Älv-Vänersborg (-A=46,830 km²) (1807-1979), Kymijoki-Pernoo (-A=36,500 km²) (1900-1979), and Kemijoki-Taivalkoski (-A=50,877 km²) (1911-1979; cp. Fig. 1).

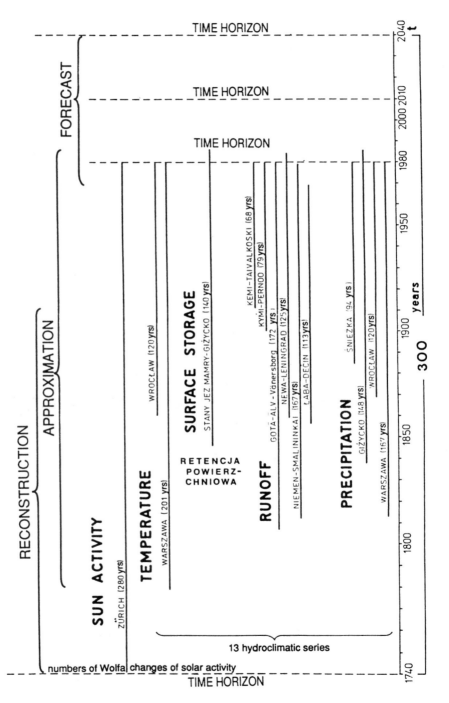

Fig. 2   Hydroclimatic time series used in scientific investigations

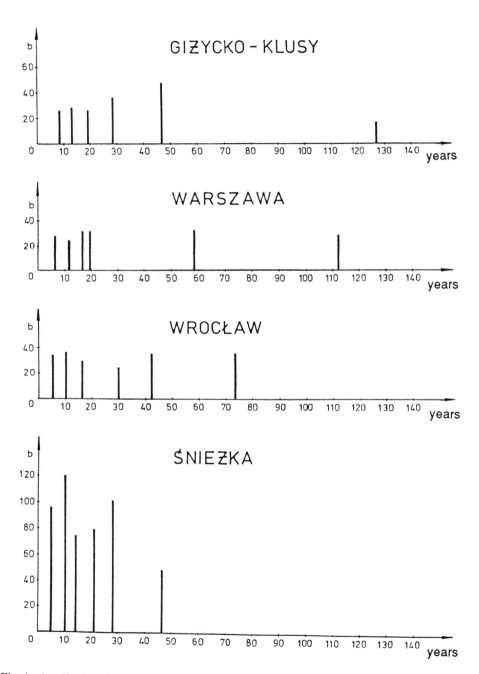

Fig. 4   Amplitudes of periodical precipitation changes at selected gauges in Poland

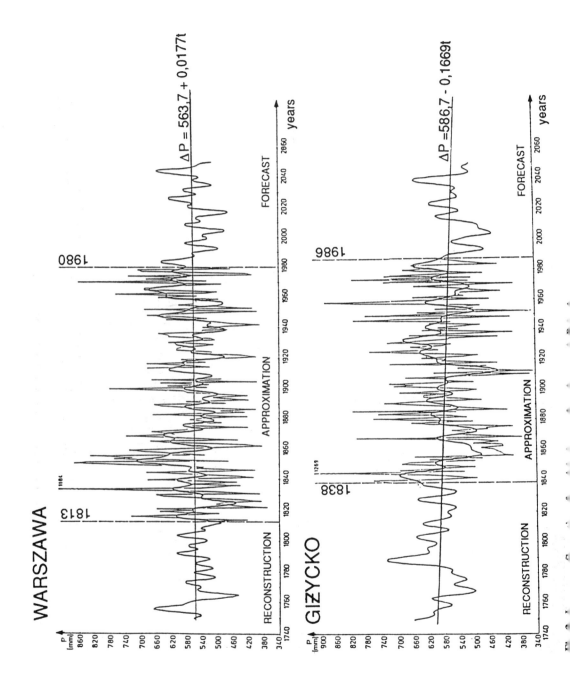

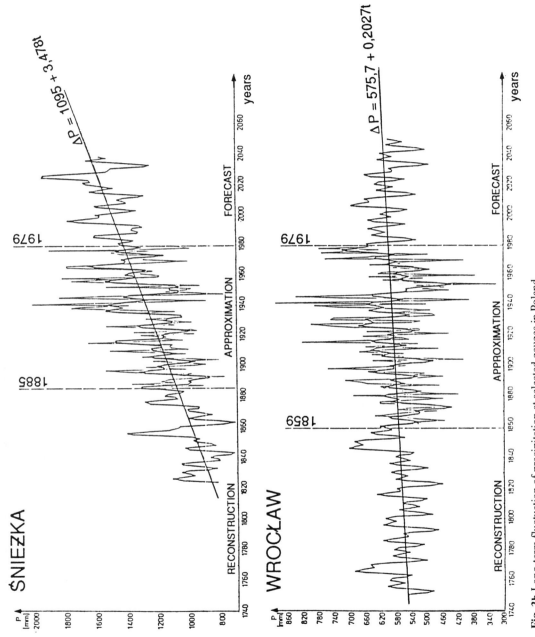

Fig. 3b Long-term fluctuation of precipitation at selected gauges in Poland

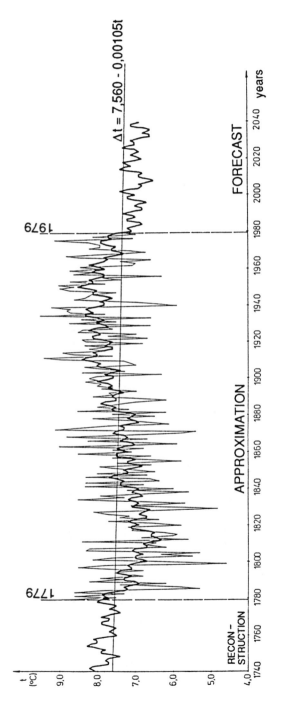

Fig. 5 Long-term fluctuations of air temperature in Warsaw (1779-1979)

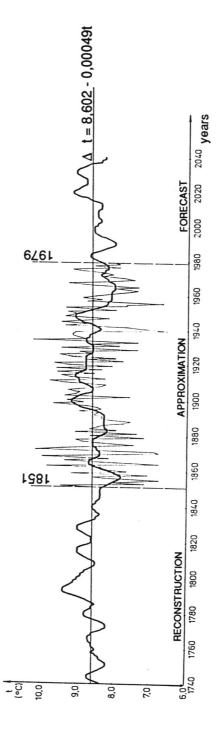

Fig. 6 Long-term fluctuations of air temperature in Wrocław (1851-1979)

2. Theoretical approach

The periodicity of the hydroclimatic elements Y has been examined using Boryczka's model (1984) which helps to disclose the optimum (real) periods. These optimum periods T in the secular changes are found by eliminating regression sine curves from among T = 1,2,3 to n (n=number of data, b=amplitudes, c=phase shifts).

$$Y = a_0 + b * \sin \left(\frac{2\pi}{T} * t + c \right) \qquad (1)$$

The optimum periods T_j which are to be calculated include local residual variance minima ε^2 and correspond to the multiple correlation factor maximum R where s is the standard deviation of the variable y (Boryczka, 1989).

$$R = \left(1 - \frac{\varepsilon^2}{s^2} \right)^{1/2}$$

The optimum period detection model is verified with the Fisher-Snedecor test F with 2 and n - 3 degrees of freedom (Zieliński, 1972).

$$F = \frac{n-3}{2}, \frac{R^2}{1-R^2}$$

Boryczka's optimum period model can be used to determine the regression sine curve segment with its period longer than T > n (instrumental data sequence). It can also be used in the case of uncomplete records (no observation data available for some of the years).

While knowing the optimum T_j period, we can try to calculate the time-related trend of any hydroclimate element with the help of equation (2) by minimizing the residual variance ε^2 since the T_j periods are incommensurable.

$$Y = f(t) = a_0 + \sum_{j=1}^{k} b_j * \sin \left(\frac{2\pi}{T_j} * t + c_j \right) \qquad (2)$$

$$\varepsilon^2 = \frac{1}{n} * \sum_{i=1}^{n} \left[Y_i - f(t_i) \right]^2$$

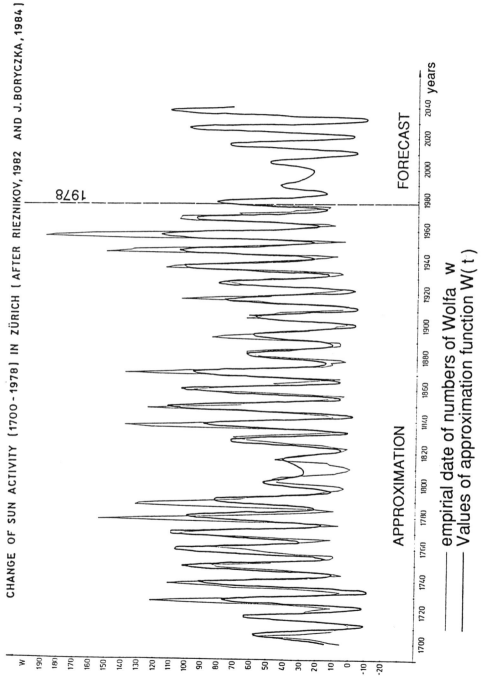

CHANGE OF SUN ACTIVITY (1700-1978) IN ZÜRICH (AFTER RIEZNIKOV, 1982 AND J.BORYCZKA, 1984)

——— empirial date of numbers of Wolfa w
——— Values of approximation function W(t)

APPROXIMATION   FORECAST

Fig. 7 Long-term fluctuations of solar activity in Zurich (1700-1978)

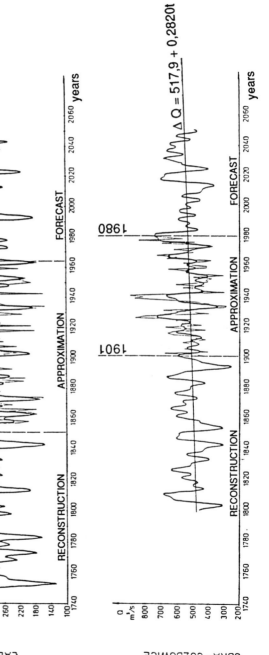

Fig. 9a Long-term run-off fluctuations of selected rivers in Northeastern Europe

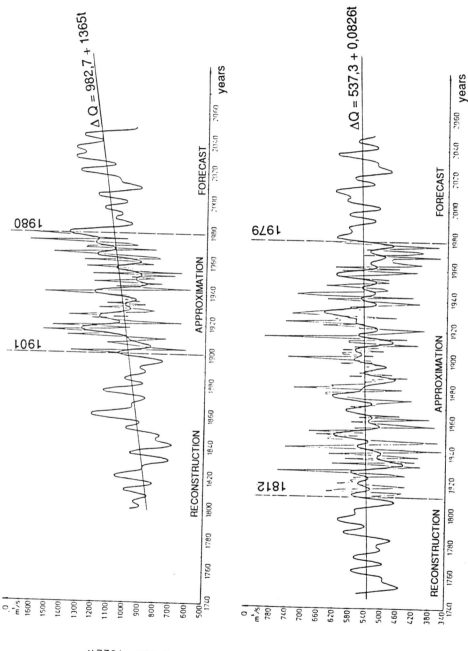

Fig. 9b Long-term run-off fluctuations of selected rivers in Northeastern Europe

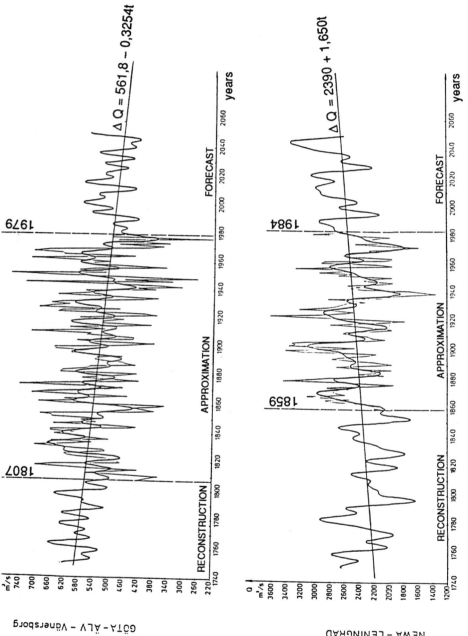

Fig. 9c Long-term run-off fluctuations of selected rivers in Northeastern Europe

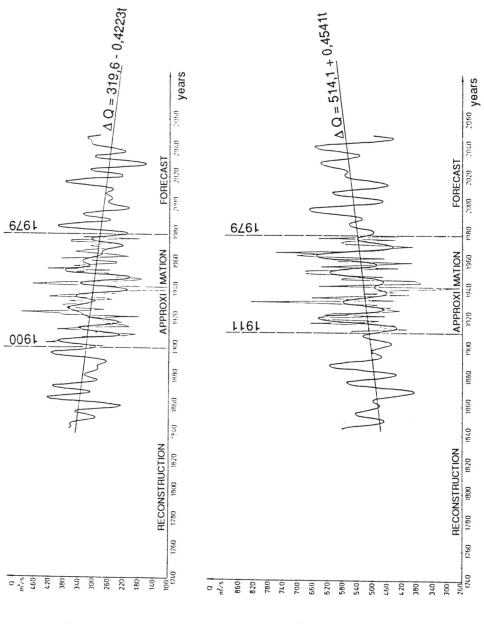

Fig. 9d Long-term run-off fluctuations of selected rivers in Northeastern Europe

By extrapolating the time-related trend function f(t) of the analyzed variables one can complete their reconstruction (t<0) or obtain forecasts (t>0) with any time advance desired.

Up till now, the time-related trend f (t) of hydroclimate elements in Poland was expressed with the FOURIER series in which fictional periods, functionally dependent on the length of a chronological sequence of precipitation (KACZOROWSKA, 1962; EWERT, 1984) or discharge (MITOSEK, 1970, 1984; KRASNODĘBSKI & GADKOWSKI, 1978), are introduced.

If we try to add a linear component $\Delta y = at$ to the periodic (natural) changes $\Delta y = f(t)$ resulting from the imposition of real cycles, the time-related model F (t) will be divided into two components:

$$Y = F(t) = a_0 + at + \underbrace{\sum_{j=1}^{k} b_j * \sin\left(\frac{2\pi}{T_j} * t + c_j\right)} \tag{3}$$

$$\underbrace{}$$

Anthro-   Natural changes resulting
pogenic   from actual (optimum)
changes   changes T_j

Linear components with a lasting tendency of $\Delta y/\Delta t = a = $ const. may indicate the effect of the successively progressing changes of anthropogenic nature. If the partial regression factor a is >0, the anthropogenic changes will show a rising tendency; and if a<0, a falling tendency.

3. Precipitation

The annual sums of precipitation at selected gauges are liable to periodical changes (Fig. 3, 4). These are short half-period 5-8 year cycles, solar 10-14 year cycles, double 16-21 year cycles, triple 26-34 year cycles, quadruple 42-58 year and longer (secular) cycles: Warsaw (112 years), Wrocław (73 years), and Giżycko (120 years).

For the time-related trend curves of annual precipitation sums with the linear anthropogenic components also being taken into consideration compare Fig. 3.

The *a* regression factor values are as follows: Warsaw: 1,8 mm per 100 years; Wrocław: 20,3 mm per 100 years; Giżycko: 16,7 mm per 100 years; Śnieżka: 3,5 mm per year. The rising tendency as regards annual precipitation sums for Warsaw and Wrocław may result from an increase in the content of dust (Condensation nuclei) in the urban atmosphere. The markedly rising tendency for precipitaion at Śnieżka is most probably an outcome of the straight-line approximation over the sine curve section with a long unknown period - a period which could not be determined because of a short measurement interval only. We also do not know what is likely to be the cause for a lasting drop in local precipitation at Giżycko.

4. Air temperature as an index of evaporation

Air temperature has a great effect on evaporation, which forms one of the hydrological components. Evaporation depends on periodical short-term and long-term fluctuations (Fig. 5, 6), which are synchronous with the short (11 and 12 year) and long (94 and 180 year) sun activity cycles (cp. BORYCZKA, 1984; BORYCZKA & STOPA-BORYCZKA, 1986). Two main air temperature cycles have been reconstructed in Warsaw (89-year and 217-year cycles with 0,5°C and 1,4°C amplitudes) which have been influencing Poland's climate for more than two centuries. The absolute air temperature minimum in Warsaw occurred during the years coinciding with the least sun activity (1810-1811); the maximum was observed to correspond with the dates of the absolute sun-spot maxima (1957; Fig. 7, 8).

The anthropogenic linear[1] components indicate a consistently diminishing air temperature tendency in Warsaw (0,1°C per 100 years) and in Wrocław (1,5°C per 1000 years). These very small anthropogenic influences on the mean annual temperature (practically unimportant from a statistical point of view) in all probability result from the fact that in winter we have a dominating greenhouse effect (due to higher CO_2 contents in the atmosphere), whereas in summer a greater part of the incoming radiation is absorbed by dust particles deriving from secondary emission effects.

5. River run-off

An attempt was made to single out periods and tendencies of run-off fluctuations in Polish rivers in comparison with eight selected rivers in Northeastern Europe, and provide explanations for their cause.

Run-off of all the rivers under investigation was found to depend on periodical high-amplitude fluctuation between more or less 95 or 90% levels (Fig. 9, 10). The largest amplitude cycles of such Polish rivers as the Vistula (13, 20, and 55 years) and Oder (10, 19, and 54 years) resemble sun activity cycles with 11, 21-22, and 56 sun activity years. The long river run-off cycles have attracted the attention of KRASNODĘBSI & GADKOWSKI (1978) as well as of STACHÝ (1970).

The run-off data of eight main rivers point to rather short cycles, lasting for 5-8 and 10-15 years respectively, vaguely approaching the 11-year sun activity cycle. A somewhat longer

---

[1] assumed simple linear model of change

cycle, 17 to 22 years, is noticeable in the run-off of six rivers, i.e. the Elba, Oder, Vistula, Niemen, Neva, and Göta. The triple BRÜCKNER cycle of 27-22 years occurs in the case of seven rivers, except the Oder. The longest cycles disclosed so far are: Neva (132 years), Elba (101 years), Göta (87 years), and Niemen (67 years). Most of the rivers with long run-off cycles, i.e. the Elba (101 years), the Göta (87 years) and, quoted from the literature (cp. STACHÝ, 1970), the Veltava (86 years), Niemen (82 years), Elba (85 years), and Dniepr (88 years), are more or less in line with the 94-year century-long sun activity cycle (Fig. 10).

Of some interest are the time-dependent river flow tendencies resulting from the linear component $a_0 + at$ imposed upon the natural (periodical) cycles in which one can easily trace the anthropogenic influence (Fig. 9).

Anthropogenically induced increments in river run-off (a) expressed as $m^3/s/100$ years are given in the following:

river	Elba	Oder	Vistula	Niemen	Neva	Göta	Kymijoki	Kemijoki
$m^3/s/100$ yrs	12,8	28,2	13,6	8,3	165,0	32,0	-42,2	45,4

The run-off data of six rivers exhibit a rising tendency (>0), those of the two Scandinavian ones a decreasing tendency (a<0). The Scandinavian rivers of Kymi and Göta with their negative flow tendencies are characterized by a high retention level which results from the number of lakes within their basin area, exceeding 15% (VATTENFÖRING, 1979; UNESCO, 1987).

The relative 100-year anthropogenic influence increments $\dfrac{\Delta Q}{\overline{Q}}$ and $\dfrac{\Delta Q}{\overline{Q}^*}$ when compared with the mean century-long discharge and with the scope of natural changes $\Delta Q^* = \sum\limits_{i=1}^{k} Q_j$ are given in the following:

river	Elba	Oder	Vistula	Niemen	Neva	Göta	Kymijoki	Kemijoki
$\dfrac{\Delta Q}{\overline{Q}}$ (%)	4,3	5,3	1,3	1,5	6,6	-6,1	-14,1	8,5
$\dfrac{\Delta Q}{\overline{Q}^*}$ (%)	6,6	9,8	3,8	5,1	17,2	-19,8	-32,4	33,2

The highest increments due to anthropogenic influence are found to be those of the rivers Kymi and Kemi. They constitute 14,1% and 8,5% of the average run-off these rivers have - rather high percentages amounting to 1/3 of their natural (periodical) variation.

The even higher rising tendency of the Vistula run-off might be the consequence of additional inflow, i.e. due to mining activities (pit waters), or of other anthropogenic influences.

6. Storage capacity

The storage capacity of lakes has been characterized with reference to the water level sequence of the Great Masurian Lakes (Giżycko). Water storage undergoes fluctuations resembling the cycles of precipitation, temperature, and run-off of the Polish and other North-East European rivers (Fig. 11, 12). The cycles mentioned (13, 18, 28 years) resemble the cycles of single and double sun activities. The 26, 34, and 47-year cycles show the highest amplitude. They proved to be essential on the 99% confidence level according to the FISHER-SNEDECOR test. Moreover, there is also a 34-year and a longer 73-year BRÜCKNER's cycle resembling the Wrocław precipitation cycle. In this chronological series, the most clearly "recorded" natural and anthropogenic changes are changes in water storage.

Decreasing water levels due to anthropogenic factors amount to -24 cm per 100 years. This represents $\Delta H / \bar{H}$ nearly 20% of an average water level ($\bar{H} = 120$ cm) for the Great Masurian lakes in the 1846-1986 time interval. This lake may dry up completely in 500 years (recording from 1846 on), if the linear component $\Delta H = a*t$ fails to approximate the sine curve segment of an unknown longer interval cycle.

The progressive lowering of the water levels of the Great Masurian Lakes has been attracting MIKULSKI's attention (1966) ever since. In MIKULSKI's opinion, the adverse storage trend of the lakes is an outcome of the natural changes in water circulation and of artificial water level regulation.

7. Conclusions

To sum up, we can conclude that such hydroclimate variables as precipitation, air temperature, river run-off, and surface storage, are liable to periodical high-amplitude (statistically significant) changes. Both the single 10-13 year, double and triple BRÜCKNER cycles as well as some longer ones are found to be synchronous with the solar activity cycles. Thus, solar activity seems to have some influence on natural changes of the hydroclimate elements.

Long secular cycles can most easily be distinguished in air temperature and certain river run-off processes.

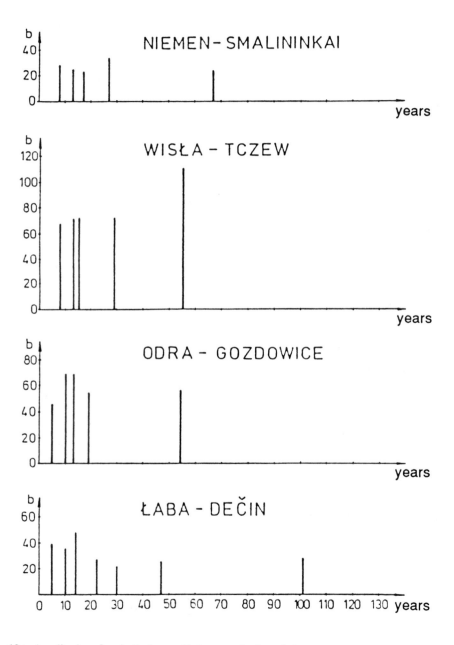

Fig. 10a Amplitudes of periodical run-off changes of selected rivers

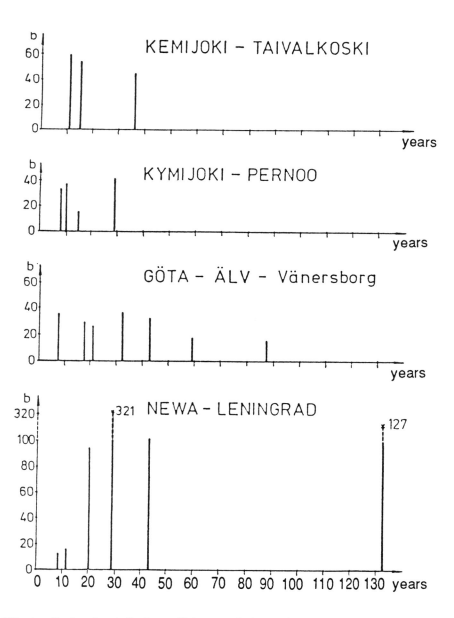

Fig. 10b Amplitudes of periodical run-off changes of selected rivers

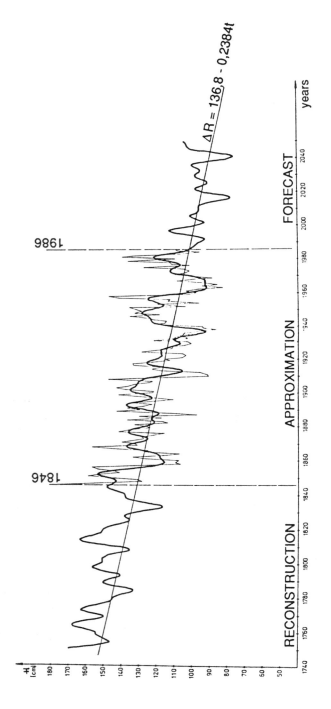

Fig. 11 Long-term fluctuations of storage capacity of the Great Masurian Lakes (1846-1986)

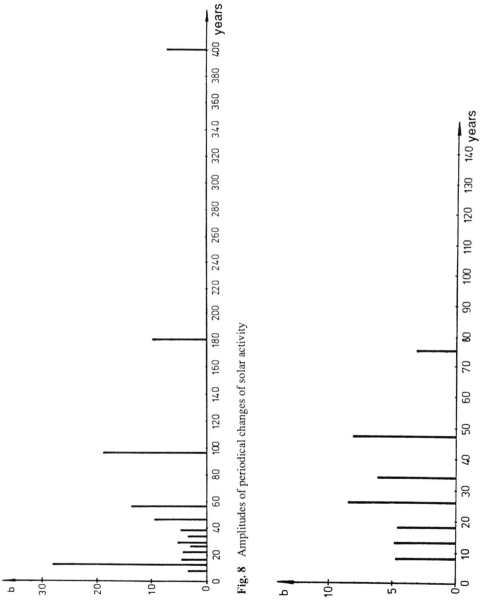

Fig. 8 Amplitudes of periodical changes of solar activity

Fig. 12 Amplitudes of periodical changes of storage capacity of the Great Masurian Lakes

Sums of annual precipitation and annual mean temperature undergo a process of cyclic changes, the anthropogenic components of their trends being nevertheless quite negligible (statistically unimportant). Most probably this results from an adverse effect the anthropogenic factors tend to exert in winter (CO_2 domination) and in summer (domination of radiation absorbed by dust).

The accelerated discharge rates, increasing over centuries due to human activity, are statistically significant because they may amount to more than 12% of the long-term average discharge.

River discharge and storage capacity are factors strongly influenced by human impact. Run-off from a highly inertial basin shows a decreasing trend most probably due to land reclamation or hydro-engineering development projects etc.

For further investigations of the problem it is recommended to make use not only of annual but also of monthly empirical sequences.

References

BORYCZKA, J. (1984): Model deterministyczno-stochastyczny wielookresowych zmian klimatu. Rozpr. U.W., Wyd. U.W.

BORYCZKA, J. & STOPA-BORYCZKA, M. (1986): Matematyczny model klimatu Polski. Mat. I Sesji INFG UW, Wyd. U

EWERT, A. (1984): Opady atmosferyczne na obszarze Polski w przekroju rocznym. Wyd. W.S.P., Slupsk

HERMAN, J. R. & GOLDBERG, R. A. (1978): Sun weather and climate. N.A.S.A., Washington

KACZOROWSKA, Z. (1962): Opady atmosferyczne w przekroju wieloletnim. Prace Geogr. Inst. P.A.N. 33, Warszawa

KRASNODĘBSKI, R. & GADKOWSKI, M. (1978): Statystyczna analiza cykliczności zmian średnich rocznych przepływów w dziewięciu przekrojach Wisły. Prz. Geof., t. 23/31, Nr. 1

MIKULSKI, Z. (1966): Bilans wodny Wielkich Jezior Mazurskich. Mat. P.I.H.M., Warszawa

MITOSEK, H. (1970): Przebieg standaryzowanej funkcji autokorelacyjnej i funkcji gęstości widmowej średnich przepływów rocznych w terminach początku roku w wybranych profilach hydrometrycznych. Prz. Geof., t. 15/23, Nr. 2

MITOSEK, H. T. (1984): Stochastyczna struktura przepływu rzecznego. Monogr. K.G.W. P.A.N., Wyd. Geol., Warszawa

STACHÝ, J. (1970): Wielotnia zmienność odpływu rzek polskich. Mat. P.I.H.M., Warszawa

UNESCO (1969-1985): Discharge of selected rivers of the world. Vol. I, II, III, part 1-4, Paris

VATTENFÖRING i Sverige (Streamflow records of Sweden) 1979. The Swedish Meteorological and Hydrological Institute, Stockholm

ZIELIŃSKI, R. (1972): Tablice statystyczne. P.W.N., Warszawa

Addresses of the authors

Dr. M. Gutry-Korycka, Department of Hydrology, Faculty of Geography and Regional Studies, Warsaw University, ul. Krakowskie Przedmieście 30, PL-00-927 Warsaw, Poland
Dr. J. Boryczka, Department of Climatology, Faculty of Geography and Regional Studies, Warsaw University, ul. Krakowskie Przedmieście 30, PL-00-927 Warsaw, Poland

Spatial variability of climatic change in Europe 1780-1960

Christian Pfister & Andreas Lauterburg

Summary

In order to define areas of similar year-to-year fluctuations of temperature and precipitation in Europe, correlation matrices of long temperature and precipitation series from 27 stations were submitted to cluster analysis (WARD's method) for two subperiods 1841-1900 and 1901-1960. For temperatures the similo-fluctuative areas or clusters emerging from the procedure turned out to be relatively stable over the two subperiods (except autumn), even when the test was extended to the period of early instrumental measurements prior to 1840. For precipitation the number of clusters was greater and the correlations were weaker. This procedure is particularly useful, if climate is to be reconstructed for periods of low data density, such as the Middle Ages. However, trends and extremes do not coincide within similo-fluctuative areas and have to be assessed separately.

Zusammenfassung

Zur Gliederung Europas in Räume ähnlicher interannueller Klimafluktuation wurden lange Temperatur- und Niederschlagsreihen von 27 Klimastationen in Form von Korrelationsmatritzen für die beiden Subperioden 1841-1900 und 1901-1960 nach der Methode der WARD'schen Clusteranalyse untersucht. Bei den Temperaturen erwiesen sich die Räume ähnlicher jahreszeitlicher Temperaturschwankungen für die beiden Subperioden und die Zeit vor 1840 als relativ stabil (die Herbste ausgenommen). Bei den Niederschlägen war die Zahl der Cluster grösser, und die Korrelationen waren schwächer. Die Definition von Räumen ähnlicher interannueller Klimafluktuation ist eine unabdingbare Voraussetzung, um in Perioden geringerer Materialdichte Klimarekonstruktionen anhand von Daten aus historischen Quellen vorzunehmen. Die Elemente "Trend" und "Extremwerte" sind neben den Fluktuationen gesondert zu analysieren.

1. From time series analysis to spatial analysis over time

Most reconstructions of climate from natural or man-made archives tend to produce results which have the form of time series. They show variations of climatic parameters for one particular region that may have the dimension of a German Bundesland, or an Italian Province, or a small state such as Switzerland. New methods tend to improve the time resolution of the findings down to seasons and months. The statistical tools and the software for sophisticated kinds of time series analysis is improved and refined. To sum up - time is the dominant, in most cases the only, dimension in our analyses of climatic change.

Our image of weather, on the other hand, has changed dramatically over the last decades. Films from weather satellites have become an ingredient of daily TV news. Weather is increasingly perceived as a two dimensional or three dimensional process. We have become familiar with the move and the rotation of cyclones and the typical form of clouds which are associated to certain air masses. We are beginning to get a feeling for the spatial dimension of climatic anomalies and for the behaviour of the weather machine as a system.

In order to understand the nature of the climate system, we must acquire detailed knowledge on how it has fluctuated or changed over the last centuries. The image of climatic change in one particular region is therefore just a first step to reconstruct climate history on a continental dimension. To put it clearly: the pieces of information we get from time series analyses at a regional level, are in fact parts of a large coherent puzzle. They cannot be properly interpreted, unless they are merged with results obtained from other, more distant regions to provide a picture of climatic patterns in space and over time. Series of historical weather maps for the main trends and the most outstanding anomalies, that are obtained from such a procedure, may be useful for calibrating climatic models and for investigating climatic anomalies. In any case, this kind of a spatial approach is needed for exploring climatic patterns in the Late Middle Ages, where data densities are too low for setting up time series within regions of a certain climatic homogeneity.

Whether this goal of a weather history on a European scale might ever be attained, depends on the future international cooperation between scholars in historical climatology on the one hand, and from working out an appropriate methodology for merging evidence from various parts of Europe on the other.

Our paper summarizes the main results of the thesis by LAUTERBURG (1990), as far as they are related to the reconstruction of the climate of Europe from documentary data. The main goal of this thesis was to set up evident statistical procedures for defining regions of similar year-to-year fluctuations of measured temperature and precipitation in Europe and to test their consistency over time. The data were mainly drawn from the Data Bank of the U.S. Department of Energy, which includes some 1200 long precipitation series and some 800 long temperature series from around the globe (DOE, 1985). In a first step similarities were explored for the period 1901-1960 and then compared to those for the preceding sixty year period 1841-1900, both for temperature and precipitation. In a final step the six decades from 1780 to 1841 and the period from 1700 to 1779 were included, for which data density is considerably lower.

2. Cluster analysis

In the following some basic characteristics of the approach will be explained, in order to contribute to the understanding of the similo-fluctuative areas.

Temperature fluctuations for summer, 1841-1900 and 1901-60 (Fig. 1)

Fig. 1 displays fluctuations of summer temperatures within the two subperiods 1841-1900 and 1901-1960 at four so-called key stations - Bergen, Oxford, Geneva and Vienna - which are representative for the areas. If we compare the four curves, we will detect both similarities - such as the cool period from 1900 to 1920 or the warm period around 1950 - as well as contrasts, e.g. between Geneva and Vienna from 1841 to 1878.

How may those curves be compared? The most widely used measure of association is the PEARSON product moment correlation coefficient R (LOETHER & MCTAVISH, 1974).

Lines of iso-correlation, related to A and correlation matrix (Fig. 2)

A correlation matrix shows the relationship between every combination of variables in a hypothetical data set. In our model matrix we have included for the sake of demonstration four hypothetical stations A through D. Taking A as the basis, the relationship to the remaining three stations is expressed through their distance. The iso-correlation lines indicate distances of equal correlation.

Lines of iso-correlation, related to D and correlation matrix (Fig. 3)

Taking D as the basis of the same matrix, a new chart must be drawn which corresponds to a new level of analysis. This holds also for B and C. In order to represent all measures of association contained in the matrix in form of maps, we would therefore need four levels of analysis.

Cluster analysis is a procedure that summarizes mutual relationships between a large set of stations. Four basic steps may be distinguished (SPSS-X User's Guide, 1988: 405):

(1) The similarities or "distances" between the individual cases are computed. In our example the similarity between cases is expressed through the coefficient of correlation;
(2) the nearest cases are merged into a cluster;
(3) the similarities between the existing clusters (or cases) and the new one are recomputed. Then the nearest cases are merged into a new cluster (cp. 2), etc.;
(4) the procedure ends when all cases have been merged into one single large cluster.

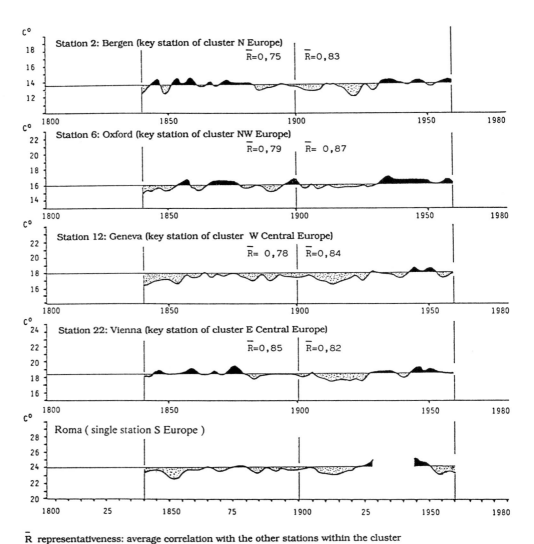

R representativeness: average correlation with the other stations within the cluster
Indicated mean = 1901-1960
Curve: five year weighted moving average (Gauss filter)   Source: Lauterburg 1990

Fig. 1 Temperatures for summer, 1841-1900 and 1901-60. The examples of Bergen, Oxford, Geneva and Vienna. The possible "warm" deviations are expressed in black, the negative "cold" ones are spotted. Source: LAUTERBURG, 1990

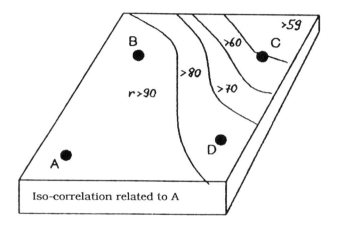

Correlation Matrix

	A	B	C	D
A	1	91	60	84
B	91	1	89	58
C	60	89	1	89
D	84	58	89	1

Fig. 2 Lines of iso-correlation related to A - correlation matrix
Source: Lauterburg, 1990

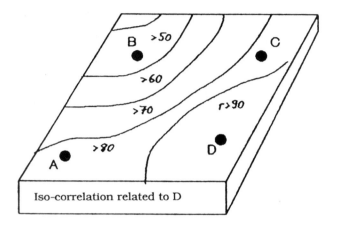

Iso-correlation related to D

Correlation Matrix

	A	B	C	D
A	1	91	60	84
B	91	1	89	58
C	60	89	1	89
D	84	58	89	1

Fig. 3   Lines of iso-correlation related to D - correlation matrix
Source: Lauterburg, 1990

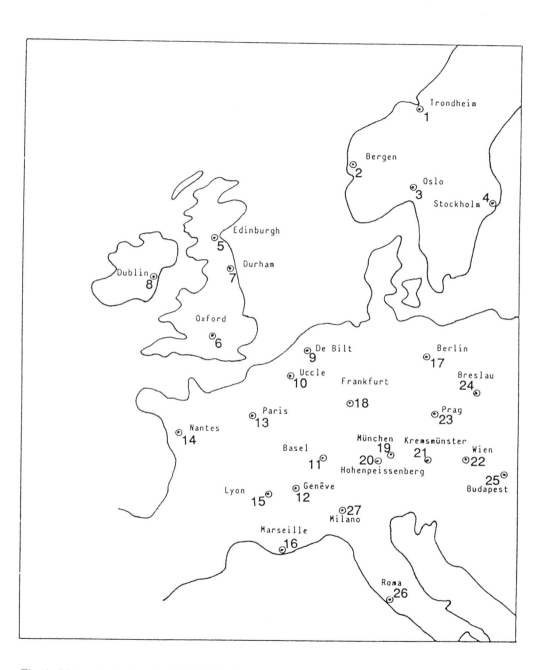

Fig. 4   Meteorological stations included in the analysis of temperature patterns.
Number of stations: 27. Source: LAUTERBURG, 1990

1841 - 1900

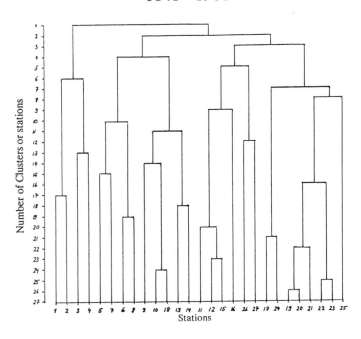

1901 - 1960

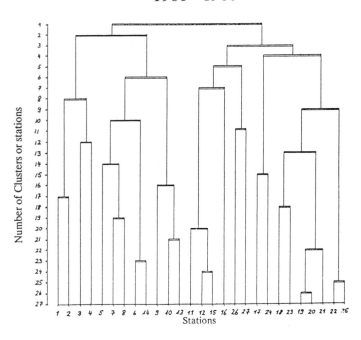

Meteorological stations included in the analysis of temperature patterns (Fig. 4)

Temperature series from 27 meteorological stations in Europe were submitted to cluster analysis (Fig. 4) the criteria for selection being the duration of measurement (the series should go back to 1841 at least), the continuity of measurement (no gaps for consecutive years) and a balanced distribution throughout the continent. (The Iberian Peninsula, Northern Scandinavia, the Mediterranean area and Europe east of the Vistula were excluded from the analysis). A correlation matrix of the 27 stations was provided for input. Because the lowest values are pertinent for the formation of clusters, whereas the coefficient of correlation R is positively related to similarity, it had to be inverted: R = 1 - R.

Hierarchical cluster analysis of summer temperatures in Europe 1841-1900 (Fig. 5)

Clustering was done according to WARD's method (KALKSTEIN et al., 1987). In this procedure the distance of cases or clusters to a clustering centre (or centroid) is computed and squared (procedure and formula in SPSSX User's Guide, 1988: 406 p.). The object, which yields the smallest increase in variance, enters the clustering process first. The greater the number of members in the cluster, the less attractive is it for "outside" members or clusters. The procedure therefore tends to produce many clusters of relatively small size. The output has the form of a dendrogram (Fig.5).

3. Mapping similo-fluctuative areas

Areas of similar year-to-year temperature fluctuations in summer, 1901-1960 (Fig. 6)

In order to understand the maps (Fig. 7-9) some terms must be introduced:

Fig. 5 Hierarchical cluster analysis of summer temperatures in Europe 1841-1900 and 1901-1960. Tree-diagram (dendrogram) for 27 stations. Number of clusters (Y-axis). Station numbers according to the survey of stations (Fig. 4). Stations 19 and 20 (München and Hohenpeissenberg) are merged in the first step; stations 22 and 23 (Wien and Praha) in the next, then stations 10 and 18 (Frankfurt and Uccle) are combined, etc. After the final step four clusters have been formed:
(1) a "Scandinavian" cluster includes Bergen, Trondheim, Oslo, and Stockholm (stations 1 to 4);
(2) a large cluster "NW Europe" contains the stations on the British isles (stations 5 to 8), in the Netherlands (stations 9, 10), in N France (stations 13, 14) and W Germany (station 18);
(3) a cluster "SW Europe" is made out of Basel, Geneva, Lyon, Marseille, Milano, and Rome (stations 11, 12, 15, 16, 26, 27);
(4) a cluster "Central-Eastern Europe" groups the remaining eight stations.
Source: LAUTERBURG, 1990

The small numerals near the stations give the **representativeness** of a single station. This term, which was coined by LAUTERBURG, is equivalent to the average correlation of a station with every other station within the cluster. Paris for instance has a representativeness of 0.73. The station with the highest representativeness is called the key station of the cluster, the four key stations being Bergen, Oxford, Geneva and Vienna. The large numerals in the frames indicate the average representativeness of all stations within the cluster. It is a measure of homogeneity. In Fig. 7 average representativeness fluctuates between 0.7 and 0.8.

The thickness of the lines is equivalent to **transgressive similarity**. LAUTERBURG has defined this term as being the average correlation of each station within a cluster with all stations of an adjacent cluster. In Fig. 6 the transgressive similarity between cluster "SW-Europe" and cluster "Central Eastern Europe" is 0.62, i.e. fluctuations in summer temperatures between stations of those two clusters tend to be rather similar. To the Northwest transgressive similarity is somewhat lower (0.54). Temperature fluctuations in Southern Scandinavia have the least co-variation with those of the remaining clusters.

We decided to call the clusters themselves **similo-fluctuative areas** rather than using the previous term "isofluctuative areas" proposed by LAUTERBURG, as the syllable "iso-" should only be related to features which are really equal.

4. No change over time?

The next step is to ask whether those boundary lines tend to vary in strength and location over time.

Areas of similar year to year temperature fluctuations in summer, 1841-1900 (Fig. 7)

In the preceding period 1841-1900 the key stations are less representative for their cluster (Fig. 7), which might be connected to the quality of measurements. As a consequence, transgressive similarities tend to be lower. Boundaries have therefore increased in strength, but their location is not changed.

Areas of similar year-to-year temperature fluctuations in spring and summer over the instrumental period, eighteenth century to 1900 (Fig. 8)

In a next step, data from the early instrumental period (1780 to 1840 and prior to 1780) were analyzed. Fig. 8 summarizes the picture of the similo-fluctuative areas for spring and summer over the entire period. The degree of spatial homogeneity is shown from the average representativeness of the four key stations Bergen, Oxford, Geneva, and Vienna. The similo-fluctuative areas, named FT1 to FT4 and ST1 to ST4, form the basic spatial scheme in which the EUROCLIM-MA data base is contained (cp. SCHWARZ-ZANETTI, PFISTER, SCHWARZ-ZANETTI & SCHÜLE, this volume).

In spring Central Europe is clearly divided into two areas "East" and "West". The spatial representativeness of the key stations is very good.

In summer the four basic similo-fluctuative areas did not change significantly over the last 250 years, though this period includes pronounced variations in summer temperatures, such as a cold trough in the first half of the nineteenth century and a very warm decade from 1943 to 1952 (cp. Fig. 1).

Areas of similar year-to-year temperature fluctuations in autumn and winter over the instrumental period, 18th century to 1900 (Fig. 9)

The similo-fluctuative areas for autumn are named HT1 to HT4, those for winter WT1 and WT2. For autumn a fundamental change in the spatial pattern is observed between the two subperiods 1841-1900 and 1901-1960 (Fig. 9). All in all, transgressive similarities are considerably lower in the nineteenth century, i.e. fluctuations are much less homogeneous.

In the earlier period one main dividing line roughly follows the shore of the North Sea and the Baltic while the other one is more or less identical with that for spring (cp. Fig. 8). In 1901-60, however, the continent and Britain - Scandinavia excluded - are contained within one large area of high representativeness. The pattern shown in Fig. 10 may therefore not be conclusive for earlier periods.

The picture for winter shows just two similo-fluctuative areas which do not change much over time. One is located in the North Sea region, the other one on the continent. This clustering procedure was also applied to series of precipitation measurements. Generally, the regions of similo-fluctuations are considerably smaller and the correlations are weaker, which is related to the more sporadic and random character of rainfall patterns.

In addition to fluctuations around a trend, the trends themselves and the extremes should be submitted to separate analysis, because it turned out that those three elements are largely independent from each other. Documentary data are most conclusive for investigating climatic extremes, because those events are frequently described in quite a detail by past observers. On the other hand it might be more difficult to discover trends from this type of evidence, because slow, gradual changes have not been noticed at the time.

5. The significance of these results for the climatic history of Europe

Within the scheme of similo-fluctuative areas, images of past climate might also be obtained for periods in which regional data density is insufficient for reconstructing past climate within relatively restricted regions, such as Bohemia, Hessen, the Lombardy, or Crete. For those periods the focus should be upon reconstructing temperature and precipitation patterns for entire similo-fluctuative areas. The image of past climate for a particular city or

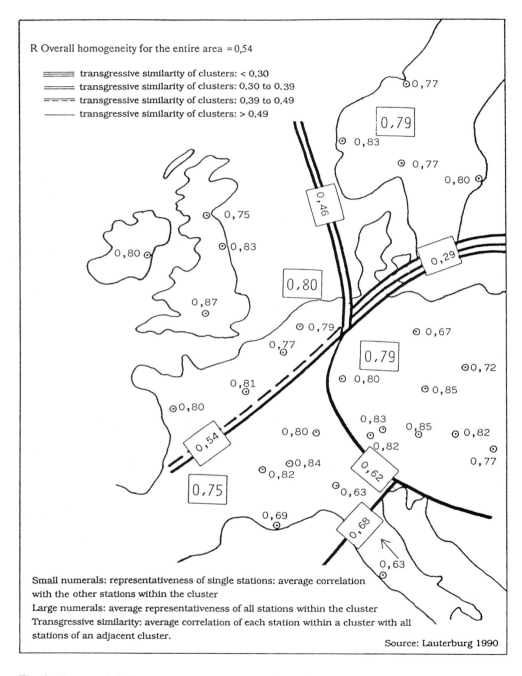

R Overall homogeneity for the entire area = 0,54

▦▦▦ transgressive similarity of clusters: < 0,30
▬▬▬ transgressive similarity of clusters: 0,30 to 0,39
= = = transgressive similarity of clusters: 0,39 to 0,49
───── transgressive similarity of clusters: > 0,49

0,77

0,79

0,83

0,77

0,80

0,46

0,75

0,83

0,80

0,29

0,87

0,80

0,79

0,77

0,79

0,67

0,81

0,80

0,72

0,85

0,80

0,83

0,85

0,82

0,54

0,80

0,82

0,77

0,75

0,84
0,82

0,62

0,63

0,69

0,68

0,63

Small numerals: representativeness of single stations: average correlation
with the other stations within the cluster
Large numerals: average representativeness of all stations within the cluster
Transgressive similarity: average correlation of each station within a cluster with all
stations of an adjacent cluster.

Source: Lauterburg 1990

Fig. 6 Clusters of similar year-to-year temperature fluctuations in summer, 1901- 1960

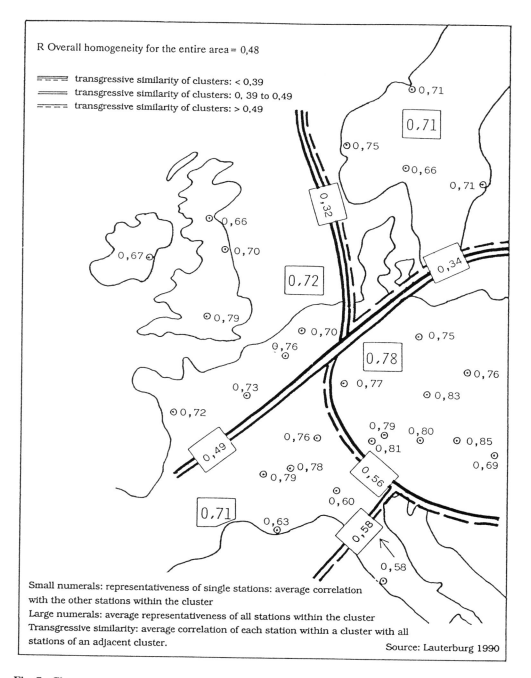

R Overall homogeneity for the entire area = 0,48

═══ transgressive similarity of clusters: < 0,39
─── transgressive similarity of clusters: 0, 39 to 0,49
════ transgressive similarity of clusters: > 0,49

0,71
0,71
0,75
0,66
0,71
0,32
0,66
0,70
0,67
0,72
0,34
0,79
0,70
0,75
0,76
0,78
0,76
0,73
0,77
0,83
0,72
0,79 0,80
0,76 0,81
0,85
0,49
0,78
0,56
0,69
0,79
0,60
0,71
0,63
0,58
0,58

Small numerals: representativeness of single stations: average correlation
with the other stations within the cluster
Large numerals: average representativeness of all stations within the cluster
Transgressive similarity: average correlation of each station within a cluster with all
stations of an adjacent cluster.

Source: Lauterburg 1990

Fig. 7 Clusters of similar year-to-year temperature fluctuations in summer, 1841-1900

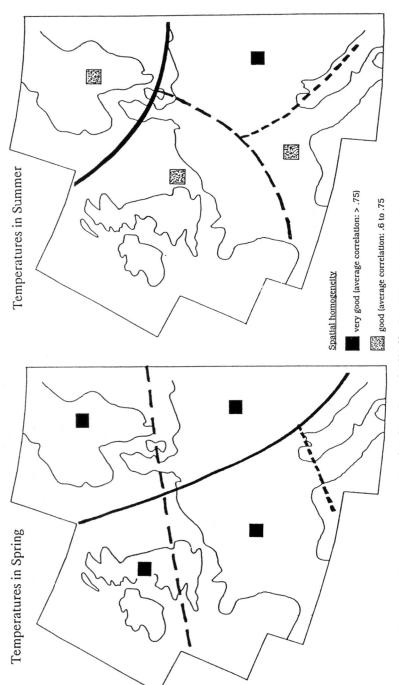

Temperatures in Spring

Temperatures in Summer

Spatial homogeneity

■ very good (average correlation: > .75)

▨ good (average correlation: .6 to .75

The location of clusters is based upon the analysis of the four sub-periods 1901-60, 1841-1900, 1781-1840, < 1781.

The boundaries indicate zones of rapid transition between iso-fluctuative areas.

The thickness of boundary lines is proportional to the inverse transgressive similarities between clusters.

Source: Lauterburg 1990

Fig. 8 Iso-fluctuative areas for spring and summer temperatures for the instrumental period

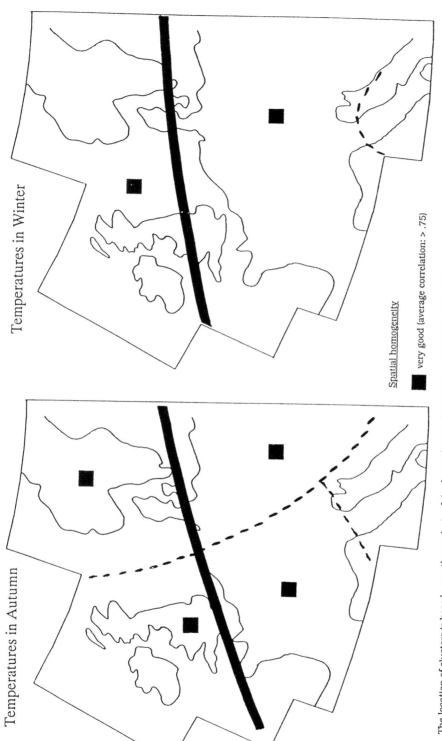

Temperatures in Autumn

Temperatures in Winter

Spatial homogeneity

■ very good (average correlation: > .75)

The location of clusters is based upon the analysis of the four sub-periods 1901-60, 1841-1900, 1781-1840, < 1781.
The boundaries indicate zones of rapid transition between iso-fluctuative areas.
The thickness of boundary lines is proportional to the inverse transgressive similarities between clusters.

Fig. 9 Iso-fluctuative areas for autumn and winter temperatures for the instrumental period

region could then be composed from those of the corresponding similo-fluctuative areas. Also the key stations of the clusters may be taken as a yardstick for calibrating proxy information where no regional series are available.

Acknowledgement

This work is supported by the Swiss National Science Foundation and the Swiss Bundesamt für Bildung und Wissenschaft (COST Programme).

References

DOE (1985): A climatic data bank for Northern Hemisphere land areas, 1851-1980. U.S. Department of Energy (DOE) TRO 17 Washington

KALKSTEIN, L. S.; TAN, G. & SKINDLOV, J. A. (1987): An evaluation of three clustering procedures for use in synoptic climatological classification. J. Climatol Appl. Meteorol. 26, 717- 730

LAUTERBURG, A. (1990): Klimaschwankungen in Europa. Raum-zeitliche Untersuchungen in der Periode 1841-1960. Geogr. Bern. G 35, Bern

LOETHER, H. & MCTAVISH, D (1974): Descriptive Statistics for Sociologists. An introduction. Boston

SPSS-X User's Guide (1988): 3rd ed. Chicago Ill

Addresses of the authors:

Prof. Dr. C. Pfister, Department for Regional and Environmental Studies at the Institute for History, University of Bern, Engehaldenstr. 4, CH-3012 Bern, Switzerland
Dr. Andreas Lauterburg, Oberdorfstraße 124, CH-9100 Herisau, Switzerland

The EURO-CLIMHIST Data Base - a tool for reconstructing the climate of Europe in the pre-instrumental period from high resolution proxy data

Werner Schwarz-Zanetti, Christian Pfister, Gabriela Schwarz-Zanetti & Hannes Schüle

Summary

30,000 proxy data from documentary sources for the period 1000 to 1525 originating from Germany, France, Northern Italy, the Benelux Countries, Switzerland, and Austria were integrated in a data base called EURO-CLIMHIST and boiled down to estimates for seasonal temperature and precipitation according to the approach by PFISTER (1984). The codebook and the software are presented and the calibration of proxy data, the interpretation and the mapping of the evidence are discussed.

Zusammenfassung

30,000 Proxydaten aus historischen Quellen aus Deutschland, Frankreich, Norditalien, den Beneluxstaaten, der Schweiz und Österreich für die Periode 1000 bis 1525 sind nach der von PFISTER (1984) entwickelten Methode in eine Datenbank namens EURO-CLIMHIST integriert und zu jahreszeitlichen Schätzwerten der Temperatur und des Niederschlages verdichtet worden. Vorgestellt werden Codebuch und Software, die Kalibrierung von Proxydaten, die Interpretation und die Umsetzung der Information in historische Wetterkarten.

1. Introduction

The present approach attempts to bridge the gap between climatic history and weather history by cross-dating different kinds of documentary proxy data with descriptive evidence. It aims at providing a combined record which includes both the quantitative estimates of temperature and precipitation needed by the scientist, the economist, and the policy maker, and the detailed weather account, needed by the historian for his reconstruction of the past. The procedure starts with collecting the smallest pieces of evidence available: weather observations, early instrumental data, and proxy information. The resulting "weather history" is coded, homogenized, and calibrated according to the type of data and stored in a data base called EURO-CLIMHIST. The evidence is then boiled down to a numerical precipitation and temperature index for each month. In the last step, this data is converted into a "climate history" by computing transfer functions for estimating temperature and precipitation (PFISTER, 1991).

The following is an intermediate report of an advanced project that aims at reconstructing weather and climate for Central Europe from the High Middle Ages to the Reformation period. It is based upon the methodology developed by PFISTER (1984) and relies on the sources collected by ALEXANDRE (1987) to some extent. The period under investigation begins around the year 1000. In the first millennium the sources are too sparse to allow estimating seasonal temperatures and precipitation or even the frequency of extremes. The spatial focus is upon the Swiss Mittelland and Germany south of the Danube, but the data base includes evidence from Northern Italy, the Benelux Countries, Austria, and France as well, in particular for the period prior to 1480. Up to the present more than 30,000 records have been stored in EURO-CLIMHIST (SCHWARZ-ZANETTI & SCHWARZ-ZANETTI, in prep.). The period investigated ends in 1525. From this year PFISTER (1984) covers the period up to the beginning of network observations (1864) for Switzerland, while GLASER provides a reconstruction from 1500 for Franconia (cp. this volume). Taken together the three investigations will cover 800 years of climate history in Central Europe and include almost 100,000 records. In the future they might become the nucleus of a larger European data base.

2. Types of climate data from documentary sources

The types of data used for the reconstruction of past climates have been described in great detail by LAMB (1981). Within the same volume INGRAM, UNDERHILL & FARMER (1981) have provided a survey of documentary sources.

PFISTER (1984) has classified the evidence firstly into natural and man-made data according to their origin. The data fall into explicit data and proxy data with respect to the kind of information they contain. Explicit data which directly refer to atmospheric phenomena and meteorological data are only contained in anthropogenic archives. The term "proxy" is used to denote any material providing an indirect measure of climate. This data comprises both natural and man-made evidence. One kind is closely related to geophysical and para-meteorological phenomena, mostly snow and ice, the second one refers to indicators of biological activity. Man-made data may also be grouped into documentary sources and material sources according to their form and to the place where they are found (cp. Fig. 1). Written sources, manuscript or printed, are mainly preserved in libraries and archives, sometimes in private ownership. Pictorial data are stored in libraries, archives or exposed in museums, objective data may be found in museums or in the field, e.g. the levels of historical floods are sometimes found to be marked on buildings or the height of low water tables may be engraved on rocks in river beds. The present investigation also includes natural proxy data in form of a series of tree-ring densities.

	MAN MADE		NATURAL	
ORIGIN INFORMATION	instrumental observations	descriptive reports	biological	geophysical
direct: weather patterns and meteorological parameters	– barometric – temperature – precipitation – water-gauge	– extreme events – rough sequence of weather situations – daily weather		
indirect (proxy (data): phenomena governed or affected by meteorological parameters	biological – time of blossoming and ripening of plants – yield and sugar content of vine – time of grain harvest and vintage	geophysical/para-meteorological – water-levels – snow falls – duration of snow-cover – freezing-over of water bodies	biological – marine plankton – pollen – tree rings etc.	geophysical – isotopes – sediments – moraines etc.

documentary sources

material sources

– paintings, prints, and photographs; maps and charts
– buildings, settlements, roads, waterways
– abandoned farms and fields
– archaeological remains

Fig. 1 A survey of evidence for reconstructing past weather and climate (PFISTER, 1992)

3. Data verification

Historians have developed a standardized methodology for evaluating sources and rejecting unreliable information. The most important critical tests are those based upon the principles of contemporaneity, propinquity and faithful transmission. Recorded statements cannot be regarded as reliable and valuable unless it can be shown: either, that the writer lived close in time and space to the events he purports to describe, and that he recorded his observations immediately or within a short time after these events had taken place; or that he had access to first hand oral or written reports and can be presumed to have accurately transmitted the information derived from them (INGRAM, UNDERHILL & FARMER, 1981). Only a decade ago, it was discovered that documentary sources of information about past climates were not equally reliable. Several scholars have pointed to the inherent weakness of compilations containing a mixture of valuable and worthless data. Their main flaws consist in inaccuracies or uncertainties in the dating of particular events, i.e. acceptance of accounts which distort or amplify original observations and spuriously multiply certain events through misdating.

Within the present investigation non-contemporary material was not completely rejected, as is recommended by INGRAM et al. (1981), because quite a detailed picture of weather patterns has already been obtained from contemporary data. Within this framework, second hand evidence was included whenever it contributed to the understanding of known weather patterns and its lower quality was clearly marked. On the other hand, it was rejected where it contradicted the contemporary evidence, for not confusing the reader.

Dating: Spurious multiplication of events through misdating is a major problem in winter because the indication of the year is ambiguous. If the source gives only one year, it must be derived from the context or from other sources, whether the "old" or the "new" year is referred to and in the analysis both years should be given in order to avoid confusion. In the Middle Ages dating is made with reference to the names of Saints. This way of dating does not fit into the scheme of calendar months. Therefore the structure of the records was arranged in such a way as to allow dating with a precision of ten days at least (cp. 5.).

For deciphering and interpreting Medieval documents some of the authors had to become familiar with hand-writings and abbreviations in Latin and Middle High German. This could only be achieved by interdisciplinary cooperation with other branches of knowledge, notably Latin philology.

4. Calibration

Calibration has to be carried out for each type of evidence before the data are processed. Data processing is performed on the basis of statistical software packages such as SAS or

SPSS-X. Much has been said on calibrating different types of evidence in a recent paper (PFISTER, in press). In the following we will only briefly illustrate the procedure by two examples:

4.1   The freezing of water bodies

From the cases documented by temperature measurements, it has been established that lakes in the Alpine foothills freeze in a specific rank order, according to their surface, depth, and individual characteristics. The freezing of lakes is primarily a function of the sum of the daily mean temperatures below the freezing point plus such other factors as wind-speed. It should also be known whether the ice was thick enough to carry men and cargoes and how long the ice-cover remained. For the freezing of the Lake of Zurich, which is the best documented example, the sum of the daily mean temperatures below the freezing point exceeded 350°C in cases people could walk on the ice-cover (PFISTER, 1984).

The freezing of rivers seems to have occurred after shorter cold spells, before their beds were dammed in the nineteenth and twentieth centuries. For rivers outside Switzerland the calibration needs to be carried out yet, comparing eye-witness reports with early instrumental measurements.

4.2   Radio-dendroclimatic data

Tree-ring data from humid Western and Central Europe do not allow very convincing climatic reconstructions, mainly because of their long climatic memory. Representative results can be expected from trees at the Alpine timberline, where the temperature of the short vegetative period controls the growth rate. Significant progress has been made through X-ray density measurements of wood, permitting the evaluation of quantitative parameters, such as the density of late wood which is produced mainly during late summer. This data is a good proxy for temperatures in July, August, and September (SCHWEINGRUBER, 1978, 1983). For the pre-instrumental period cross-correlations with other types of proxy data, notably vine harvest dates, are convincing (FLOHN, 1985). This holds primarily for the chilly summers. However, some of the hottest summers in the last 450 years - 1616, 1719, 1947 - do not stand out in the record. This suggests that we should be very cautious in using tree-ring density data as climatic indicators, unless they can be cross-checked with man-made observations or grape harvest dates (PFISTER, 1985b).

5.   Structure of the codebook

The codebook (table 1) allows to translate the descriptive weather information consisting of repetitive elements, such as "sunny", "rainy", "snowfall" etc. to a numerical code. The coding forces the researcher to focus upon the essence of the source. Our work is based upon an updated version of the software PFISTER (1981) had devised in the late 1970s, i.e.

still in the age of punched cards. In this version the record was limited to 80 columns, and the user had not only to know the codes, but the appropriate columns as well. In 1991, the structure of the codebook was adapted to the present way of programming (cp. appendix). A single coded entry is made up from the following elements:

TIME / SOURCE CODE [, SPATIAL CODE] / OBSERVATION CODE [/* TEXT]

The standard exchange file contains keys referring to the time and place of observation as well as to the source. The three keys taken together identify every particular record.

The data base is tailored to take up information from all states of Europe. The source number is linked to a number of source attributes which are stored on an external source file: name and lifetime of the observer (in order to distinguish contemporary and non-contemporary observation), name and altitude of the place of observation, its location in a similo-fluctuative region (cp. Pfister & Lauterburg, this volume), the style of dating, the reference to the bibliographical listing of sources, etc. Other external files contain statistics obtained from instrumental temperature and precipitation series for a "normal" period in the twentieth century (if possible the one from 1901 to 1960). They are used as a yardstick to compare earlier instrumental series or estimates from high resolution proxy information to "average conditions" of our century.

Daily observations are coded in the groups 11 (winds), 12 (thermal character) and 13 (sky/precipitation). A code of reliability made of one or two double crosses in brackets - (#) or (##) - indicates whether the coding is close to the explicit meaning of the text or whether it includes a small or a considerable degree of interpretation.

Impacts of weather upon the lithosphere, the hydrosphere, the biosphere, and upon human societies are coded in the groups 21 to 71. At present this section of the codebook only refers to those features which are contained in sources from Central Europe. Most obvious: marine observations are absent. For a European data base this section of the codebook needs to be amended with additional types of environmental characteristics that are typical for other regions of Europe. Thus, this version of the codebook will still have to be improved, refined and adapted to new types of data in close cooperation with its users (cp. Schüle & Pfister, this volume).

Footnotes of any length can be appended at the end of a record. Information which, according to the compiler, is unique should not only be coded, but also quoted verbally as a footnote in the original language and followed by a short English summary. At present the EURO-CLIMHIST data base already includes more than 6 000 footnotes that have been literally transcribed from documentary sources.

6. Processing data

The sequence of steps in data processing and the function of the different sub-programs and subroutines is shown in Fig. 2.

The subprogram MET1F simply counts the frequencies of weather patterns derived from daily non-instrumental diaries (cp. table 1 A). One kind of output has the form of frequency tables which allows checking the data and the results, the other one may be transferred to the "SORT-routine".

The subprogram SEPCLIM has the following two functions:

(1) Disentangling packed records:
    different kinds of observation from the same source referring to a same time interval should be coded on the same record, if possible, in order to avoid the investment of time for copying the identifying keys (time, source, place). SEPCLIM provides a separate record for every type of observation by duplicating the identifying keys;
(2) Checking the data:
-   for typing errors such as leading blanks and gaps not compatible with the codebook;
-   for observations outside a specified time period (in our case between 900 and 1550 A.D.);
-   for logical inconsistencies: e.g. cherries do not flower in December.

Errors are displayed in the output.

The SORT routine reorders the cases by sorting them in chronological order. The second and third sort keys are country and region, the fourth one is data type (cp. table 1).

The output routine SELECT allows selecting a group of the entire body of data for processing according to four criteria - country, type of observation, similo-fluctuative area, and time window - which may also be combined. It is possible to select records for August only, or just information on floods, which were noted down in Germany between 1400 and 1500. This selection routine is particularly important for the interpretation which has to be carried out on the basis of similo-fluctuative areas (cp. PFISTER & LAUTERBURG, this volume). Furthermore the language of the output can be selected from the existing routines.

The main decoding program called SORTCLIM provides an editing of the coded data (cp. Fig. 3) in two versions: the test version includes information to facilitate debugging, the handling of footnotes and interpreting the evidence, i.e. assigning the indices (cp. 8.). Errors are corrected on the level of coded input data, i.e. before the SEPCLIM step. The final version includes the indices and conforms to the accepted standards of source publication. Output is available on paper and on micro-fiches.

Table 1 Organisation of the basic record

Categ.	Subject	Details	Code	Columns[a]			
All	Chronology	NNN=year-1000	NNN	1-3			
		Month	1-12				
		Seasons	13-16	4-5			
		Entire year	17				
	Data category: A,B:	10-day intervals	1-3	6			
	A,B:	entire month	4				
	C:	precip. measure	5				
	D:	frequency counts	6				
	E:	temperature measure	7				
	Region		1-15	8-9			
	Source	Tied to author, place and altitude of observation. NNNN=reference number	NNNN	11-14			
A 16-54	Daily observations (to be processed by the program MET1K)	blanks (winds, thermal character, sky/precip.	10 three-column observations separated by	M[b]			
A,B	reliability		M	56			
	Prevailing weather in a 10-day interval, month or season (see columns	Winds	M	57-58			
			Thermal character	M	59-6C		
			Sky/precip.	M	62-63		
	4,5)	Snow cover	M	64			
	Impact of weather upon the lithosphere and hydrosphere	freezing of lakes	Landslides, glacier fluctuations, river levels,	M			
66-67							
	Phenological observations	period 58 phenophases[d]	Day within 10-day	0-9	6-8		
			M	69-70			

	Impact of weather on		Droughts, floods, frosts,	M	
71-72	the biosphere	snow etc. affecting crops or livestock			
M	Impact of weather on 71-72 Man	harvests, fluctuations of prices, dearths, famines	Epidemics, quality and quantity of		
	Type of calendar/in-clusion of footnotes			—	M 75
C	Monthly precipitation sums (NNN=actual amount in mm)			NNN	16-18
D	Monthly frequency counts based on A[c]		M	16-71	
E	Monthly mean temperatures (NNNN=temperature in °C and tenths)			NNNN	16-19

---

[a] Columns 15, 55 and 65 are blank (except possibly for data category D).

[b] M is used to denote a miscellaneous numerical code.

[c] This is the output produced by the program MET1K. It mainly contains monthly frequency counts of the items given   in the daily observations.

[d] 58 phenophases: 58 different phases of flowering an ripening for different crops and plants.

A number of external files have to be prepared for SORTCLIM:

- a source reference file containing all the elements to be assigned to a source (cp. above);
- a place reference table;
- files containing duodecile statistics (cp. 9.) for the reference period in the twentieth century, mostly 1901-1960. They are needed to compute indices from early instrumental series and from parameters obtained from non-instrumental diaries, such as the number of days with precipitation (output of MET1F). One reference file is for temperature, one for precipitation and one for the number of rainy days. For every "historical series" the most appropriate reference station must be selected for the "normal period" in the twentieth century. If no comparisons of this kind are attempted, these files may be omitted.

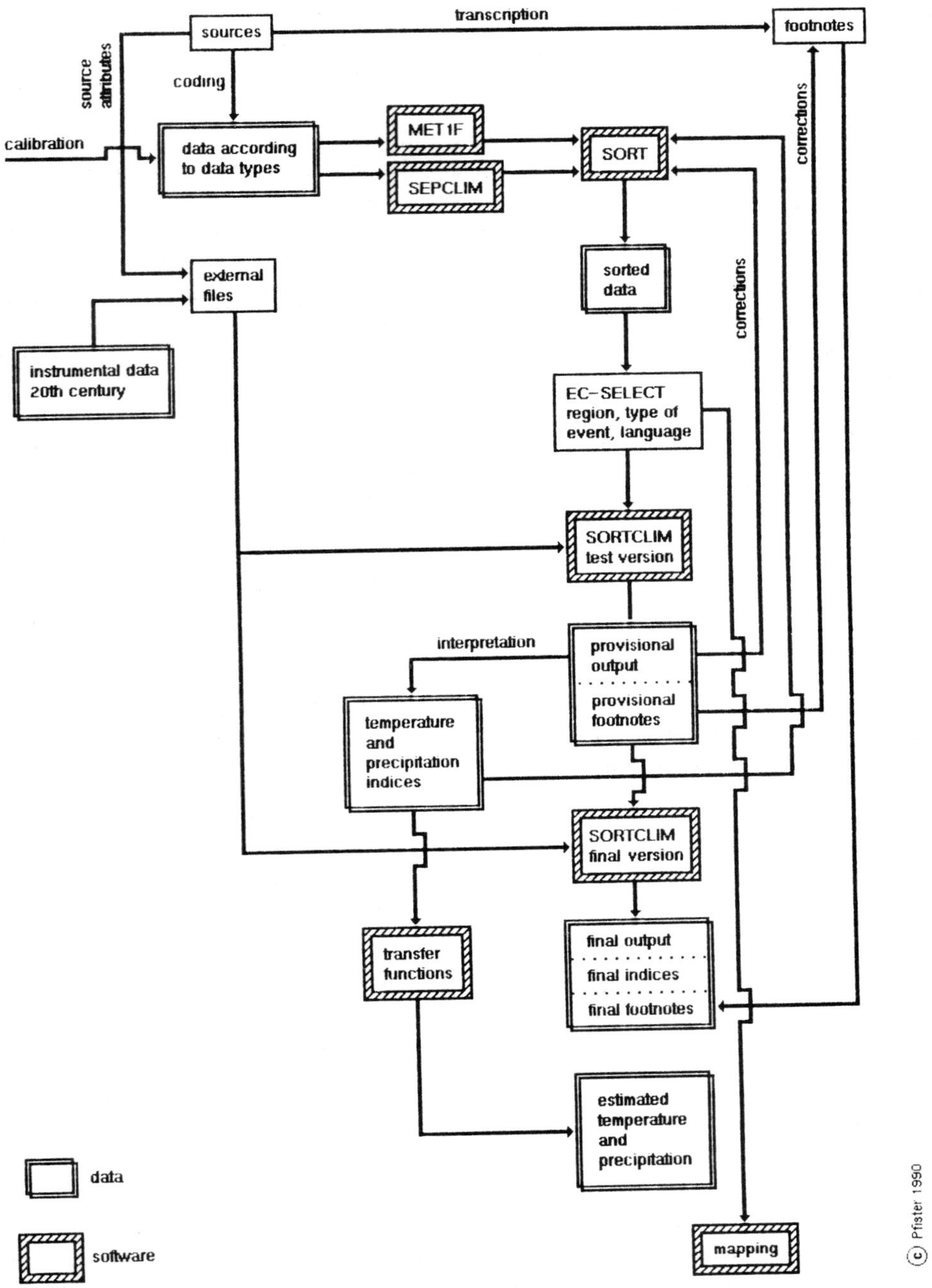

Fig. 2 A survey of steps for processing different kinds of high resolution proxy data

In the context of the present investigation, the statistics obtained from non-instrumental diaries (output of MET1F) are of particular importance (cp. SCHWARZ-ZANETTI & SCHWARZ-ZANETTI, this volume). In addition to the number of days with precipitation the subprogram MET1F provides monthly sums for the following daily entries: "variable weather"; continuous rain; thunderstorm; hailstorms; snowfall; rain and snowfall; no precipitation; cloudy; sunny; foggy all day; fog in the morning only; strong winds; wind from northerly, southerly, easterly, westerly direction; four gradations of warmth and coldness (according to the impression of the observer); the days with snowcover on the ground. Depending on threshold values set in the main program (SORTCLIM), the distinguishing meteorological quality of a month may be specified in the output. In the present version qualifying characteristics are printed: if more than 50% of the entries refer to "cloudy", "sunny", "foggy" weather or to "fog in the morning", if the number of "warm" days exceeds 12 and if it is >35% than the number of "cold days", etc.

Phenological data, i.e. observations on the timing of vegetative stages (e.g. appearance, bloom, harvest) of cultivated plants (mostly fruit trees, cereals and vines), are known to be of great value as proxy substitutes for measured temperatures. The longest series of this kind refer to the opening of the wine harvest: the series built up for Western Europe by LE ROY LADURIE & BAULANT (1980) originates in 1484; PFISTER (1988) has extended this series back to 1370. For converting the dates into numbers suited for time series analysis the SORTCLIM main program computes the number of days that have elapsed since January 1st for every phenological observation, e.g. 32 for February 1st etc.

Just to focus upon another proxy which is very important in the context of the Middle Ages, radio-dendroclimatic data (i.e. the series from Lauenen, Bernese Oberland) are pre-interpreted according to the following thresholds:

density (g/m^3)	indication
-< 880	very small
-880 - 919	small
-920 - 959	below average
-960 - 1039	average
-1040 - 1079	above average
-1080 - 1119	large
->= 1120	very large.

7. Editing the data

The data base describes the weather patterns and their impacts upon the hydrosphere, the biosphere and the anthroposphere (prices, diseases etc.) for periods of ten days, from month to month or from season to season according to the evidence available. An example of the TEST output is provided for January 1408, one of the coldest months in the last 700 years (Fig. 3).

1408 J A N U A R Y

1st TEN DAY- PERIOD
...

2nd TEN DAY-PERIOD
....

3rd TEN DAY-PERIOD
...

ENTIRE MONTH

COLD. R: 5 SOLOTHURN/CH:WT1N1: 432 M(AUF.,S 441)
 R: 1 BASEL/CH:WT1N1: 278 M(ROETELER,S 1114)**
 R: 1 BASEL/CH:WT1N1: 278 M(KOENIGS.,S 1113)**
 R: 5 BERN/CH:WT1N1: A540 M(JUSTINGER,S 1182)**

SIGNS OF STRONG COLDNESS: RIVERS FROZEN.
R: 1 BASEL/CH:WT1N1: 278 M(ROETELER,S 1114)**
COLD. R: 3 FREIBURG BR./D:WT1N1: 278 M(G.,S 425)
FROST. R: 6 KOELN/D:WT1N3: 39 M(JAHRB.,S 792)
 R: 2 REGENSBURG/D:WT1N3: 343 M(AND.,S 492)
PERMANENT SNOWCOVER.
R: 1 AUGSBURG/D:WT1N3: 490 M(ANNA.,S 400)
 R: 2 INGOLSTADT/D:WT1N3: 374 M(NOTES,S 506)

SIGNS OF STRONG COLDNESS: RIVERS FROZEN.
R: 6 KOELN/D:WT1N3: 39 M(JAHRB.,S 792).
 R: 3 ROETTELN/D:WT1N1: 415 M (R.,S 424)
FROST.SNOW. R: 3 LES DUNES/B:WT1N2: 5 M(B,S 900)
FROST.R: 6 LIEGE/B:WT1N2:115 M(B.,S 355)(F 3373).
 R: 2 BRUESSEL/B:WT1N2: 18 M (RIJMC.,S 917)

SIGNS OF STRONG COLDNESS: RIVERS FROZEN.
R: 6 LIEGE/B:WT1N2: 115 M(BAVAR.,S 355) (F 3373)
FROST. R: 6 TIEL/NL:WT1N5: 5 M (ANNALEN,S 944)
 R: 5 RATIBOR/PL:WT1N6: 192 M (ANNA., S 880)
 R: PRAHA/CS:WT1N3: 187 M (ANNALEN,S 889)
COLD. R: 13 STRASSBURG/F:WT1N2: 150 M(T.,S 470)
 R: 6 ANGERS/F:WT1N2: 14 M (NOTES,S 1230)
FROST: R: 1 ST.DENIS/F:WT1N2: 26 M (CH.,S 569)
 R: 1 PARIS/F:WT1N2: 26 M (BAYE,S 578) (F 3374)
 R: 4 ROUEN/F:WT1N2: 8 M (CHRONIQ.,S 1184)

SIGNS OF STRONG COLDNESS: RIVERS FROZEN.
 R: 4 ROUEN/F:WT1N2: 8 M (CHRONIQ.,S 1184)
FROST.COLD. R: 13 COLMAR/F:WT1N2: 193 M(C,S 456)

Fig. 3 A selection of the information contained in the EURO-CLIMHIST data base for January 1408 (Schwarz-Zanetti, Schwarz-Zanetti & Pfister, in prep.). TEST-Version

In the first three paragraphs, the information is listed according to the three ten-day periods (not displayed here). "R" gives the region within the country. The indications after the place name refer to the location within the similo-fluctuative regions (cp. PFISTER & LAUTERBURG, this volume): "W" as the first letter refers to winter, "T" as the second one to temperatures, "N" (Niederschlag) to precipitation, e.g. WT1N3 means that a location is situated in the area 1 with regard to winter temperatures and in area 3 with regard to winter precipitations.

In brackets the name of the observer or that of the source is given. If the observer or the name of the source is not mentioned, the observation is contemporary. The number after "S" (source) points to the bibliographical reference (not provided here). Two asterisks"**" are added, if considerable interpretation is involved in the coding. These can result from a single uncertainty coded in the standard exchange file, from the reliability code in the source reference table or they can be a result of the processing of the data.

"F" (footnote) followed by a number refers to the list of footnotes in the appendix. An example (F 3373):

"...in eadem hieme, gelu et frigus fuit ita intensum quod glacies inceperunt in die [Sancti] Martini, perdurantes et augmentantes continue usque ad vicesimam octabam diem mensis Ianuarii. Quo die, propter novilunum, de nocte subito ruperunt se, plura dampna pontibus et molendis inferentes, taliter quod in crastino glacies in mosa vix apparebant". (... because of hard frost and coldness in this winter (1407/08) from the 11th November (= 20th November, Gregorian Style) until the 28th January (= February 6th, Gregorian Style). In this night suddenly the ice on the Maas river broke, damaging bridges and mills.)

8. Estimating temperature and precipitation indices

Temperature estimates based on proxy data can be made with sufficient precision for periods of two or three months only, because the underlying pattern of cold or warm spells is not known in greater detail. This involves complex problems of interpretation. For example, if an observer reports the first vine buds to be bursting towards the end of May, this can be due to an exceptional heatwave in March and April succeeded by an average month of May, or to a very warm month of May, that could have followed an average April. The weather patterns underlying this event may be known in detail from weather accounts available for this same period. On the other hand the emphasis given by the observer (such as "very hot") is known to be biased. It needs to be supplemented with proxy information. As a consequence, the two types of evidence both control and supplement each other. Whereas the magnitude of a deviation can be estimated through proxy information, the qualitative observation describes the underlying weather patterns. This allows refining the interpretation and assessing the timing of the corresponding cold or warm weather spells (PFISTER, 1991).

For EURO-CLIMHIST, which refers to the early modern and early instrumental period, data density was sufficient for deriving two types of indices, a weighted index and an unweighted.

For the weighted temperature and precipitation indices the frequency distribution of monthly averages for the period from 1901-1960 was adopted as standard of comparison (Fig. 4).

The value of 0 was used for "normal" weather conditions and for all months with missing evidence. The values of +3 and -3 were applied to those cases which can unmistakably be considered as "extreme" by twentieth century standards. The values of +2/-2 were adopted for the less marked gradations. The values of +1/-1 were applied to all months for which only descriptive evidence is available as well as to those months, which, according to proxy information, fall in the corresponding range of temperature and precipitation. Admittedly, the interpretation of the observer has to face the difficulty of assigning the weights. But this subjective bias is rather small in most cases (e.g. -2 instead of -1). In order to allow an intersubjective control of the interpretation, the entire evidence is published in the EURO-CLIMHIST data base (Pfister, 1985a). Within the instrumental period, the indices were derived from measured temperature and precipitation records according to the duodecile distribution of the values. For precipitation, two separate indices for rainfall totals and for the number of rainy days have been computed in a first step. In a second step the two indices were merged.

The unweighted temperature and precipitation indices downgrade all the positive or negative weights to three gradations: +1, 0 and -1. Accordingly, this index is more homogeneous than the weighted one, but it does not fully exploit the informative potential of the data. Which of the two indices is more "realistic" depends on the quality of the evidence.

For the period 1000 to 1524 the quality and density of the material allows only estimating unweighted indices: +1/0/-1. At the level of months unweighted temperature or precipitation indices are attributed in the following way:

-1   for months unmistakably colder or dryer than the 1901-60 average;
+1   for those unmistakably warmer and wetter than the 1901-60 average;
 0   for "normal" months, roughly within the standard deviation of the 1901-1960 distribution.

Seasonal values may fluctuate between +3 and -3 for temperature and precipitation. In which way these indices will be converted into estimates for temperature and precipitation (Pfister, 1984), will be determined as soon as all of them will have been created. In any case it will be necessary to compute transfer functions for regions outside Switzerland.

9. Mapping

Mapping the evidence is of utmost importance. Up to the present studies dealing with climatic change have focussed upon the dimension of time only, and they have neglected that of space. However, climate varies according to time and space. We have, therefore, to go beyond the analysis of time series to the investigation of changing weather situations in space and over time in form of series of historical weather maps. Maps may be produced by means of a mapping routine being created at present (cp. Fig. 5).

Knowledge of the average position of cyclones and anticyclones over Europe in specific seasons of the past might be helpful in three ways.

(1) Estimating the changing frequencies of weather patterns would become conclusive evidence for investigating natural hazards in the past;
(2) it would certainly turn out to be an important input for climatic models, which could be based upon a period of 700 to 800 years in this way rather than on the short period of instrumental measurement;
(3) the image of changing weather situations in the past on a European scale might become an important tool for assessing climatic impacts upon past societies on a continental scale.

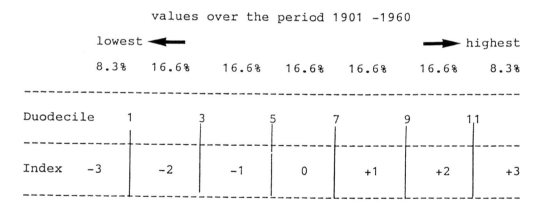

Fig. 4 The definitions of the temperature and precipitation indices (PFISTER, 1984)

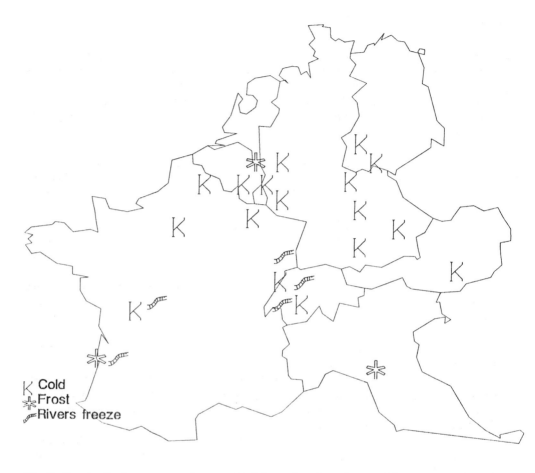

Fig. 5 Standardized computer picture with information for winter 1407/1408 (Source: EURO-CLIMHIST, Schwarz-Zanetti, Schwarz-Zanetti & Pfister, in prep.)

Acknowledgements

The EURO-CLIMHIST project is supported by the Swiss National Science Foundation and by the Swiss Bundesamt für Bildung und Wissenschaft (COST Programme). Hannes Schüle from the University of Bern has arranged the layout for the main program for the climate history data base. Stefan Ruetsch from the same university has created the mapping programs. Acknowledgments are due to David Spencer of the Swiss Federal Institute of Technology in Zurich for correcting the style of a draft version and to Petr Dobrovolny, Brno, CSFR, for reading the manuscript.

References

ALEXANDRE, P. (1987): Le climat en Europe au Moyen-Age. Contribution à l'histoire des variations climatiques de 1000 à 1425, d'après les sources narratives de l'Europe occidentale. Ecole des Hautes Etudes en Sciences Sociales Paris

BELL, W. & OGILVIE, A. E. (1978): Weather compilations as a source of data for the reconstruction of European climate during the Medieval period. Climatic Change 1/4, 331-348

BIDER, M.; SCHÜEPP, M. & VON RUDLOFF, H. (1959): Die Reduktion der 200-jährigen Basler Temperaturreihe. Arch. Meteor. Geophys. Bioklim. Ser. B/1, 360-412

FLOHN, H. (1985): A critical assessment of proxy data for climatic reconstruction. In: Tooley, M. J. & Sheail, G. M. (eds.): The climatic scene. Allen & Unwin, London, 93-103

INGRAM, M.; UNDERHILL, D. & FARMER, G. (1981): The use of documentary sources for the study of past climate. In: Wigley, T. M. L.; Ingram, M. J. & Farmer, G. (eds.): Climate and history. Studies in past climates and their impact on man. Cambridge Univ. Press, Cambridge, 180-214

LAMB, H. H. (1981): An approach to the study of the development of climate and its impact in human affairs. In: Wigley, T. M. L., Ingram, M. J. & Farmer, G. (eds.): Climate and history. Studies in past climates and their impact on man. Cambridge Univ. Press, Cambridge, 291-310

LE ROY LADURIE, E. & BAULANT, M. (1980): Grape harvests from the fifteenth through the nineteenth centuries. J. Interdisc. Hist. 10/4, 839-849

PFISTER, C. (1981a): An analysis of the Little Ice Age climate in Switzerland and its consequences for agricultural production. In: Wigley, T. M. L.; Ingram, M. J. & Farmer, G. (eds.): Climate and History. Studies in past climates and their impact on man. Cambridge Univ. Press, Cambridge, 214-247

PFISTER, C. (1984): Klimageschichte der Schweiz 1525-1860. Das Klima der Schweiz von 1525-1860 und seine Bedeutung in der Geschichte von Bevölkerung und Landwirtschaft. 2 vols. Bern, 3rd ed. 1988

PFISTER, C. (1985a): EURO-CLIMHIST - a weather data bank for Central Europe 1525 to 1863. (May be ordered from METEOTEST, Fabrikstr. 29a, CH-3012 Bern)

PFISTER, C. (1985b): Veränderungen der Sommerwitterung im südlichen Mitteleuropa von 1270-1400 als Auftakt zum Gletscherhochstand der Neuzeit. Geogr. Helv. 4, 186-194

PFISTER, C. (1988): Variations in the spring- summer climate of Central Europe from the High Middle Ages to 1850. In: Wanner, H. & Siegenthaler, U. (eds.): Long and short variability of climate. Springer, Berlin, 57-82

PFISTER, C. (1992): Monthly temperature and precipitation patterns in Central Europe from 1525 to the present. A methodology for quantifying man-made evidence on weather and climate. In: Bradley, R. S. & Jones, P. D. (eds.): Climate since 1500 A.D. (in print)

PFISTER, C.; SCHWARZ-ZANETTI W. & SCHWARZ-ZANETTI, G. (1986): Ein Programm- und Methodenpaket zur Rekonstruktion von Klimaverhältnissen seit dem Hochmittelalter.

Datenbanken und Datenverwaltungssysteme als Werkzeuge historischer Forschung, Hist.-Sozialwiss. Forsch. 20, 75-92

SCHWEINGRUBER, F. H.; Fritts, H. C.; Bräker, O. U.; Drew, L. G. & Schär, E. (1978): The X-ray technique as applied to dendroclimatology. Tree-Ring Bull. 38, 61-91

SCHWEINGRUBER, F. (1983): Der Jahrring. Standort, Methodik, Zeit und Klima in der Dendrochronologie. Paul Haupt, Bern

Addresses of the authors:

Prof. Dr. C. Pfister, Department for Regional and Environmental Studies at the Institute for History, University of Bern, Engehaldenstr. 4, CH-3012 Bern, Switzerland
H. Schüle, Department for Regional and Environmental Studies at the Institute for History, University of Bern, Engehaldenstr. 4, CH-3012 Bern, Switzerland
G. Schwarz-Zanetti, Florastraße 29, CH-8620 Wetzikon, Switzerland
W. Schwarz-Zanetti, Florastraße 29, CH-8620 Wetzikon, Switzerland

EURO-CLIMHIST - outlines of a Multi Proxy Data Base for investigating the climate of Europe over the last centuries

Hannes Schüle & Christian Pfister

Summary

It is suggested creating a data base to investigate climate dynamics in Europe over the past 700-800 years from various kinds of high resolution proxy data. This approach enables going beyond time series analysis to attempt a spatial reconstruction of past atmospheric conditions in form of Multi Proxy Mapping. A pilot study of this kind of European research cooperation is being attempted for the "Maunder Minimum" period (1675-1715).

Zusammenfassung

Es wird angeregt, die zur Rekonstruktion der Klimageschichte Europas in den letzten 700-800 Jahren verwendeten hochauflösenden Datentypen aus natürlichen und historischen Archiven in eine Datenbank zu integrieren. Dieses Vorgehen wird es erlauben, neben den üblichen Zeitreihen ein raum-zeitliches Bild der Klimaentwicklung in Form einer Reihe von "Paläo-Klimakarten" zu entwerfen. Eine pan-europäische Zusammenarbeit im Hinblick auf diese Zielsetzung soll am Beispiel eines Pilotprojekts für die Zeit des "Maunder Minimums" (1675-1715) erprobt werden.

1. The whole is more than a sum of its parts

The aim of investigating weather patterns and climate variations for the pre-instrumental period from documentary data, season by season or even month by month, involves both a regional and a universal approach. Reconstructing past climate on a regional level is accomplished by scholars familiar with the historical geography and the environment history of their country (cp. BRADLEY & JONES, 1991, and the examples provided in this volume). Results are mainly presented in form of time series which are graphically or statistically compared, and in most cases conclusions are restricted to the coincidence of "cold" and "warm" phases. Since different procedures were applied for getting and handling the data, it is not possible to standardize this evidence in a mapping procedure which would enable spatial images of past situations to be derived. Moreover, systematic investigations of this kind are lacking in many parts of Europe. The mapping approach is not entirely new of course: LAMB (1977) was probably the first to derive weather charts for the pre-instrumental period from proxy information. Later on KINGTON (1988) drew daily synoptic maps for the 1780s from the instrumental series obtained within the observational network of the Societas Meteorologica Palatina. Recently TAGAMI & FUKAISHI (in press) have systematically mapped non-instrumental daily weather observations in eighteenth century Japan. But for the pre-instrumental period a systematic Multi Proxy Mapping involving documentary data and proxy data from natural archives has not yet been attempted. Such a project could yield an inventory of large-scale spatial images of severe anomalies over the last 700 or 800 years, and possibly provide clues to the variations in the frequency of weather situations with a time resolution for seasons or months over the last 500 years. These results would certainly be useful for interpreting the present situation and for improving the calibration of climatic models. They might even become the nucleus of the global Multi Proxy Mapping approach: an attempt promoted by the Past Global Changes (PAGES) project, which is part of the International Geosphere Biosphere Programme IGBP (IGBP, 1990). In this way, regional investigations could yield the building blocks enabling past climates on a continental or a global scale to be ultimately reconstructed. This example demonstrates once again that the whole is more than just the sum of its parts.

However, in the present situation we are not able to gain such a macro-history of European weather patterns for the pre-instrumental period. This is accounted for by the following reasons:

(1) Quite often regional studies do not include an extended data appendix, because this would have added exceedingly to the cost of the book. This involves two shortcomings:
- the procedure is not open to thorough criticism, because it cannot be traced back to the original sources. The reader has simply to believe or reject the conclusions of the authors;
- the basic evidence that would be needed in the context of a European study is not readily available. Thus, the time spent on locating and transcribing sources in the archives has to be invested again in the context of a subsequent study.
(2) Even in those cases where primary data are stored in machine-readable form the files are often deleted after publication or they are not sufficiently documented for outsiders. Moreover, methodologies and coding systems are often incompatible with those of other studies.

The best way to overcome these shortcomings would be by creating an international data base as a common research platform based upon a common standard and a common software. In a similar way, a European palynological data base is being established in Arles under the direction of J.-L. DE BEAULIEU (cp. the "Newsletter" publications). This requires a preliminary consensus in the research community on standards for data coding and processing, on the academic property and on the rules for redistributing the data contributed by others, as well as the readiness of every partner to submit his data to the data base.

2. How EURO-CLIMHIST could work

How a fictitious data base of this kind could be organized will be outlined in the following in the form of a mental image. Let us call it EURO-CLIMHIST.

EURO-CLIMHIST includes all kinds of data which are known to contribute to our understanding of climatic change for the period from the Middle Ages to the present: the bulk of the evidence is made up of information from historical archives. It is complemented with tree-ring data, pollen data, ice core data etc., coming from the specific data bases EURO-CLIMHIST is linked with. The framework of a general codebook for historical data and the corresponding software is set up. EURO-CLIMHIST maintains an extended bibliographical documentation on climate history for the present millennium. The cooperation between the data bank and the research partners works along the following lines:

(1) The data base staff already provide support in the planning phase of an investigation, which is the most decisive one. Prior to submitting a research proposal for a regional climate reconstruction to his national funding agency, a scholar gets in touch with the data base administrator to be informed about the possibilities of cooperating with EURO-CLIMHIST. He then works out a detailed project. If this is approved by the funding agency, a contract regarding all aspects of the cooperation is to be agreed upon and signed;
(2) the research partner is assisted by the data bank staff in adapting the codebook to specific characteristics of his sources as necessary (e.g. for including observations on sea-ice in Iceland or reports on processions for obtaining rain in Spain). Then a simple coding program is written and additional software modules are set up to deal with this new kind of evidence;
(3) if necessary, he translates the codebook in his language to set up a translation module. Any language a translation module has been created for may be selected for output;
(4) processing is done according to one of the following three options:
- the researcher processes his data on his own computing facilities under the guidance of the EURO-CLIMHIST staff. A member of this staff has access to the data base software by network and processes the data;
- the researcher integrates his data into the data base, running the necessary proceedings on his own but assisted by the staff;
- the researcher sends his data to the data base for processing either on a floppy disk or on tape or through the network. Afterwards the results and the data are handed back.

For his investigation the research partner has full access to all "public" data stored in EURO-CLIMHIST. The processed data handed back to him may include additional evidence for "his" region, "his" time, and "his" topic. From the knowledge of large-scale weather patterns he might be able to interpolate gaps in his region and he might discover conclusive links to studies from neighbouring regions. He also has access to the bibliographical documentation associated with the data base. Of course he has to provide the interpretation himself; the brain work cannot be done by the computer...

(5) after publication of the results, EURO-CLIMHIST provides means for publishing the data under the name of the author. In order to reduce the costs, this is done in the form of computer print-outs and micro-fiches, which are available on request only. This allows the production of one English version and one in the language of the region the data refer to. This procedure has already been explored in the context of Swiss data (PFISTER, 1985);

(6) only when a scholar has published both his regional study and his data, his evidence will be integrated in the "public" part of the data base. This will enlarge the data basis for future studies.

3. A beginning is made

Preliminary steps for creating a data base for climate history in Europe have been made at the University of Bern:

(1) The methodological framework for the spatial analysis of climatic change has been created by LAUTERBURG (cp. PFISTER & LAUTERBURG, this volume);

(2) PFISTER (1984) has elaborated a sequence of computer programs enabling the sources from historical and natural archives to be processed. W. and G. SCHWARZ-ZANETTI have adapted this software to handle evidence from all European countries (cp. SCHWARZ-ZANETTI, PFISTER, SCHWARZ-ZANETTI & SCHÜLE, this volume);

(3) at present a 40-page standard codebook is available in English, Czech, French, German, Italian and Hungarian. Translation routines for additional European languages are being made (cp. appendix);

(4) the nucleus of "public" data for EURO-CLIMHIST has already been set up:

-   34,000 records referring to Switzerland in the period between 1525 and 1860 (PFISTER, 1985);

-   a considerable number of long temperature and precipitation series from stations in Europe (LAUTERBURG, 1990).
    In the early 1990s the data base will be enlarged by more than 30,000 records collected by G. and W. SCHWARZ-ZANETTI for Germany, France, Northern Italy, the Benelux Countries, Austria, and Switzerland for the period from the Middle Ages to 1525. Part of the data collected by the colleagues contributing to this volume will further enlarge our data base;

(5) the Swiss National Science Foundation has approved funding the data base located in Bern, the creation of which was suggested at the Second EPC Workshop in Mainz (March 1990). The team of historians and computer scientists at the Department for Regional and Environmental Studies at the Institute for History, University of Bern, has experience in the handling of complex data bases for various and often inconsistent historical entities of any type (e.g. PFISTER & SCHÜLE, 1992);

(6) The EPC Working Group is closely cooperating with IGBP (International Geosphere Biosphere Programme) which has recently decided to set up a Multi Proxy Mapping

Project including dendroclimatological, palynological, and documentary evidence. This project will start with a pilot study concentrating on the so-called "Maunder Minimum", i.e. the period from 1675-1715 (cp. Fig. 1). The pilot study provides an excellent opportunity for a scientific cooperation between EPC and IGBP. Within this framework EPC will organize a second workshop on "Documentary data and high resolution proxy data" to be held in September 1992 in Bern.

4. A new kind of cooperation in research is needed

The main obstacles in dealing with this approach are associated with the traditional ways of research cooperation. How can somebody, willing to submit his data to a data base for processing, be sure that he will indeed be the first to reap the rewards of his work? Who makes sure that his data will not be included in some global analysis even before he has completed his own regional study? A researcher who has taken the trouble of source gathering, of transcribing and coding his data, relies on a publication to gain academic credit. The latter cannot only be regarded as a selfish support for our tender ego; it is, and will remain, an important component influencing our income and future prospects.

Therefore, it must be ensured that the "owner" of a regional data set has the exclusive right for a first interpretation of his data in a regional context and for publishing the results. Cooperation between a researcher and EURO-CLIMHIST has to be based on a contract according to law, in which all the relevant points are to be agreed upon. This involves the services provided by EURO-CLIMHIST, the rights of the owners of data, and the conditions under which the data are to be integrated into the "public" part of EURO-CLIMHIST later on. This agreement should make sure that both partners will benefit from their cooperation.

The research partner will not be busy just inventing the wheel again. Instead of struggling to get an appropriate scheme for his analysis and spending a considerable amount of his time on computing work, he will be able to focus on a careful and subtle interpretation. At the end he will gain his academic credit from two publications: the regional study and the published version of the data. Additional credits will flow from his contribution to the reconstruction of weather patterns on a European basis, because he will also become a co-author of the synthesis to be made.

The data on which regional studies rely can be merged to reach a synthesis at the continental level. This attempt should be undertaken by an interdisciplinary group of historians, geographers, climatologists, botanists, and geophysicists etc. The main results could take the form of a synoptic mapping of outstanding anomalies and an analysis of shifts in the frequency of synoptic weather situations. From this evidence large-scale impacts upon the ecosystems and the societies could be assessed in a next step. Both studies could contribute to our understanding of the European climate system in the past - and in the present.

1689 August   English

2nd 10-day period (August 1689)
　　　Hungary: mostly sunny (11.) R:1359 (Kucajna T0P0) (S:RA-7716)
　　　CSFR: rain: heavy (11.) R:VA (Varnsdorf (CB: Central Bohemia) T2P3) (S:DO-0033)
　　　Hungary: mostly sunny (14.) R:1359 (Kucajna T0P0) (S:RA-7716)
　　　Hungary: warm (14.) R:1359 (Kucajna T0P0) (S:RA-7716)
　　　Hungary: rain: continuous (15.) R:1359 (Kucajna T0P0) (S:RA-7716) (->5624)
　　　Hungary: rain: continuous (16.) R:1415 (Majden (Torontál megye) T0P0) (S:RA-7716)
　　　Hungary: rain: continuous (17.) R:1415 (Majden (Torontál megye) T0P0) (S:RA-7716) (->5625)
　　　Hungary: mostly sunny (20.) R:679 (Orsova (Torda megye) T0P0) (S:RA-7716) (->5626)
　　　Switzerland: mainly rainy: some brightening R:06 (ZH,LU,AG-Mittelland T1P1) (S:PF-1871)

1689 August   German

zweite Dekade (August 1689)
　　　Hungary: vorwiegend sonnig (11.) R:1359 (Kucajna T0P0) (S:RA-7716)
　　　CSFR: Regen: stark (11.) R:VA (Varnsdorf (CB: Central Bohemia) T2P3) (S:DO-0033)
　　　Hungary: vorwiegend sonnig (14.) R:1359 (Kucajna T0P0) (S:RA-7716)
　　　Hungary: warm (14.) R:1359 (Kucajna T0P0) (S:RA-7716)
　　　Hungary: Regen: dauernd (15.) R:1359 (Kucajna T0P0) (S:RA-7716) (->5624)
　　　Hungary: Regen: dauernd (16.) R:1415 (Majden (Torontál megye) T0P0) (S:RA-7716)
　　　Hungary: Regen: dauernd (17.) R:1415 (Majden (Torontál megye) T0P0) (S:RA-7716) (->5625)
　　　Hungary: vorwiegend sonnig (20.) R:679 (Orsova (Torda megye) T0P0) (S:RA-7716) (->5626)
　　　Switzerland: vorwiegend Regen: vereinzelte Aufhellungen R:06 (ZH,LU,AG-Mittelland T1P1) (S:PF-
　　　　　　　　1871)

1689 srpen   Czech

druhá dekáda (srpen 1689)
　　　Hungary: vetsinou slunecno (11.) R:1359 (Kucajna T0P0) (S:RA-7716)
　　　CSFR: dést: sily dést, liják (11.) R:VA (Varnsdorf (CB: Central Bohemia) T2P3) (S:DO-0033)
　　　Hungary: vetsinou slunecno (14.) R:1359 (Kucajna T0P0) (S:RA-7716)
　　　Hungary: teplo (14.) R:1359 (Kucajna T0P0) (S:RA-7716)
　　　Hungary: dést: stály, dlouhotrvající dést (15.) R:1359 (Kucajna T0P0) (S:RA-7716) (->5624)
　　　Hungary: stály, dlouhotrvající dést (16.) R:1415 (Majden (Torontál megye) T0P0) (S:RA-7716)
　　　Hungary: stály, dlouhotrvající dést (17.) R:1415 (Majden (Torontál megye) T0P0) (S:RA-7716) (->5625)
　　　Hungary:vetsinou slunecno (20.) R:679 (Orsova (Torda megye) T0P0) (S:RA-7716) (->5626)
　　　Switzerland: prevázne destivo: ojedinelé vyjasnení R:06 (ZH,LU,AG-Mittelland T1P1) (S:PF-1871)

Fig. 1 Layout of a EURO-CLIMHIST printout (current version) in English, German, Czech, and Hungarian (output is also available in French and Italian). The example includes data from Hungary (L. Racz), C.S.F.R. (P. Dobrovolny), and Switzerland (C. Pfister) for the period from August 11 to 20, 1689. (The handling of the special characters for Czech and other European languages will be possible from spring 1992)

Footnotes

5624. <Eng,Time> exact hours: nuit;
5625. <Eng,Time> exact hours: nuit;
5626. <Eng,Time> period(to_date): 1689.08.23;

1689 Augustus   Hungarian

2. tiz napos szakasz (Augustus 1689)
    Hungary: többnyire napos idö (11.) R:1359 (Kucajna T0P0) (S:RA-7716)
    CSFR: esö: erös (11.) R:VA (Varnsdorf (CB: Central Bohemia) T2P3) (S:DO-0033)
    Hungary: többnyire napos idö (14.) R:1359 (Kucajna T0P0) (S:RA-7716)
    Hungary: meleg (14.) R:1359 (Kucajna T0P0) (S:RA-7716)
    Hungary: esö: tardòs (15.) R:1359 (Kucajna T0P0) (S:RA-7716) (->5624)
    Hungary: esö: tardòs (16.) R:1415 (Majden (Torontál megye) T0P0) (S:RA-7716)
    Hungary: esö: tardòs (17.) R:1415 (Majden (Torontál megye) T0P0) (S:RA-7716) (->5625)
    Hungary: többnyire napos idö (20.) R:679 (Orsova (Torda megye) T0P0) (S:RA-7716) (->5626)
    Switzerland: többnyire csapadékos: szòrvànyos derült idö R:06 (ZH,LU,AG-Mittelland T1P1) (S:PF-
        1871)

Sources
DO-0033: [Dobrovolny, Petr, Brno, CSFR] Palme Alois: Warnsdorf mis seinen historischen Denkwürdigkeiten
    von dessen Grundüng an bis zum Jahre 1850. In Comission bei dem J. Hamann in B. Leipa u.
    M. Adam in Rumburg, sowie bei dem Verfasser selbst zu haben. 49P

PF-1871: [Pfister, Christan, Bern, CH] Fries, Johann Heinrich (1639-1718). Weltliche, meist vaterländische
    geschichten. Zürich, Zentralbibliothek: B 186 a-f.

RA-7716: [Rasz, Lajos, Kecskemét, H] TöKöLI (Thököly) Imre és némely föbb híveinek naplói és emlékezetes
    írásai 1686-1705., közli Thaly Kálmán (Magyar Történelmi Emlékek II. oszt. írók XXIII. kötet),
    Pest 1868 (Tatalmazza Almády István, Bay Mihály és Dobay Zsigmond naplóit is)

In brackets are the individual days e.g. "(11)" = Aug. 11. "R" indicates the number of a region or a
place of observation; in brackets the corresponding names are provided. The numbers associated with
"T" (=temperature) and "P" (=precipitation) refer to the similo-fluctuative regions (cp. PFISTER &
LAUTERBURG, this volume). "S:" refers to the sources,"->" to the footnotes

Acknowledgement

This research is supported by the Swiss National Science Foundation and by the Swiss Bundesamt für Bildung und Wissenschaft (COST Programme).

References

Bradley, R. & Jones, P. (eds.) (1992). Climate since 1500 A.D. London

IGBP (1990): The International Geosphere-Biosphere Program. Global Change Report Nr. 12, Roy. Acad. Sci., Stockholm

Kington, J. (1988): The weather of the 1780s over Europe. Cambridge Univ. Press, Cambridge

Lamb, H. H. (1977): Climate: present, past and future. Vol. 2, Climatic history and the future. London

Lauterburg, A. (1990): Klimaschwankungen in Europa. Raum-zeitliche Untersuchungen in der Periode 1841-1960. Geogr. Bern. G 35, Bern

Pfister, C. (1984): Klimageschichte der Schweiz 1525-1860. Das Klima der Schweiz von 1525-1860 und seine Bedeutung in der Geschichte von Bevölkerung und Landwirt-schaft, 2 Vols., 3rd ed. 1988, Bern.

Pfister, C. (1985): EURO-CLIMHIST - a weather data bank for Central Europe 1525 to 1863. (May be ordered from METEOTEST, Fabrikstr. 29a, CH 3012 Bern, Switzer-land)

Pfister, C. & Schüle, H. (1992): Encompassing "Geo- Histoire". Methodological dimensions and historiographical implications of the BERNHIST interdisciplinary information system. In: van der Voort, R. (ed.): Proc. Tindberg Conference on History and Computing, July 1989, Amsterdam (in press)

Tagami, Y. & Fukaishi, K. (in press): Seasonal relationship and phases of climatic variation in Japan from the 17th to the 19th century. Proc. Int. Symp. Little Ice Age Climate organized by Tokyo Geographical Society, The Association of Japanese Geographers and the Study Group for the Past Climate Reconstruction, Tokyo

Addresses of the authors:

Prof. Dr. C. Pfister, Department for Regional and Environmental Studies at the Institute for History, University of Bern, Engehaldenstr. 4, CH-3012 Bern, Switzerland
H. Schüle, Department for Regional and Environmental Studies at the Institute for History, University of Bern, Engehaldenstr. 4, CH-3012 Bern, Switzerland

The climate as a factor of historical causation

Helge Salvesen

Summary

The starting point of the paper is the close connection between socio-cultural systems and the surrounding environment. The proposition is that the environment of a people is not exclusively characterized by the given natural conditions, but also by the structured ways in which a people organizes its existence. The climate belongs, however, to the more prominent given natural variables in diachronic investigations of socio-economic change in the long term. An account is given here of a number of methods, sources, and results concerned with climatic reconstruction in Scandinavia, and the problem of how climate relates to ideas on historical causation is discussed with reference to the importance attributed to the different types of cultures involved. The contention is that it is necessary to consider the climate as an impact factor limiting or offering possibilities of cultural choice, but which in itself does not determine a culture's response to climatic change. The climate may nevertheless function as a catalyst or have a retarding effect on the line of action chosen. Then, too, it is important to distinguish between the climate as a real factor of causation and a motive for institutionalized cultural changes.

Zusammenfassung

Ausgangspunkt des Aufsatzes ist die enge Verbindung zwischen sozio-kulturellen Systemen und der Umwelt. Hieraus folgt die Annahme, daß die ökologische Anpassung des Menschen nicht nur von den Naturverhältnissen abhängt, sondern auch von der strukturellen Kulturorganisation. Das Klima jedoch zählt zu den bedeutendsten Rahmenbedingungen für die kulturelle Anpassung. Es wird ein methodischer, quellenkritischer und realhistorischer Beitrag zur Rekonstruktion des Klimas von Skandinavien geliefert, wobei das Klima als historischer Erklärungsfaktor behandelt wird. Kulturunterschiedliche Anpassungsformen sind hierbei wichtige Variablen; das Klima muß jedoch als bestimmende Variable angesehen werden, die den Rahmen für die Möglichkeiten kultureller Entscheidungen absteckt, kulturelle Änderungen aber nicht determiniert. Das Klima kann die gewählte Kulturentwicklung fördern oder hemmen, es muß jedoch differenziert werden zwischen dem Klima als Ursache und dem Klima als Motiv für kulturellen Wandel.

1. Introduction

Man's situation within and relationship to his given natural surroundings are no field of research limited to natural scientists, nor are they open to the views of natural science alone. Using biology as the starting point, it seems to have been within social anthropology that culture and ecology first were aligned on a broader basis and considered in terms of their mutual possibilities and limitations, this even being the achievement of a Norwegian. In 1956 BARTH published his study on the ecological relations between ethnic groups in Swat (Northern Pakistan). Several Norwegian socio-ecological studies have later acquired the status of classics, among these KLEIVAN's (1962) short study "Ecological Change in Labrador" and BROX's (1966, 1969) process-analytical studies based primarily on Northern Norwegian material. These studies clearly show that social and cultural systems do not only exhibit close interrelationships and an inherent order, but also that they are closely linked to the surrounding natural environment.

This approach consequently breaks with the convention that "culture" and "society" exist in sharp contrast to "nature". On the other hand, their interrelationship may not be considered in terms of a simple natural determinism. Hence the social milieu of a particular people is not exclusively characterized by the given natural conditions, but also by the structured ways in which it organizes its existence and by those of other peoples and their activities.

By introducing the term "niche", defined as the situation of a group within the total environment and its relationship to the available resources and its fellow players, BARTH is able to explain how and why several ethnic groups can co-exist within the same area while exploiting different resources and reacting differently to external factors. Culture gives man the possibility to exploit certain niches in various ways, at the same time that it can render the utilization of other resources difficult or impossible, even though they are available. This implies that changes in the natural environment, e.g. climatic changes, do not affect all groups in the same manner.

Historians in particular have focussed on one of the given natural forces within the ecological spectrum, that is, on climate. To a great extent this can be explained with reference to the fact that historians, too, during the last 60-70 years have begun to show an interest in society as a whole, including social and economic history, that is, how people relate to one another and how in the widest possible sense they manage to stay alive.

Naturally, the number of people in an area, the area itself, the technological level, and the patterns of social organisation are important variables within this perspective. But among the variables of nature itself, the climate is - together with the soil and the topography - among the most important socio-economical premises. Together they form the social and natural resources exploited by man. A typical trait of the variables of nature itself is their relative stability with respect to the area chosen, at least they are more stable than social and technological factors normally are. In some respects the climate still occupies a special position, because it tends to vary more in time than other natural factors. If we get to know what the weather was like at different times, the historian will catch a glimpse of the side scenes on the stage of cultural history.

This perspective involves considering the climate both as a resource and a limitation for human enterprise and adaptability. UTTERSTRÖM (1955: 3) was among the first historians to arrive at this conclusion with respect to the relationship between climate, food production, and population figures.

Ever since MALTHUS and RICARDO, all discussions about the pressure on food supplies have started with the assumption that population is the active factor and nature the fixed one. This interpretation, however, can hardly be reconciled with modern scientific thought, especially if the problem is viewed in the long term.

Systematically considered, two possible approaches are available to the historian when studying the climate: firstly, it is comparatively simple to contribute to the reconstruction of the contours of meteorological change in the long term, secondly, there is the study of the climate as a means of finding explanations for economic, social or even political conditions in the past. The French historian LE ROY LADURIE (1973) can be seen as an exponent of the former approach, when he argues that the historian of the climate should come up in front and establish interdisciplinary cooperation between natural scientists aiming at the reconstruction of long-term climatic variations.

At first, the natural scientists may possibly consider the historian of climate an intruder, a confused son of Klio, but without nothing of value to tell them? Be this as it may. In that case the historian must try to overcome this irritation and endeavour to gain a reputation for his exclusive contribution.

The second application of climate history involves considering the relevance of the climate as a factor of historical causation: on the basis of established theories of climatic development, scientists of culture obtain data facilitating the discussion of the causes of social, economic, and political change. This is the approach which provides the focus of the present investigation. But I wish, nevertheless, to present some examples which will show that with respect to work with traditional historical sources, the expertise of the historian may offer valuable contributions to climatic history. Also, the historian's training in the study of sources may be useful both when evaluating the reliability of facts of climatic history, and when assessing whether they are independently based or based on circular arguments. When adopting the approach outlined above, it becomes necessary to consider the concepts of "climate" and "historical causation" in greater detail.

2. Methods, sources, and results in historical studies of the climate

The English climatologist LAMB (1982: 8) defines climate as follows: "By climate we mean the total experience of the weather at any place over some specific period of time". In the following, we will survey some of the relevant groups of sources, their proof value, and inherent margins of unreliability, offering examples of what they may disclose about the history of the climate in the Nordic countries. There is no room in the present paper, however, to give a full account of all the kinds of existing data; to serve that purpose there exist voluminous works of a general kind.

Apart from meteorological instrument readings (data) there are two main categories of "soft" testimonies to the climate in the past: (1) documentary material and (2) physical and biological data. Examples of documentary material are records in annals, chronicles, diaries, old inscriptions, records made by the Civil Service and the local administration concerning the State, the regions, individual communities, etc.

There probably are numerous such "inofficial" weather observations which are yet to be made accessible to research. In fact, it ought to be part of the historian's task to collect and interpret these data, rendering most of them accessible to the international research community. These data may then be collected in an international bank of meteorological data. This is probably one of the most important areas where historians can contribute directly to climatological research.

At this point I wish to mention an example of this kind of registration work undertaken at the University of Tromsø. the sources examined with a view to locate explicit and indirect information about the climate are *Diplomatarium Norvegicum* (D.N.), Norges gamle Love (N.G.L.), Islandske Annaler indtil 1578, and Konungs skuggsjá (Mirror for Kings). The registered data cover the time span from about 1200 and virtually till about 1430. Though the representativeness of the examined material is qualified by a considerable amount of uncertainty, examining the weather information provided by the Norwegian Medieval sources may nevertheless be an interesting pilot study. We do not, therefore, intend to emphasize the results, wishing instead to suggest some possible interpretations. We intend, however, to go further in this direction in future studies.

Generally speaking the Islandske Annaler can be said to contain a considerable number of explicit data referring to the weather, whereas D.N. and N.G.L. basically provide such information indirectly. All in all the survey does not seem to yield much information about climatic conditions in Medieval Norway. It may, however, be of interest to see how Medieval Norwegian men reflected on the climatic conditions. The information coming up in the examined materials concerns extreme conditions on a particular day or an entire summer or winter (Fig. 1). Most commonly there is talk about bad weather, often combined with talk about many dead cattle. Surprisingly often the winter weather is mentioned, and often in the form of severe frost or great quantities of snow, not uncommonly linked with the occurrence of large quantities of sea-ice during spring and early summer. Only quite rarely a good summer is mentioned. We should bear in mind, however, that the annals basically offer information about Iceland. The data can not readily be extended to refer to the conditions on the Scandinavian mainland, although it is reasonable to assume that a possible deterioration of the climate would have affected the entire Northeastern Atlantic area, when considering the large-scale meteorological conditions of circulation.

From about 1275 till about 1400 there are as many as twenty-four registrations of bad winters in a total of about fifty testimonies referring to winters with heavy snowfall or extreme cold. This hardly provides a firm basis for contrasting these registrations with those from the preceding and the succeeding periods. In fact, the registrations do not turn out to be equally complete for other periods, but for the period providing these data, it is evident that people quite frequently find that the snowfall is heavy in the extreme. To those who can reduce this to a system, these data possibly give contemporary reflections on the gradually more accepted, assumed fact that the last part of the thirteenth century and the fourteenth century were characterized by an unstable climate with frequent extreme weather conditions. It is also possible that reiterated statements to this effect dating from the middle of the thirteenth century and onwards, together with records of people being exempted from holiday prohibition in order to save their corn and hay, and the difficulties the Church had towards the end of the thirteenth century when collecting its tithe, may be interpreted to reflect a deteriorated climate for agriculture. In this respect, the mentioned shortages of grain in Hedmark and at Toten in 1293 are more convincing, because - provided it was conditioned by the climate - it would presuppose a bad climate over a period of several years. The reports from 1340 of a large number of abandoned farms and fellings close to the glaciers at Olden and Loen support this material, and the latter may be seen as an expression of glacier growth which parallels the problems in the areas adjacent to the Jostedal Glacier in the early eighteenth century. It is possible that a reduced production capacity on coastal farms before about 1700 can be coupled with a lowering of the water temperature, which may contribute to strengthening the documentation about the Little Ice Age.

In this connection it may be worth mentioning the attempts at coupling climate and economy in the long term. In particular one has attempted to couple climatic development with fluctuations in grain prices. The problem raised by the resulting fluctuations mainly consists in the difficulty of calculating the degree of climatic influence in relation to other variables which influence grain prices. These variables may briefly be summarized in terms of the size of the population in relation to the arable land available, mentality in food preference, political problems involving the distribution of grain, and the fact that many farmers were transferred from agricultural production to military service, etc. It is probably wise to resist relying too exclusively on any one kind of explanation, which is the danger incurred by experts in one particular field, be the chosen factor of causation the climate, the plague, or demographical developments. Social reality is determined by the interplay of a number of differently weighted factors.

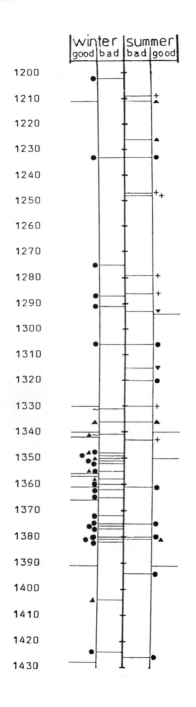

snowy winter
wet summer

cold winter
cool summer/with sea ice

dry winter
dry summer

considerable losses
of cattle

+ famine years

Fig. 1 Years with reports on good and/or bad summers and winters in the northern parts of the Nordic countries, especially in Iceland. "Good" and "bad" are my own standardized terms respectively for expressions like "the best winter within the memory of man", "mild winter", "good crops", on the one hand, and expressions like "severe frost", "snowy winter", "heavy rains", "much sea-ice", on the other. There is no particular reason to emphasize the number of registrations, as the figure must be considered in an overall perspective. It may reflect the time's reflections on the generally accepted fact that the latter part of the thirteenth century and the fourteenth century were chracterized by an unstable climate with frequent eruptions of extreme weather conditions

Among the physical and biological data about the climate in the past, one also finds the "fossile" remains of supposed connections between climatic fluctuations and the periodic fluctuations of certain physical natural phenomena, e.g. the attempts made to correlate climatic variations with the eleven-year cycle of the fluctuations in sun spot activity. Also, it has been noted that several changes in natural geography on earth influence the climate. The increase of CO_2 in the atmosphere caused by the burning of fossilized fuel is assumed to generate an increase in temperature, because the reflected heat radiation from the earth is partially assorbed by CO_2 and aqueous vapour (the so-called greenhouse effect). However, this does not necessarily imply a rise in temperature, because increased temperature will result in increased evaporation of the oceans which again will result in a thicker cloud cover, which finally may prevent too much radiation to pass through so that a cooler climate may be the result. Nor is it certain that the polar ice cap will be reduced so as to cause a rise in the water-level by several meters. The effect may also be a lowered sea level in the oceans if the temperature will continue to remain below 0°C at the poles. In that case the increased world-scale evaporation of the oceans would cause glacier growth around the poles. Additionally, we must consider that the entire global pattern of air and ocean water circulation will be influenced by temperature conditions in such a complex manner that a further discussion along these lines would easily turn this paper into an exercise in geophysics.

At this point something must be said about research in climatic history in general. The reconstruction of past climate is one of the most comprehensive interdisciplinary projects ever. In the same manner as the weather and the climate affect almost every aspect of our lives and environment, testimonies concerning climate become visible in a number of different sources. This does not imply that the climate by necessity offers an explanation that is equally valid as other accounts of human behavioural patterns. The research results seem moreover to cover large geographical areas in a fairly general manner, often extending to an entire country, or an entire continent. In addition, topography is of substantial importance to local historical conditions.

3. Historical causational thought related to climate

Descriptions of climatic history are primarily interesting to the historian in so far as climatic conditions correlate with social, economic, and political conditions, enabling the historian to follow the right track to viable explanations of social change. Let us consider how the climate enters into the thought of historical causation.

All statements on causes by necessity imply the counterfactual hypothesis that if the proposed cause was absent, the effects under discussion would not have occurred. This holds true regardless of whether we hold something to be the sole or a contributing cause. When a factor merely is a general premise at almost any time and in every place, it often becomes redundant as a factor of historical causation, no matter how necessary it may be. In this respect, even a concomitant factor of causation must in the least function as a catalyst or possess a retarding or reactionary effect. Provided that a deterioration of the climate is to be adduced as a factor of causation, say, in relation to the agrarian crisis in the Late Middle Ages, it must have (1) contributed to a surplus in the mortality rate exceeding that caused by the plagues, and/or (2) counteracted population growth. Also, a deteriorated climate must have been more marked after the plagues than before, if it were to produce these results, because - in the wake of a plague - people naturally moved to the best farms, as these had the richest soil and the largest safety margin with regard to climate variation.

Regardless of the counterfactual implication inherent in all arguments of historical causation, the recognition that there rarely exists a compelling logic to link perceived effects to causes implies that deciding on priorities always will involve an element of opinion and evaluation, or as it were, carry ethical implications. An example taken from historiography will illustrate this: writing an obituary for EDVARD BULL, senior, KOHT (1933) criticized his materialistically inclined colleague of having considered the climate as a factor of historical causation when treating the Late Medieval agrarian crisis.

At this point many will object that if the climate changes, this will influence social conditions. KOHT realized this, of course, but when deciding on the priorities among the factors of causation, we immediately reveal what powers we hold to be active in social change. Strong emphasis on climatic influence instil notions of human powerlessness: we are mere pawns in nature's grand game. Anyone who wishes to change the development of society, however, is not dissuaded by the natural conditions. The climate poses certain limits in the choices available, but several options generally exist. The selection of options is culturally conditioned, as the existing social, economic or political circumstances conditioned the particular response to the climatic change. We cannot stop the chain of historical causation by reference to the climate, but rather consider the climate as a datum of observation, inserting it as an impact factor on an equal footing with e.g. the level of taxation, and then look for the more fundamental factors of causation in the social, economic, or political conditions. This was probably the reasoning behind KOHT's critique of BULL's enthusiasm about climatic historical explanations of causality.

Contemporary agents only rarely perceive changes which emerge so gradually that they are not automatically reflected in the source materials. They would rather explain the patterns of their actions on the basis of motives relating to future expectations or fears, and not in terms of a natural scientific effect of a given cause. Within natural science it is an absolute requirement that cause precedes effect. To hear a thunderclap, it must have lightened. To the historian this becomes more complex. Because his objects of study, human beings, reflect on past and future, patterns of human activity and social change may even be determined by causes supposed to occur in the future, or even by causes which never appear, i.e. actions may be initiated by motives and not by causes. Thus human activities may as well have been motivated by expected or feared changes, as being the direct effect of past causes.

Within this context both an improvement in the climate and a climatic deterioration will be viewed differently depending on the way it is experienced by people in different social, economic and political situations. If in a pre-industrial farming community it is assumed to be feasible to continue production as of old, possible responses to a worsened climate may be to increase the cultivated area to compensate for the drop in productivity or to change the operational structure. If this is considered unrealistic, e.g. migration could become another pattern of response. Only in extreme cases people would die as the direct effect of climatic deterioration. The patterns of response to a climatic change may thus vary greatly depending on how people at the time consider their future prospects. Reversely, a given observable effect could be explained e.g. in terms of a deteriorated climate, a contraction of the cultivated area, a change in the operational structure, say from an emphasis on crop farming to cattle herding, or in terms of a migrational pattern from marginal to more favourable areas. What constitutes the problem is that the climate alone rarely offers an indication of the direction in which human adaptation will move. This is to a greater extent determined by the political, social, and economic conditions existing at a particular time. If this proves to be the case, the climate must be considered as a variable of pressure since it quite obviously can reinforce, slow down, or further a particular development.

In spite of this it is evident that the distribution of settlements is conditioned by the climate, when e.g. slopes facing south are more attractive than those facing north and the productivity of farms on high ground is lower than that of farms situated at sea level. These, however, are basically statistical priorities which seldom can contribute to elucidating historical changes, and they will apply in general whether the climate changes or not. But had changes in the climate been accompanied by corresponding significant changes in the pattern of settlement, this would have been sufficient to use the climate to account for changes of settlement. The correlations are, however, too uncertain to support such conclusions. To account for the actual settlement pattern and changes within it we need additional explanations.

Even though there turns out to be a high degree of correlation between climatic deterioration and changes in Norwegian agriculture after about 1950 both with regard to abandonment of farms and discontinuance of grain growing, very few people are likely to establish any direct causal relations between them. One set of factors, not least the political ones, has generally been operative to a greater or lesser extent. If we are to explain the situation of the individual farm and its possible discontinuance, individual factors of time and place must also be assessed. The usefulness of discriminating between causal explanations at different levels, demonstrating that the explanatory power of a single factor also depends on the chosen level of individuality, may be illustrated as follows.

The prospects of good fishing combined with certain possibilities for subsistence motivated commerce provide a sufficient explanation of why people in the Late Middle Ages migrated towards Northern Norway and its coasts. Other resources Northern Norway could offer were more easily accessible elsewhere, and within a society where the population figures already had been drastically reduced, the population was not driven towards the north owing to lack of space. When considering the settlement pattern formed in Northern Norway, the prospects offered by fishing become an insufficient factor of explanation. Fishing is possible almost everywhere and hence does not become a generally necessary premise. To explain the actual pattern of settlement one must therefore turn to additional explanations within a scale graded according to the degree of optimal resources a fisher-farmer culture is able to exploit. It is e.g. to be expected that the prospects of finding arable land and pasture for cattle are favoured to the prospects of fishing, if one presupposes a subsistence economy or a relatively weak subsistence motivated trade economy. Prospects of farming and pasture possibilities thus become sufficient explanations of the settlement pattern within the parts of Northern Norway where this is a realistic possibility in combination with fishing. This also holds true even when fishing is a highly important economic factor and the most important condition for any settlement at all. At the macro-level, however, the agricultural conditions only become a general necessary premise, when combined farming-fishing operations provide the only real alternative. Fishing thus becomes the most important factor of explanation. When we are to account for the location of individual farms, references to general factors of localisation will not suffice. Not all farms have equally optimal production conditions. The general preference of localisation can only be considered as the framework of the given conditions, but it cannot provide an adequate account of the location of a particular farm. This is also determined by other factors such as the soil at precisely this site: if it is in the vicinity of good fishing grounds for domestic fishing and good grazing lands for cattle and sheep, etc. These examples indicate how factors of causation can be relevant at an aggregational level, but redundant at another. If the climate remains unaltered, it therefore acquires power of explanation of social conditions at the same general level as bacilli which are the cause of a cold. In the same manner as fishing explains the shift in the settlement to Northern Norway in the Late Middle Ages, the climate may contribute to our understanding of the cultural differences existing between the various natural geographic zones. But changed climatic conditions within the same zone would possess virtually no force of explanation with regard to preferences in settlement localisation, which e.g. would be analogous to the number of cold-producing bacilli altering the factors which characterize the risk groups. That the number of people within the risk groups who catch a cold may change, is another matter. This phenomenon is interesting when the climate changes, too.

Whether the short-term climatic fluctuations with frequent extreme manifestation or the long-term fluctuations in the climate are the most decisive ones, is a much debated issue. Even in this case I believe the answer to depend on the options provided by the ecological margin with respect to social, economical, and political adaptability. A grain-growing economy react differently from a cattle herding economy, which again responds differently than a fishing or a hunting economy.

But in all arguments of this kind it is important to remember that the actual development would have become different without a possible change in the climate, if the climate is to be relevant in an account of historical causation. This is an important point of consideration e.g. in discussions of causal relationships concerning the Late Medieval agrarian crisis. Would people have migrated from the poorest to the richest and most central areas of settlement when the population was severely decimated during the Late Middle Ages if the climate had not become worse?

Most human societal structures are likely to be more vulnerable during frequent, recurring extreme anomalies of climate. So long as people face well-known challenges, they most often develop methods for tackling them. It is when the unexpected manifests itself with increased frequency, it becomes more difficult to meet the challenges. In a vulnerable society such frequent extreme manifestations could even become the direct triggering effect of social and economic change. On the other hand there is reason to believe that long-term climatic fluctuations, through their effects on the ecosystem in a more indirect way will lead to more fundamental structural changes in the organization of society. If e.g. a climatic change causes the stock of fish to increase in a region, this may cause people to adapt to an economy where fishing becomes more important than before. An explanation of such possible changes in the economic structure is not sufficient, if reference is made exclusively to the climate. Other social and economic factors must be taken into consideration. Local conditions must e.g. either lend themselves to the sale of or trade for other goods or the taxation must be sufficiency severe and require large payments in fish to make people interested in catching more fish than they themselves manage to consume. This is an elementary *conditio sine qua non* no matter how rich the fishing is. In this connection long-term fluctuations in the climate can only contribute to establishing possible or probable limits to human activity. In the same manner - and as mentioned above- the natural conditions, including climate, may offer good factors of explanation to understand cultural variation in terms of geography, which often may be equally important to the climatic historians as to the geographer. However, in this paper the focus of interest is the climate as a factor of explanation of long-term social, economic, and political changes within the individual culture forms established by different ethnic groups.

As a matter of fact the cultural conditions will figure fairly prominently and condition how people adapt to the natural environment. And what happens when established cultural forms are given other natural conditions under which to exist? The Icelandic geographer and geologist THORARINSSON (1958) has - albeit in an essay rather than a research paper - written an analysis of Icelandic communities of the Saga period, in which he presents a stimulating approach to the relationship between nature and culture. His point of departure is the unique position of Iceland in being the only large area on earth without an indigenous population to be colonized by Europeans. Hardly any herbivorous mammals existed on the island in the Postglacial period. Furthermore, greater and more substantial physical-geographical changes have taken place in this country than in almost any other country during the preceding 1000 years. THORARINSSON still warns against overestimating these natural factors when attempting to understand Icelandic culture, though Iceland in terms of its natural geographic placing lies on the extreme limits for habitation in civilized societies.

In the majority of new areas colonized by Europeans, they encountered natives who had adapted to the natural environment. The native had lived in a situation of ecological equilibrium and they were able to teach the newcomers a lot. This was not the case in Iceland, where the newcomers could only rely on their own imported culture. Many of the settlers came from areas where grain-growing formed the basis of economic life. Their first effort upon arrival therefore was to till the land and sow grain, sometimes after having burned the birch woods as they often had done at home. Pollen analyses show that they first tried to grow oats, but later turned to barley. Gradually grain growing came to take place exclusively in the south and the southwest, but even here it gradually declined to the point of almost disappearing in the middle of the sixteenth century. The natural scientist would easily be able to produce arguments in support of this being caused by a demonstrably deteriorating climate from the thirteenth century and onwards.

THORARINSSON does on the other hand view this in a more humanistic perspective, as it were. Without rejecting the possible effects of a deteriorated climate, he draws attention to the situation arising when people adapted to a natural environment capable of bearing a substantially tougher exploitation entered into this extremely marginal arena. The inevitable result we see in the serious consequences for the Icelandic natural resources. He rather prefers, therefore, to connect the Icelanders' slow abandonment of grain-growing with their lack of teachers and the accordingly slow process of learning and changing their mental outlook, than to interpret it as the direct effect of a deteriorated climate. The culture pattern of the settlers, therefore, was as badly suited to the Icelandic natural conditions in terms of ecology, as that of the Icelanders of later centuries has been.

According to THORARINSSON, the Icelanders were stubborn and slow learners, and one may well ask how willing man is to learn a new culture. In his opinion the Norse settlement in Greenland gives an indication of man's low adaptability, and the differences between the natural conditions at Austerbygd and Vesterbygd in Greenland and the settlements in Northwestern Iceland are small. One cannot but observe that the Inuits are much better adapted to the natural conditions in terms of their pattern of living, clothing, etc., than the Norse settlers. For cultural reasons the Inuits were therefore much more able to cope with a tougher climate than the settlers. Lower temperatures would lead the arctic animals which they hunted closer to their settlements, thus increasing their supply of food, whereas the Norse population without a comparable flexible ability to adapt would face deteriorating living conditions. THORARINSSON argues that the technological culture in Iceland never became fully national in the sense that it never learnt how to adapt to the Icelandic natural environment. Neither did the Icelanders learn to dress according to the wet and cold climate. Their shoes were less suitable than those of other peoples living in a correspondingly cold climate. Neither did they in times of famine completely learn how to utilize the Icelandic larder, nor were their fishing tackles particularly advanced. Perhaps they sought, THORARINSSON proposes, refuge from reality in their pursuit of the Muses...

If the climate, so it appears to me, is to be counted as a relevant factor of historical causation, it must be weighted according to the relevant type of climatic change and the specific

type of culture should also be considered. Short-term fluctuations in the form of frequent extreme manifestations may trigger off society changes by causing the closing down of old ecological niches. People being unprepared to face what hitherto has been considered to be improbable, will not find time to adapt their social, economic, and political organization to the changing conditions. This type of climatic change will acquire the same status as a causal explanation as other disaster theories involving plagues, important political decisions, natural disasters, etc., i.e. as a *diabolus ex machina*. In these cases there will often be a direct relationship of cause and effect between climatic change and the social consequences, but - as indicated above - the culture pattern of a few ethnic groups makes them better prepared than other to tackle such frequent extreme weather conditions. The effects of the same climatic changes may therefore vary between one culture pattern and the other. It becomes particularly important to remember this when different ethnic groups stay in one area, say, a Sámi nomadic economy and a Scandinavian agricultural economy.

Long-term variations in climate will contribute to bringing about more fundamental structural changes. This is the case when the climate influences the ecosystem so as to make people consider their situation and future prospects in order to find a way to adapt structurally to the changes in the short term.

The way to adapt to new natural conditions depends on the degree of pressure on the resources inscribed into the culture pattern practised by the particular ethnic group. Then, too, long-term climatic variations will in the main function as a catalyst or a restraining element in changes in the culture pattern, posing theoretical boundaries for possible options of culture without being neither *diabolus* nor *deus ex machina*. This in turn entails realizing the problem of inferring from effect back to cause, i.e. the difficulty of reading climatic changes directly in the changes observed in human societies. A different issue is the fact that long-term fluctuations are constituted by aggregated individual occurrences, so that systematic changes often will appear in the form of short-term variations. This will also place short-term variations in a somewhat different category than other disaster factors. If several bad years are the effect of systematic changes, it will be more difficult to resume the former economic activities upon a spell of bad years, than e.g. after an earthquake.

In this connection it is important to realize that variations in the culture pattern within a given culture form may be restricted, but also to see that cultural barriers are so great that an ethnic group may well see how another culture pattern manages to cope more successfully with a shared problem, without even reflecting on the possibility of changing its own culture pattern. Examples that come readily to mind are the Inuit hunting culture and the Norse agricultural culture in Greenland. We consequently find very few cultural shifts recorded in human history; important examples are the agrarian revolution and the industrial revolution. The normal situation is to find few changes involving structural reorientation within a culture pattern. The fact is that people practise a given culture form as long as possible hoping that the conditions will change for the better. When in the end the shift becomes inevitable, it is uncertain whether there are time and sufficient resources left for a reorientation.

I disassociate myself from classical natural determinism and take exception to the existence of a mechanical connection between nature and culture, where nature is given a privileged position in explanations. I rather wish to view nature as a pressure variable which establishes boundaries and opens up possibilities of cultural choice. Of course, this does not imply that to the historian climatic history is given low priority, nor that it is insignificant in questions of culture.

Still, it is important to distinguish between the climate as an actual factor of causation and the climate as a motive behind institutionalized changes. Because the patterns of human activity are culturally conditioned, it is essential to separate the probable from the possible. All cultures do not race and bet on all horses. If the climate facilitates a particular social adaptation, it does not necessarily follow that the adaptation is probable. In the same manner, the motive behind a social action need not be initiated according to a simple pattern of action and reaction. Often the climate will be a concomitant causal factor, functioning either as a catalyst or a restraining element in the process, without determining *per se* the solution the particular culture will choose in its response to climatic change.

It is not possible to explain the drama of culture history solely in terms of action and reaction on a simple formula of 1:1. Climate and culture must be located within a model of complex interplay on a par with arguments about how cultural conditions will influence it and how fast a population increases after an epidemic plague. The potential procreative powers and the potentially available food resources merely provide a theoretical framework.

Acknowledgement

Reinhard Mook, Stein Aanderaa, and Jörn Sandnes greatly assisted me in constructive discussions. Geir Remen carried out the registration work which is the basis of Fig. 1. Roy Eriksen rendered the article into English. All are herewith cordially thanked.

References

BARTH, F. (1956): Ecological relationship of ethnic groups in Swat, North Pakistan. Am. Anthropol. 38, No. 6
BROX, O. (1966): Hva skjer i Nord-Norge? En studie i norsk utkantpolitikk. Pax, Oslo.
BROX, O. (1969): Norsk landbruk og verdens matproblem. In: Brox, O. (ed.): Norsk landbruk, utvikling eller avvikling. Pax, Oslo
KLEIVAN, H. (1962): Økologisk endring i Labrador. Naturen 86/4, 200-213
KOHT, H. (1933): Edv. Bull. Scandia, Vol. VI
LAMB, H. H. (1982): Climate, history and the modern world. Methuen, London & New York

LE ROY LADURIE, E. (1973): Le climat: L'histoire de la pluie et du beau temps. Le territoire de l'homme, Paris

THORARINSSON, S. (1958): Iceland in the Saga Period. Some geographical aspects. Third Viking congress Reykjavik 1956. 'Arbók hins íslenzka fornleifafélags fylgirit, Reykjavik, 13-24

UTTERSTRÖM, G. (1955): Climatic fluctuations and population problems in early modern history. Scand. Econ. Hist. Rev. 3/1

Address of the author:

Dr. H. Salvesen, University Library, University of Tromsø, N-9000 Tromsø, Norway

Coding climate proxy information for the EURO-CLIMHIST Data Base

Hannes Schüle & Christian Pfister, University of Bern, with amendments by Gabriela and Werner Schwarz-Zanetti and Stefan Militzer

CONTENTS

1. Introduction

The EURO-CLIMHIST data base is a comprehensive tool for managing, analyzing and displaying climatic high resolution proxy information from natural and documentary archives. The exchange of data between individual researchers and between data bases on different levels of analysis (regional, national, continental, global) requires a general agreement on certain standards. This codebook describes the preliminary steps required for setting up the processing of information from documentary sources within the EURO-CLIMHIST data base. A numerical code was conceived to facilitate the analysis of descriptive information contained in documentary sources and to make it independent of the source language. The EURO-CLIMHIST data base procedures allow coded information to be displayed together with its interpretation in a comprehensive way in any language for which a translation routine has been previously created.

The original version of this codebook and the underlying software was devised by CHRISTIAN PFISTER in the late 1970s. In the 1980s it was adapted to data from Medieval Europe by GABRIELA and WERNER SCHWARZ-ZANETTI. This version restructured the codebook to make its application easier, to rationalize the creation of new language routines and to allow a coding which is closer to the source content. Flexible solutions were deliberately sought, because it is evident that this version will have to be amended in close cooperation between the users and the EURO-CLIMHIST staff.

Depending on the type of data, partners of EURO-CLIMHIST will have to prepare the following files (see Fig. 1)

(1) a data file
(2) a source reference file
(3) a place reference file
(4) several statistics reference files (optional).

The data file contains the coded observations, the source reference file contains the attributes that define the source and its author, the place reference file contains the attributes needed to define the place of observation. Statistics reference files are required to include the result of statistical analyses that have been made on time series outside EURO-CLIMHIST (see section 5). If no analyses of this kind are involved, these files may be omitted.

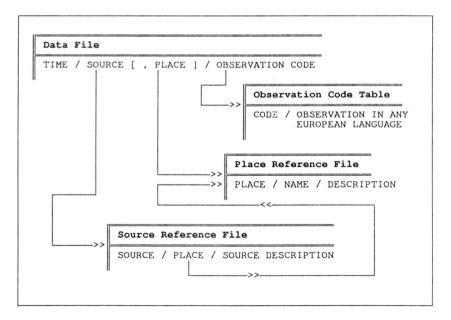

Fig. 1 Relations between data file, source reference file and place reference file

2. The standard data file

2.1 General structure and main conventions

2.1.1 Set option

At the beginning of a standard data file general defaults that refer to all cases (records) in the file may be specified using a **Set Option**: e.g. set COUNTRY = Denmark for a data file which contains mostly data from Denmark (see section 4). Consequently: Set OWNER = XXXX designates the "owner" of the source.

The user can also create short codes for observations that occur frequently in his sources and have a complex structure. e.g. set 31.112 = 91 to refer to winter wheat (see section 6.9).

2.1.2 General structure

A record can be of unlimited length. It ends when a line feed sign is encountered (<CT><LF>). Any **record** is made of several **fields** that are separated by a slash (/). Square brackets ([,]) are used in the following examples for designating optional fields. Square brackets can also be used in the footnotes according to standard editing rules of textual sources.

TIME SPECIFICATION / SOURCE CODE [, PLACE CODE] / CODED OBSERVATIONS [/* FOOTNOTE]

Thus, a record comprises at least a time specification, a source code and a coded observation (see the hypothetical example 1):

Example 1   **1709.S1 / 3332 / 12.1.1**

Any field contains one **code** at least, that may be made of several **code groups**. Code groups are linked by a full stop.

Within a field, several codes may be enumerated, separated by a comma (,). Because the author of the source (see example 2) specifies that his report refers not only to the place of observation, but to Switzerland and Germany as a whole, two country codes - 41,49 - were added to the source code. Additional information (such as a footnote) is always introduced with slash and star (/*) at the end of a record.

> **Example 2**   1709.S1 / 3332, 41, 49 / 12.1.1 /* <S,G> Dieser Winter war
> entsetzlich kalt allhier bei uns und auch in allen
> deutschen Landen <SA,E> This winter was extremely
> cold all over Switzerland and Germany

2.1.3 Delimiters

In addition to the slash (/) and the comma (,) the following delimiters are used: the semi-colon (;) precedes **code amendments** such as the **hour** in the time specification (see section 2.2) and the **scale** or **intensity** parameters in the coded observations (see section 2.4.2).

Text specifications referring to **footnotes** or **other text** are included in cornered brackets, e.g. <SA,E> which means that the following is an abstract of the source in English (see section 2.5).

Blanks are not required before and after a delimiter.

2.1.4 Copying options

Usually, a large number of details contained in a specific source are coded at the same time. In the EURO-CLIMHIST coding system the source code has only to be entered if a new source starts. Similarly, when observations from the same year or the same month are coded in chronological order, year and month must not be repeated unless they deviate from those in the previous record(s). Furthermore, all observation codes that refer to the same time and to the same place from the same source can be included in one record.

Elements of the time specification field may be copied using the full stop (.) or the double full stop (..) option (see section 2.2): the two full stops in the time parameter copy year and month from the previous record. A quotation mark (") copies the text from the first record. It is necessary to use different structures to copy time, source and textual information from the previous record. If a researcher enters a personal comment regarding a specific time and a specific place, the source code "0" must be used, followed by a comma and the code for the place.

Source codes may be copied using the double slash (//) (see example 3). If no source code is entered, the system assumes that the source code from the previous record is still active.

> **Example 3.1**   1709.S1 / 3332 / 12.1.1

> **Example 3.2**   .S4 / / 41.2.15;4

The same source provides two observations for 1709. In example 3.2 the year is copied by (.) and the source is copied by (//) from example 3.1.

A SOURCE text may contain both details with regard to another time or to another place. If more than one observation coded refers to the same TEXT, the text is entered with the first observation, and a quotation mark (") can be used for the following one(s).

The quotation mark (") is used to copy a footnote (see example 4)

Example 4.1	1709.S1 / 3332, 41, 49 / 12.1.1. /* <SA,E> This winter was extremely cold all over Switzerland and Germany and the Rhine was frozen at Basel in early January

Example 4.2	.01.P1 / / 22.7 /* "

In example 4.1 and 4.2 the year and the source are the same. Therefore they are copied (see example 3). Because the English summary of the footnote refers to both observations, it is copied using (/* ").

2.2 Time specification

TIME can be an exact date or another time interval (e.g. week, month, season, etc). It must refer to a dating style (explicitly or by default) and can include an indicator of uncertainty.

Time parameters are coded as follows: (see example 5)

Year:	to be given A.D. For years before the beginning of the Christian style a solution will be sought.
Month:	From 1 to 12 (January to December);
Season:	S1 (winter: December till February); winter is always coded in the year in which January falls. S2 (spring: March till May) S3 (summer: June till August) S4 (autumn: September till November)

Ten day periods within a month: D1 (1st to 10th), D2 (11th to 20th), D3 (21st to 31st); If a ten day period does not result from a statistical analysis of daily observations, it is assumed not to be precise.

Five day periods within a month: P1 (1st to 5th), P2 (6th to 10th)..... to P6 (26th to 31st).

| Days: | day of a month (from 1 to 31). |

| Parts of day: | ;m (morning), ;d (daytime), ;p (afternoon), ;e (evening), ;n (previous night) |

| Hours: | 0-24, introduced by a semicolon (see example 5.6) |

Example 5.1	"winter": 1709.S1
Example 5.2	"December": 1708.12
Example 5.3	"Christmas" 1708.12.D3
Example 5.4	"Christmas" 1708.12.P5
Example 5.5	exact date: 1708.12.24
Example 5.6	date and time: 1708.12.24;14

Example 5 displays the graduation for time specification: its accuracy depends on the quality of the observation: if the source just specifies the season -i.e. winter - the year is that in which January falls - (see example 5.1). If the date is given by a Saint's name or by a religious festival (e.g. "Christmas") the date is assumed to be approximate. The researcher then decides whether he prefers the ten day period (example 5.3.) or the five day period (example 5.4). If the hour of the observation is given, such as in some early instrumental diaries, a semicolon has to precede the indication (example 5.6)

Dating Style: Is defined in the source reference file (see 3.). It has only to be given if it deviates from this definition for a particular observation.

If a period between two dates is indicated, only the changing parts of the date have to be re-specified:

Year.month.day1-day2 (example 6.1)
year.month.day1-month2.day2 (example 6.2)

Example 6.1	1708.12.24-31
Example 6.2	1708.11.2-1708.12.24
Example 7.1	1708.12.24-2.14 [of 1709]/
Example 7.2	1708.12.D3-2.P3 [of 1709]/

If the month specified in the second position - i.e. February (see example 7.1) - precedes the one specified in the first place -i.e. December- in the calendar year, it is assumed that the second date refers to the following year - i.e. 1609. In the same way the indication with ten day periods and five day periods may be used (see example 7.2).

Example 8.1	1708.11.14/
Example 8.2	.12.24/
Example 8.3	.. 25/

The repetition of the year and the month may be avoided by using a full stop (.) or a double full stop (..) of the copying option (see section 2.1.4). In example 8.2 the year is copied from the preceding example 8.1, in example 8.3 both the year and the month are copied from the preceding observation.

2.3 Specification of source code and place of observation

SOURCE CODE is a numerical code pointing to a source in the source reference file (see section 3.). A two letter code for every user (assigned by the EURO-CLIMHIST staff) is added as a prefix - e.g. PF-1871 or RA-7716. This composite code not only unmistakably identifies any source in the whole data base, but it also designates "ownership" of a source which is important for the exchange of data.

PLACE CODE is a numerical code pointing to a spatial unit in the place reference file. This code is already defined by the SOURCE CODE via the source reference file (see section 3.). It needs only to be specified if it deviates from this definition (see example 2). The COUNTRY CODE defined by the SET option (see section 2.1.1) is automatically assigned.

2.4 The coding of observations

2.4.1 General structure

OBSERVATIONS are coded according to the list of observations (see section 6). The codes are built up from groups that are linked together by a full stop (see section 2.1). Every **key group** comprises all features of the same nature e.g. 13: "precipitation" or 41: "weather impacts". Every key group is subdivided by specifications, that may be subdivided again in specifications of specifications. In addition special codes may be added after a semicolon (see section 2.4.2). The general form is as follows:

"GROUP"."SPECIFICATION_1"[."SPECIFICATION_2"] [; Special Codes]

The report of an observer that it was bitterly cold from "Christmas" to "mid February" reads in the code as follows (see example 9).

Example 9   **1708.12.D3-2.P3 / 4556 / 12.3**

The key group 12 designates temperatures, 3 is for "cold" (see section 6). The emphasis given by the observer should not be expressed in the code unless it is corroborated by a proxy indicator e.g. the freezing over of a lake or river.

2.4.2 Special codes

There are three kinds of special codes: the intensity code, the relative time code and the amount or quality indicator. The intensity code and the relative time are always preceded by a semicolon.

The intensity code is used to indicate the relative intensity of a feature such as the magnitude of damage from a weather impact, the relative increase or slump of prices or the amount of imports or exports. It extends from 1 to 4. The default is 2 which is assumed if no specification is made in the source and need not be coded.

An observer reports that many vines in his region were completely destroyed by the harsh frost during the winter of 1708/09. The coded version of this observation would be as follows (example 10):

Example 10   **1709.S1 / 0045 / 41.2.15;4**

The code is made up by 3 components: the key group 41 (weather impacts), a specification_1 for the cause of the impact -i.e. frost - and a specification_2 for the material or the living structure that suffered from the impact - i.e. grapevines (see section 6.). The intensity code 4 is set, because the death of many plants is reported.

The same observer reports, that in the following autumn the price of wine rose sharply (see example 11) because considerable amounts of foreign wine had to be imported (see example 12).

Example 11	1709.S4 / 0045 / 53.35;4
Example 12	1709.S4 / 0045 / 54.35;3

The key group 53 designates a rise in prices, the key group 54 stands for imports; specification_1 - wine- is the same for both. Example 11 and example 12 may of course be merged in the coding (see section 2.4.3.).

The intensity code may also be used to qualify a weather spell (see example 13)

GENERAL CONDITION.[SECONDARY CONDITION] [[,-"OTHER ADDITIONAL DETAILED INFORMATION]] [;INTENSITY]

Example 13	1616.6 / 0878 / 17.1;4

The author of source 0878 emphasizes that he saw hardly a cloud during the entire month of June, 1616. Thus, the intensity code 4 is attributed.

This system is quite flexible but does on the other hand allow nonsense codes, such as

> 17.generally cloudy.some clouds;
> 17.generally sunny.some sunshine;

Thus, the entered codes are to be checked for such illegal combinations (see section 6).

The **relative time code** is used to indicate the interpretation which the author of a source attributes to an event compared to his standard for "normal conditions". It extends from 1 (extremely early) to 9 (extremely late), 5 being the average time. The relative time code may only be used if the source mentions it. Otherwise the relative time is to be computed from the analysis of time series.

An author has noted that in 1783 cherry trees were in full bloom on February 17. According to his experience, this is "very early" (see example 14).

Example 14	1783.2.17 / / 31.23.12;2

Because his statement might be subjective the code ;2 is given; code ;3 is only used if objective information is found, e.g. from the analysis of phenological time series! The relative time code can be used whether a precise date is known or not.

The relative amount/quality indicator has the same structure as the relative time code, except that it refers to the amount or to the quality of a crop (see section 6., key group 56); it is part of the code and has not to be added with a semicolon.

Example 15.1	1709.S4 / 0045 / 56.1.2

The author of example 15.1 has stated that in 1709 the grain harvest was very small.

For the vinegrapes both quantity and quality -i.e. the sugar content - are used as climatic proxy information. The key group 57 (see section 6) allows the combination of two parameters (see example 15.2).

Example 15.2	1709.S4 / 0045 / 57.1.5

This author specifies that whereas only a few grapes were obtained in an entire vineyard, quality was mediocre.

2.4.3   The enumeration of observations

In the context of a climatic anomaly, a long range of unusual effects is often reported for the same time interval. In order to prevent duplicating time specifications and source codes, groups may be enumerated in the following general way:

TIME SPECIFICATION / SOURCE CODE / X1.Y1.Z1, GX2.Y2.Z2

The observations are separated by a comma. If a new group begins a "G" has to precede the observation, to make the statement clear (see example 16).

Example 16	1817.6.D3 / 0957 / 71.2.92., G25.3., G25.8

An author reports for the last ten day period of June, 1817, that a lake flooded its lakeside and a large river overflowed its banks as a consequence of an extraordinary strong snowmelt in the mountains. When enumerating observations, the intensity code has always to be repeated (see example 17).

Example 17	1709.S4 / 0045 / 53.35;4, G54.35;3

Example 17 is a combination of the examples 11 and 12.

2.5   Footnotes and other text

Notice that the transcription of a footnote is not to be included in quotation marks, because this sign is used as cascade sign for duplicating footnotes (see section 2.1, example 4).

SOURCE TEXT is any textual extract from the source and is always entered, as the text might give hints for the interpretation or evaluation of the observation concerned later on. Source text not containing codeable observations can be entered too, using a "zero" weather code (see example 18).

Example 18	1709.12.24 / 0045 / 0 /* <PC,E> On Christmas evening the city was attacked by the French army

Such a text is always carried through the programs and edited as a footnote in chronological order.

OTHER TEXT is any textual information other than original source text. It is handled the same way as SOURCE TEXT, but it can be entered with a "zero" source code and a "zero" weather code at the same time (see example 19).

Example 19	1709/0/0 /* <C,E> Check the accuracy of all sources

Additionally TEXT can be classified to allow a selective suppression of parts of it for the final edition. TEXT can be preceded by **classifying** information within <>-brackets. The first classification always states the type of text: <S> for "source", <SA> "source abstract", <ST> "translated source", <C> "comment", <PC> "personal comment" etc.), the second the language of the text (see example 2). TEXT can also contain editing information such as <new_line> <tab> etc.

2.6 Uncertainty in time, place or observation code

Uncertainties of any kind are indicated with one or two hashes in brackets following the date, time, place or observation code concerned: (#) or (##). The uncertainty in the examples concern:

19.1a	the date
19.1b	the year (the source states a precise day of a month, the year is uncertain)
19.1c	the period as a whole
19.1d	the starting date of a period (" ... during last week the cherries came in full blossom ... ")
19.2	the place (a place mentioned cannot be assigned with certainty)
19.3a	the observation code
19.3b	the plants concerned (" ... the trees came in full blossom ..."; only from the context can it be assumed that cherry trees are meant)

Example 19.1a	1783.2.17 (#) / / 31.23.12;2
Example 19.1b	1783(#).2.17 / / 31.23.12;2
Example 19.1c	1783.2.10-17 (#) / / 31.23.12;2
Example 19.1d	1783.2.10(#)-17 / / 31.23.12;2
Example 19.2	1783.2.17 / ,645(#) / 31.23.12;2
Example 19.3a	1783.2.17 / ,645 / 31.23.12;2(#)
Example 19.3b	1783.2.17 / / 31.23(#).12;2

3. Source reference file

The file with the source references contains all the relevant information about the source and the author in the form:

SOURCE CODE / PLACE CODE / RELIABILITY / YEAR OF BIRTH AND DEATH OF THE AUTHOR / STYLE OF DATING / BIBLIOGRAPHICAL REFERENCES /* COMMENTS

Sources are numbered from 0001 to 9999.

The PLACE CODE is defined in the place reference file (see section 4).

The RELIABILITY code contains an assessment of the reliability of the author:

0 not yet classified
1 first class source
2 second class source
3 unreliable.

The author's year of birth and death are separated by a slash ("/") (uncertainties are indicated by a hash in brackets). In processing the data the system then checks and indicates automatically whether a source is contemporary or not. If the author is not known, a shortened name of the source is entered instead and its time of origin is given as a substitute for the year of the author's death. A life time of 30 years is assumed by the system for an unknown author.

Example 20	8023 / PLZ5300 / 2 / 1584(#)-1645 / J / Spangenberg, Carl, Sächsische Chronica. - Frankfurt 1635. Edited by Hans Staufer. Leipzig 1878 /* Spangenberg was chaplain at the court of the Count of Mansfeld. See: Allgemeine Deutsche Biographie. München 1967ff.

In this example, the German postal code (PLZ=Postleitzahl) for Frankfurt is used which points to the place reference file (see section 4). The year of birth is not certain. The dating style is Julian (J) and a short text about the author includes a bibliographical hint for further information.

Dating Style: The default is Gregorian (not to be specified). Other dating styles such as Julian (J) will have to be defined in cooperation with the users of the codebook.

4. The place reference file

The file with the place references contains all the relevant information about the place in the form:

COUNTRY / PLACE CODE / PLACE NAME / METEOROLOGICAL REGION / ALTITUDE A.S.L. / SIMILO-FLUCTUATIVE AREA / COORDINATES /* FURTHER INFORMATION

Some information contained in this field will be used for improving the interpretation: the meteorological region within the country, the altitude (in m above sea-level) and the similo-fluctuative area. The meteorological regions should be provided by the meteorological services. Similo-fluctuative areas are spatial units in which year-to-year fluctuations of seasonal temperature and precipitation were similar over the last 150-200 years (LAUTERBURG, 1990; PFISTER & LAUTERBURG, 1992). They are used to comprise data within certain parts of Europe in a comprehensive way. The similo-fluctuative areas are provided by the EURO-CLIMHIST staff according to the location of a given place.

The coordinates are provided to permit an automatic mapping. For this reason the place codes should be transferred from spatial codes that are already defined from geographical or statistical surveys of the country concerned. A large number of data such as coordinates can be transmitted from existing data bases.

The coordinates refer either to the internal coordinate system of a country or to world coordinates. No example is given here since the spatial coding system, the division of a country into climate regions, the assignment of similo-fluctuative areas, the coordinate system and the mapping facilities still need to be discussed with each researcher or research group for each country.

5. The statistics reference files

Statistics reference files are required to compute temperature and precipitation indices from early instrumental series and from parameters obtained from non-instrumental diaries (such as the number of rainy days). They define duodecile distributions for a "normal period" in the twentieth century, if possible the 1901-60 period. For every "historical series" a reference station must be selected and the values of its duodecile distribution have to be included in the statistics reference file.

6. List of observation codes (version 1.0)

6.0 Early instrumental measurements

Prior to being included in EURO-CLIMHIST early instrumental measurements will have to be submitted to statistical analysis. For this reason no code is provided at the moment. Special cases should be discussed with the EURO-CLIMHIST staff.

6.1   Direct weather observations

6.11   *Air /Sky*

11.1	wind
11.2	cloud cover
11.3	fog
11.4	thunderstorm
11.5	aurora borealis
11.6	other atmospheric phenomena

6.1.1 a)   Specification

11.1	wind
11.1	direction;intensity

Indicate the direction with letters (N, NE, S, SSW etc), the intensity using the ;1..;4 codes (see section 2.4.2). Intensity ;4 should only be coded if considerable damage is reported.

Example 21	1616.6.9 / 0089 / 11.1.S;3(=very strong S wind)

Use set options to code the three to four wind directions in your region (see section 2.1.1.)

11.2.2	sunny
11.2.3	mostly sunny
11.2.5	partially cloudy
11.2.51	variable
11.2.7	mainly cloudy
11.2.8	totally cloudy
11.3.1	morning fog
11.3.2	fog all day
11.4	thunderstorm
11.5	aurora borealis
11.6	other atmospheric phenomena

6.1.2   *Thermic conditions*

12.1	extremely cold'
12.2	very cold
12.3	cold
12.3.1	frost
12.3.2	hoar frost

12.4	cool
12.5	average
12.6	mild
12.7	warm
12.8	hot
12.9	extremely hot

6.1.3   Precipitation

13.0	dry
13.1	rain
13.2	snowfall
13.3	snowfall and rain
13.4	hail
13.5	sleet
13.6	drizzle

6.1.3 a) Specification

13.1.0	rain of unknown duration and intensity
13.1.1	short rain
13.1.2	long rain
13.1.3	continuous rain
13.2.0	snowfall of unknown duration and intensity
13.2.1	short snowfall
13.2.2	long snowfall
13.2.3	continuous snowfall
13.3.0	snowfall and rain

6.1.7   General character of atmospheric conditions

This group describes the general weather situation over a period of several days (five or ten day period), over an entire month or an entire season. It allows both the coding of the general conditions and additional occurrences of other weather (such as "some rainy days" in a period of "mainly sunny" weather) as well as making use of the intensity codes (see section 2.4.2). The latter can be used for the dominant weather condition (see example 22)

Example 22.1	1540.S3/0989/17.1;3 (= entire summer very sunny) or for the secondary weather condition
Example 22.2	1617.10.D3/8787/17.1.71;1 (= whole ten day period mainly sunny with some fog in the morning).

If a secondary weather condition is coded, the intensity code relates to this one.

6.1.7 a)   General weather description

17.0	unknown
17.1	mainly sunny
17.2	mainly cloudy
17.3	variable
17.4	mainly rainy
17.5	mainly snowfall
17.51	mainly snowfall and rain
17.6	mainly windy
17.61	mainly stormy
17.65	mainly windy and rainy
17.7	mainly foggy
17.71	mainly fog in the morning
17.8	...

6.1.7 b)   Derivation from the general weather condition

17.x.0	not ascertainable
17.x.1	some sunshine
17.x.11	sunny above the fog (inversion)
17.x.12	some brightening
17.x.2	cloudy at times
17.x.3	
17.x.4	some rain
17.x.41	some hail
17.x.5	some snowfall
17.x.51	some snowfall and rain
17.x.6	some storms
17.x.61	some thunderstorms
17.x.62	several hailstorms
17.x.7	fog at times
17.x.71	shorter periods with fog in the morning
17.x.8	without any precipitation
17.x.9	some frost

6.2 Special natural events

All the following codes can have an intensity add code (;1 .. ;4).

6.2 a)   *Group survey*

21	signs of dryness
22	signs of coldness
23	signs of low water
24	signs of warmth
25	signs of high water
26	landslides and rockslides
27	movement of glacier tongues

6.2 b)   *Specification*

21   signs of dryness
21.0 soil dried out
21.1 low water level (of springs, brooks or small rivers)
21.2 drought: very low water, soil fissures
21.3 extreme drought
21.4 mills closed

22   signs of coldness
22.0 small lakes and soil frozen
22.1 larger lakes partially frozen
22.2 larger lakes frozen and passable
22.3 frost
22.4 mills closed
22.6 large delay of vegetation
22.7 rivers frozen
22.8 very cold

24   signs of warmth
24.1 vegetation very early
24.2 warm lakes and rivers
24.5 lake thaw

23   signs of low water
23.1 low water; but no signs of dryness

25   signs of high water
25.0 high water
25.1 flood (water in streets and buildings)
25.2 strong flood
25.3 large rivers overflowing the banks
25.4 small rivers overflowing the banks
25.7 high level of lakes
25.8 lakes flood lakeside

26   landslides and rockslides
26.0 some landslides
26.1 frequent landslides
26.2 rockslide

27   glacier tongues
27.1 glacier tongues melting back
26.4 glacier tongues advancing

6.3 Phenological observations

This is the most delicate part of the codebook. Direct phenological observations are to be coded as follows

---

31.PLANT.OBSERVATION;RELATIVE TIME CODE (SEE SECTION 2.4.2)

For relative time codes see section 6.31

6.3.1 a)   Plants

31.1	grain
31.2	fruit trees
31.3	other useful trees
31.4	wild trees
31.5	cultivated shrubs
31.6	wild shrubs
31.7	herbs
31.8	grass, pasture
31.1	grain
31.11	wheat {*Triticum sp.*}
31.111	spring wheat
31.12	spelt {*Triticum spelta*}
31.121	spring spelt
31.13	rye {*Secale cereale*}
31.131	spring rye
31.14..	other winter grain (make subcodes if specified!)
31.15	rice (make subcodes for varieties) {*Oryza sp.*}
31.16	oat {*Avena sp.*}
31.17	barley {*Hordeum sp.*}
31.171	spring barley
31.172	winter barley

31.18	maize {*Zea mays*}
31.2	fruit trees (make subcodes for varieties)
31.21	apple {*Malus sp.*}
31.22	pear {*Pyrus sp.*}
31.23	cherry {*Prunus avium*}
31.24	plum (Zwetschge) {*Prunus domestica*}
31.241	cherry plum (Pflaume) {*Prunus cerasifera*}
31.25	chestnut {*Castanea sativa*}
31.26	olive {*Olea europaea*}
31.27	walnut {*Juglans regia*}
31.3	other useful trees
31.4	wild trees
31.41	beech {*Fagus sylvatica*}
31.42	cornelian {*Cornus mas*}
31.43	horse-chestnut {*Aesculus hippocastanum*}
31.5	cultivated shrubs
31.51	grapevine {*vitis sp.*}
31.511	early burgundy grapes ("Äugstler")
31.52	potato {*Solanum tuberosum*}
31.56	strawberry {*Fragaria sp.*}
31.6	wild shrubs
31.61	hazelnut {*Corylus avellana*}
31.62	hip {*Rosa sp.*}
31.7	herbs
31.71	dandelion {*Taraxacum officinale*}
31.72	coltsfoot {*Tussilago farfara*}
31.73	hepatica {*Hepatica nobilis*}
31.8	grass
31.81	first hay cut
31.82	second hay cut
31.83	pasture
31.831	pasture in lowlands
31.832	pasture on the mountains

6.3.1 b) Phenological observations

31.x.1	in blossom (without precision)
31.x.11	blossom start
31.x.12	in full bloom
31.x.13	end of blossom
31.x.2	leaves
31.x.21	leaves start to unfold
31.x.22	leaves fully unfolded

31.x.25	leaves begin autumn colouring
31.x.26	leaves coloured (in autumn)
31.x.27	defoliation
31.x.28	fully defoliated (leafless)
31.x.3	stages in maturity
31.x.31	first fruit, grapevine berry, ear
31.x.32	beginning of coloring of grapevine berries
31.x.33	first colored grapevine berries
31.x.34	first ripe fruit, grapevine berry, ear

6.3.1 c)   *Paraphenological observations (plant codes see group 31)*

32.x.4	harvest
32.x.41	harvest begins
32.x.42	harvest ends
32.x.5	pasture
32.x.51	pasture begins
32.x.62	pasture ends
32.x.69	lack of fodder
32.x.7	sowing

6.3.1 d)   *Relative time codes for observation of phenology*

;1	extremely early
;2	very early
;3	early
;5	normal
;7	late
;8	very late
;9	extremely late

The relative time code should only be used if the source mentions it! Otherwise the relative time is to be computed from time series. Be careful with expressions from the sources: if an author states "very early" use the code ;2 only if you find other, more objective information for "very", otherwise make use of the ;3 code!

6.4 Damage

Damage coding is divided into two main groups:

41	physical impacts (e.g. through a storm)
42	biological impacts (through epidemics, epizootics, parasites, fungi, etc.)

Often it is not possible to clearly separate the two, because most biological impacts are related to certain weather conditions.

Impacts can in general be followed by code of intensity after a semicolon (;):

41.x.x;1	slight impacts
41.x.x;2	(default assumption)
41.x.x;3	heavy impacts
41.x.x;4	very heavy impacts

6.4.1   Physical impacts

6.4.1 a)   Origin of impact (by):

41.1	drought
41.2	coldness, frost
41.3	snow (except avalanches)
41.4	water, flooding
41.5	storm
41.6	humidity (long rain periods)
41.7	avalanches
41.8	hail
41.9	lightning

6.4.1 b)   Damage to: (main groups)

41.x.0	general (not specified)
41.x.1	crops (fields, any crops)
41.x.2	livestock
41.x.3	stored nutrition and fodder
41.x.4	forest
41.x.5	infrastructure
41.x.6	humans

6.4.1 c)   Damage to: (groups in detail)

41.x.0	general (not specified)
41.x.1	agriculture general (fields, any crops)
41.x.11	grain (fields!)
41.x.12	potatoes
41.x.13	grass, hay, pasture
41.x.14	other crops
41.x.15	vines
41.x.16	fruit trees and other useful trees

41.x.17	vegetables
41.x.18	harvest
41.x.19	fish
41.x.2	livestock
41.x.21	interruption of mountain pasture
41.x.22	delayed beginning of mountain pasture
41.x.25	death of animals
41.x.3	stored nutrition and fodder
41.x.31	grain
41.x.32	potatoes
41.x.33	grass, hay, other stored fodder
41.x.34	stored food
41.x.35	vines
41.x.36	fruit
41.x.37	vegetables
41.x.5	infrastructure
41.x.51	houses, barns
41.x.52	bridges
41.x.53	churches
41.x.54	other buildings
....	
41.x.6	humans
41.x.61	injuries
41.x.62	death

6.4.2   *Impacts by animals, parasites, etc (bioimpact)*

42.1	parasites / diseases
42.2	locusts

the "damage to" codes are the same as above (in group 41)

6.5.1   *Illness and famine (of man)*

51.1	dysentery
51.2	plague
51.3	bronchial diseases
51.4	smallpox
51.5	malaria
51.6	famine

6.5.2   *Fall in prices*

6.5.3   Rise in prices

Price codes are generally followed by a code of intensity (see section 2.4.2)

x.x;1	slight change
x.x;2	(default assumption)
x.x;3	great change
x.x;4	very great change

x.0	general
x.2	livestock
x.3	food
x.31	grain
x.32	potatoes
x.33	hay
x.34	livestock products
x.341	butter
x.342	cheese
x.343	milk
x.349	meat
x.35	vines
x.36	fruit
x.37	vegetables
x.38	spring crops
x.39	fish
x.2	livestock
x.4	wood

6.5.4/6.5.5 Import / export

Import: 54.product;intensity
Export: 55.product;intensity

The code for the products concerned is the same as in the price codes (52 and 53). Import or export can in general be followed by code of relative intensity after a semicolon (;):

x.x;0	none (embargo)
x.x;1	some additional imports/exports
x.x;2	(default assumption)
x.x;3	large additional imports/exports
x.x;4	very large additional imports/exports

These codes are always relative to "business as usual" according to the source.

6.5.6   *Harvest (except vine harvest):*

---

quantity (relative time of harvest: code in group 32)56.CROP-
CODE.AMOUNT-CODE

Just to recall: the amount code ranges from 1 to 9, with 5 denoting "average"; codes 4 and 6
are usually not used; 0 stands for uncertain or unknown (see section 2.4.2).

6.5.6 a)   *Crop*

56.0	all crops (incl. grass and pasture)
56.1	grain
56.2	potatoes
56.3	grass, hay, pasture
56.31	first cut
56.32	second cut
56.33	grass
56.331	grass on mountain pasture
56.35	pasture (duration)
56.4	other crops
56.6	fruit
56.7	vegetables
56.8	harvest general

6.5.6 b)   *Amount of harvest*

56.x.1	catastrophic (once per century)
56.x.2	very small
56.x.3	small
56.x.5	average
56.x.7	abundant
56.x.8	very abundant
56.x.9	extremely abundant (once in a century bumper crop)

6.5.7   *Vine harvest (vintage)*

57.quantity.quality
The codes for quantity and quality range from 1 to 9, with 5 denoting "average";
codes 4 and 6 are usually not used; 0 stands for unknown.

6.5.7 a)   Quantity of vine harvest

57.0.x	unknown
57.1.x	catastrophic (once in a century)
57.2.x	very small
57.3.x	small
57.5.x	average
57.7.x	abundant
57.8.x	very abundant
57.9.x	extremely abundant (once in a century bumper crop)

6.5.7 b)   Quality of vine harvest

57.x.0	unknown
57.x.1	catastrophic (once in a century)
57.x.2	very bad
57.x.3	bad
57.x.5	mediocre
57.x.7	good
57.x.8	very good
57.x.9	excellent (once in a century)

6.6   Other Observations

61.1	comet
61.2	air dark
61.3	earthquake

6.7.1   Observation of snow (except impacts!)

71.1	snowcover (relating to periods shorter than a month)
71.2	snowcover (relating to months)
71.3	snowcover (relating to seasons)
71.5	snow masses & avalanches (no damage reported)
71.6	snowfall (related to time such as early snow, late snow, first snow etc.; daily observations of snowfall are to be coded in group 13).

For snowing up and melting, precise dates (e.g. snowing up October 14th) can be used as well as relative time codes (snowing up early); these go together with months, seasons or even years in the time parameter. Today a snowcover is reported if the area surrounding the station is half covered at the time of the morning observation!

71.1	snowcover (relating to periods shorter than a month) (+ relative time code)
71.1.0	no snow
71.1.1	one day of snow cover (snowing up and melting again)
71.1.2	snowcover of several days (snowing up and melting again)
71.1.3	deep snowcover of several days (snowing up and melting again)
71.1.4	snowed up (not melting again)
71.1.5	deeply snowed up
71.1.6	permanent snowcover
71.1.7	complete melting
71.1.9	snow melting in the mountains
71.1.91	delayed snow melting in the mountains
71.1.92	advanced snow melting in the mountains
71.2	snowcover (relating to months) (+ relative time code)
71.2.0	no snow
71.2.1	little snow
71.2.3	deep snowcover of unknown duration
71.2.4	snowed up
71.2.5	snowed up deeply
71.2.6	permanent snowcover
71.2.7	complete melting
71.2.8	complete melting and snowed up again
71.2.9	snow melting in the mountains
71.2.91	advanced snow melting in the mountains
71.2.92	delayed snow melting in the mountains
71.3	snowcover (relating to seasons)
71.3.0	no snow
71.3.2	little snow
71.3.3	deep snowcover of unknown duration
71.3.4	rich in snow
71.3.6	long snow duration
71.3.7	short snow duration
71.3.	great masses of snow
71.5	snow masses & avalanches (+ intensity code) (no reported damage)
71.5.1	great masses of snow
71.5.2	avalanches
71.6	snowfall (+ relative time code ;1 .. ;9)
71.6.1	snowfall
71.6.2	snowfall on the mountain summits
71.6.3	snowfall in the mountains down to lower levels
71.6.9	beginning of winter

6.8 Time parameters and other necessary terms for translation

In addition to the codes, some other terms need to be translated into all the languages:

> First of all the time parameters (months, season, "ten day period", "five day period",
> then "1st" ... "6th",
> terms like "place", "country", "region",
> "author", "contributor", "source",
> "footnote", "comment", "translation"
> and some others.

6.9 Frequent codes

For entering frequent codes, the user can define any short codes, starting with "9" in the set option right at the beginning of the file.

Acknowledgement

This research is supported by the Swiss National Science Foundation and by the Swiss Bundesamt für Bildung und Wissenschaft (COST Programme). Acknowledgements are due to R. Brázdil (Brno), J. Kington (Norwich), and E. Wishman (Stavanger) for reading the draft version of the code book and for making helpful suggestions. Improvements of the present version are also due to the first users: P. Dobrovolny (Brno), L. Rácz (Kecskemet), and S. Militzer (Leipzig).

References

LAUTERBURG, A. (1990): Klimaschwankungen in Europa. Raum-zeitliche Untersuchungen in der Periode 1841-1960. Geogr. Bern. G 35, Bern
PFISTER, C. & LAUTERBURG, A. (1992): Spatial variability of climatic change in Europe 1780-1960. Paläoklimaforschung / Palaeoclimate Research 7, 177-192

Addresses of the authors:

Prof. Dr. C. Pfister, Department for Regional and Environmental Studies at the Institute for History, University of Bern, Engehaldenstr. 4, CH-3012 Bern, Switzerland
H. Schüle, Department for Regional and Environmental Studies at the Institute for History, University of Bern, Engehaldenstr. 4, CH-3012 Bern, Switzerland

PERIODICAL TITLE ABBREVIATIONS

Abh. Königl. Preuß. Meteor. Inst.	• Abhandlungen des Königlich-Preußischen Meteorologischen Institutes
Acad. Helv.	• Academica Helvetica
Acad. Sci. Bohem.	• Academiae Scientiarum Bohemoslovacae
Akad. Wiss. Lit.	• Akademie der Wissenschaften und Literatur
Am. Anthropol.	• American Anthropologist
Am. J. Archaeol.	• American Journal of Archaeology
Ann. Hum. Biol.	• Annals of Human Biology
Ann. E.S.C.	• Annales des Economies, Sociétés et Civilisations
Ann. Meteor.	• Annalen der Meteorologie
Arch. Meteor. Geophys. Bioklim.	• Archiv für Meteorologie, Geophysik und Bioklimatologie
B.A.R.	• Bulletin de l'Academie Royale de Belgique
Ber. Dtsch. Wetterdienst.	• Berichte des Deutschen Wetterdienstes
Boll. Geofis.	• Bolletino di Geofisica
Bull. Hist. Phil. Com. Trav. Hist. Sci.	• Bulletin Historique et Philologique du Comité des Travaux Historiques et Scientifiques
Cah. Hist. Mond.	• Cahiers d'Histoire Mondiale (Journal of World History)
C.N.R.	• National Research Council
Coll. Antropol.	• Collegium Anthropologicum
C.T.A.I.H.S.	• Collection des Travaux de l'Académie Internationale d'Histoire et des Sciences
Czech. Acad. Sci.	• Czechoslovak Academy of Sciences
Econ. Hist. Rev.	• Economic History Review
Geogr. Abh.	• Geographische Abhandlungen
Geogr. Arb.	• Geographische Arbeiten
Geogr. Bern.	• Geographica Bernensia
Geogr. Helv.	• Geographica Helvetica
Geogr. J.	• Geographical Journal

Geogr. Ann.	• Geografiska Annaler
Glasn. Antropol. Društ. Jug.	• Glasnik Antropoloskog Društva Jugoslavije
Hist. Geogr.	• Historická Geografie
Hist. Sozialwiss. Forsch.	• Historisch-Sozialwissenschaftliche Forschungen
H.M.Ú.	• Hydrometeorologického Ústavu
I.A.G.A.	• International Association of Geomagnetism and Aeronomy
Int. Ser.	• International Series
Int. Symp.	• International Symposium
Interdiv. Comm.	• Interdivisional Commission
Izv. A.N. S.S.S.R., Ser. Geogr.	• Izvestiya Akademii Nauk S.S.S.R., Seriya Geograficheskaya
J. Climatol Appl. Meteorol.	• Journal of Climatology and Applied Meteorology
J. Climatol.	• Journal of Climatology
J. Europ. Econ. Hist.	• Journal of European Economic History
J. Field Archaeol.	• Journal of Field Archeology
J. Geophys. Res.	• Journal of Geophysical Research
J. Interdisc. Hist.	• Journal of Interdisciplinary History
Mat. I Sesji I.N.F.G. U.W., Wyd.	• Materiały I Sesji Instytutu Nauk Fizycznogeograficnych Uniwersytetu Warszawskiego, Wydawnictwa
Mat. P.I.H.M.	• Materiały Państwowego Instytutu Hydrologiczno-Meteorologicznego
Mém. Acad. Roy. Belg.	• Mémoires de l'Académie Royale de Belgique
Meteor. Zpr.	• Meteorologické Zprávy
M.G.H.	• Monumenta Germaniae Historica
Monogr. K.G.W., P.A.N., Geol.	• Monografie Komitetu Gospodarski Wodnej, Polska Akademia Nauk, Wydawnictwa Geologiczne
Mus. Helv.	• Museum Helveticum
N.F.	• Neue Folge
Österr. Akad. Wiss.	• Österreichische Akademie der Wissenschaften
Phys. Earth Planet. Inter.	• Physics of the Earth and Planetary Interiors
Prace Geogr. Inst. P.A.N.	• Prace Geographical Institute of the Polish Academy of Nauk

Prace Geogr. Inst. P.A.N.

Proc.
Prz. Antropol.
Prz. Geof.
Prz. Geogr.
Č.S.A.V.
Publ. Comp.
P.W.N.

Quart. J. Roy. Meteor. Soc.

Quat. Res.
Renc. Int. Archéol. Hist.

Rev. Hist.
Roy. Acad. Sci.
Rozpr. U.W., Wyd.

Sb. Pr.
Scand. Econ. Hist. Rev.

Sov. Geophys. Com.
Spraw. Tow. Nauk.

Tijdschr. Econ. Soc. Geogr.

Trav. Géophys.
Trav. Sci.
Tree-Ring Bull.
Trudy G.G.O.

Vierteljahresschr. Naturf. Ges.

Wiss. Mitt.
Wyd. W.S.P.

Z. Papyr. Epigraph.

Z. Agrargesch. Agrarsoz.

- Prace Geograficzne Instytut Geografii, Polska Akademia Nauk
- Proceedings
- Przegląd Anthropologiczny
- Przegląd Geofizyczny
- Przegląd Geograficzny
- Československá Akademie Ved
- Publishing Company
- Państwowe Wydawnictwo Naukowe
- Quarterly Journal of the Royal Meteorological Society
- Quaternary Research
- Rencontres Internationales d'Archéologie et d'Histoire
- Revue Historique
- Royal Academy of Sciences
- Rozprawy Uniwersytetu Warszawskiego, Wydawnictwa
- Sborník Prací
- Scandinavian Economic History Review
- Soviet Geophysical Committee
- Sprawozdania Towarzystwa Naukowego
- Tijdschrift voor Economische en Sociale Geografie
- Travaux Géophysiques
- Travaux Scientifiques
- Tree-Ring Bulletin
- Trudy Gluvnoiy Geophysicheskoiy Observatorii
- Vierteljahresschrift der Naturforschenden Gesellschaft
- Wissenschaftliche Mitteilungen
- Wydawnictwa Wyższej Szkoły Pedagogicznej, Słupsk
- Zeitschrift für Papyrologie und Epigraphik
- Zeitschrift für Agrargeschichte und Agrarsoziologie

Paläoklimaforschung

Herausgegeben von der Akademie der Wissenschaften und der Literatur, Mainz.
Mathematisch-naturwissenschaftliche Klasse, Prof. Dr. Dr. Burkhard Frenzel, Stuttgart

Band 1: Klimageschichtliche Probleme der letzten 130 000 Jahre
Herausgegeben von Prof. Dr. Dr. B. Frenzel
1991. 451 Seiten, 159 Abbildungen, 22 Tabellen, kt. DM 128,–

**Band 2: Zur Rekonstruktion des Klimas im Bereich der Rheinpfalz seit Mitte des
16. Jahrhunderts mit Hilfe von Zeitreihen der Weinquantität und Weinqualität**
Von Prof. Dr. Wilhelm Lauer und Prof. Dr. Peter Frankenberg
1986. 54 Seiten mit 10 Abbildungen, 3 Tabellen und 1 Falttafel, kt. DM 34,–

Band 3: Beiträge zu einer quantitativen Paläoklimatologie des Holozäns
^{2}H-, ^{18}O- und ^{13}C-Gehalt von Holz-Cellulose rezenter und fossiler Bäume
Teil 1: Einführung Methodik
Mit Beiträgen von B. Frenzel, H. Moser, B. Becker, R. Geranmayeh, K. Haas, K. Loris,
W. Stichler und P. Trimborn
**Teil 2: Pflanzenphysiologische und pflanzenökologische Grundlagen der unterschied-
lichen Isotopengehalte**
Mit Beiträgen von B. Frenzel und H. Moser unter Mitwirkung von B. Becker,
R. Geranmayeh, K. Haas, K. Loris, W. Stichler und P. Trimborn
In Vorbereitung

**Band 4: Zur Paläoklimatologie des letzten Interglazials im Nordteil
der Oberrheinebene**
Herausgegeben von Prof. Dr. W. von Koenigswald.
Unter Mitarbeit zahlreicher Fachautoren
1988. 327 Seiten, 137 Abbildungen, 25 Tabellen, kt. DM 96,–

**Band 5: Klimarekonstruktion für Mainfranken, Bauland und Odenwald anhand
direkter und indirekter Witterungsdaten seit 1500**
Von Dr. Rüdiger Glaser
1991. 175 Seiten, 5 Abbildungen, 31 Figuren, 10 Tabellen, kt. DM 48,–

Band 6: Evaluation of Climate Proxy Data in Relation to the European Holocene
Edited by Prof. Dr. Dr. B. Frenzel, Prof. Dr. A Pons and Dr. B. Gläser
1992. XII, 309 pages, 84 figures, 10 tables, softcover, DM 96,–

Preisänderungen vorbehalten.

SEMPER BONIS ARTIBUS GUSTAV FISCHER

Samuel Thomas Soemmerring:
Schriften zur Paläontologie

Samuel Thomas Soemmerring-Werke Band 14.
Bearbeitet und herausgegeben von Dr. Manfred **Wenzel**, Gießen.
Veröffentlichung der Akademie der Wissenschaften und der Literatur, Mainz.

1990. 434 S., 4 Falttafeln,
geb. DM 198,–

Inhaltsübersicht: Wissenschafts-historische Einführung · Die Originalschriften Samuel Thomas Soemmerrings: Über die in Leibnitz *Protogaea* abgebildeten fossilen Thierknochen · Einfluß der Bestimmung der Zoolithen auf die Geschichte der Menschheit · Über einen Ornithocephalus, oder über das unbekannte Thier der Vorwelt · Über einen Ornithocephalus brevirostris der Vorwelt · Über die fossilen Reste einer großen Fledermausgattung · Über den Crocodilus priscus oder über ein in Baiern (!) versteint gefundenes schmalkieferiges Krokodil, Gavial der Vorwelt · Über die Lacerta gigantea der Vorwelt · Bemerkungen über einige in der Naturaliensammlung der königlichen Akademie der Wissenschaften befindliche fossile Zähne von Elephanten, Mastodonten, Rhinoceros'n und einem Tapire · Über die geheilte Verletzung eines fossilen Hyänen-Schedels (!) · Stellenkommentar

Mit diesem Band liegt der erste einer auf 24 Bände angelegten Ausgabe von Werken S. Th. Soemmerrings vor, des bedeutenden Naturforschers der Goethezeit. Die Ausgabe publiziert neben medizinischen, physikalisch-chemischen, paläontologischen und anthropologischen Schriften auch Soemmerrings Tagebücher, Briefe und Rezensionen.
Band 14 verdeutlicht, daß Soemmerring auch ein bedeutender Paläontologe war. Schon als junger Mediziner galt sein Interesse den Fossilien. Nach seinem Wechsel an die Bayerische Akademie der Wissenschaften in München (1805) widmete sich Soemmerring systematischen Studien zu den Flugsauriern und Krokodiliern. Weitere Arbeiten galten den Zähnen von Rüsseltieren sowie einem Hyänenschädel. Schon vor Georges Cuvier, der die Paläontologie als wissenschaftliches Fach begründete, wandte Soemmerring konsequent die vergleichende Methode zur Bestimmung fossiler Fundstücke an. Seine Interpretationen, oft modern anmutend, entsprechen den zeitgenössischen Erkenntnismöglichkeiten.